WELCOME

Firstly, I would like to show my appreciation to you, the American Football fan. We know you come in all different shapes, sizes, ages and ethnicity, but you all share a common bond - a passion for the greatest game on earth. Whether you just watch the game, play the game in some form, or if you are able to multi-skill like my wife, and can do more than one thing at the same time, by purchasing this inaugural Full10Yards NFL Season Guide you have helped contribute back to the grassroots game in the UK.

Here at the Full10Yards, our mission is to raise funds that help grow the game in the UK. We'll do this by helping those wanting to get involved with officiating or coaching. You can find more details about how we are giving back on our website or social media platforms. All content we produce, either through our website (www.full10yards.com) or through our podcasts, is all with the aim of helping our game get better, and getting more people involved. By just buying this guide, you have actively helped us help the game of American Football in the UK. So for that, I thank you.

In this guide you will find lots of different flavours of the game, giving you ample information to help get you excited for the upcoming 2020 season, that will be like no other. It also includes aspects of our other content we create throughout the year, including fantasy football projections, college football spotlights, a betting overview and a nod to the past in our retro section.

If that wasn't enough, we'll give you a few articles to get your teeth into. We are taking a look at a Miami Dolphins legend, and taking a look at some of the British players flying the flag for the UK in the NFL in 2020.

I would like to dedicate this guide to the Full10Yards team, and I would like to express my never ending gratitude to them. Without them, this season guide would never have got off the ground. There are not enough words to articulate how humbled and thankful I am that the team continue to help the Full10Yards grow into what started out three years ago with me sitting on my bedroom floor recording my first podcast.

Finally, I would like to dedicate this season guide to my wife, who has unreservedly supported me throughout this journey, and allowed me to pursue a dream. My incredible wife continues to remind me that she is the (unofficial) CEO/Chairman. Well, I guess she did come up with the name after all!

I hope this guide provides you with enough content to keep you entertained over the next few weeks as this unique season approaches. If you have any feedback on how we can improve, please feel free to contact us or myself personally.

As we like to say at F10Y HQ, keep those #EyesPeeled.

Tim Lambert Monk

Full10Yards Founder
contact@full10yards.com
@Tim_MonkF10Y/@Full10Yards

CONTENTS

ROOKIE'S GUIDE TO THE NFL
OFFENSIVE POSITIONS

Quarterback (QB)

Viewed as the team leader, he (along with the offensive co-ordinator) calls the plays & throws the ball or hands it off. Only player to touch the ball on every snap on offence (unless the offence is bringing out a trick play!)

Running Back (RB)

Clue is in the name, the guy who runs with the ball out of the backfield when handed to him by the quarterback. Also referred to as a Half-Back (HB)

Wide Receiver (WR)

All shapes and sizes, lined up all over the formation and all with their main job being to catch the ball when thrown in their direction from the quarterback with some wide receivers attempting a rush attempt too.

Tight End (TE)

A jack of all trades, blocks on running plays but also acts as a receiver at times. A very underrated position

Fullback (FB)

A dying bread of player who acts as the battering ram in front of the running back.

Offensive Line

Center (C)

The player who snaps the ball to the quarterback. He anchors the middle of the offensive line.

Guard (LG/RG)

The inner two members of the offensive line, whose jobs are to block for and protect the quarterback andball carriers.

Tackle (LT/RT)

The outer two members of the offensive line. Often tasked with blocking the oppositions best pass rushers.

The **shotgun** offense is often used on passing downs. This formation gives the quarterback (QB) more time to visualize the defense, particularly the secondary's alignment. Here's what you'll see: The QB lines up 5 to 7 yards behind the center. The center makes a long snap to the QB.

Before the play, you'll see why this formation is called the "I". The QB, FB & RB form an I, with the FB between the QB and RB. This lineup allows the RB to have complete vision of his blockers & the defenders reaction to the run. The RB can be 7yds deep so he can be in full stride when he nears the line of scrimmage.

Teams use the **split-back** formation as it's difficult for the defense to gauge whether the offense is running or passing. The runners are aligned behind the two guards about 5 yds behind the line of scrimmage. The backfield is balanced (i.e. it's not aligned toward one side or the other). This makes it more difficult for the defense to anticipate what the play is.

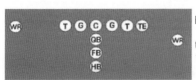

ROOKIE'S GUIDE

1

FULL 10 YARDS

ROOKIE'S GUIDE TO THE NFL
DEFENSIVE POSITIONS

Defensive Tackle (DT)

Big guys in the middle of the defensive line whose job is to maintain their positions in order to stop the run or exploit gaps to get after the QB.

Defensive End (DE)

As the name suggests, these guys line up on the end of the defensive line. Generally they get after the QB but they also try and force running plays in a certain direction to help the rest of the defence.

Linebacker (LB)

Tackle machines in the second level of the defence. Linebackers often have the dual role of defending the run and the pass while "outside" linebackers also rush the passer regularly.

Cornerback (CB)

The players who line up on the wide parts of the field, generally opposite the offensive receivers. In today's game you will hear more about the "nickel" corner whom lines up in the slot against the slot receiver of the opponent.

Safety (FS/SS)

The players who line up the deepest in the secondary — the last line of defense. There are called either Free Safeties (FS) or Strong Safeties (SS), and they must defend the deep pass and the run. The free safety tends to watch the play unfold and follow the ball as well as be the "defensive quarterback" of the backfield. The strong safety tends to play closer to the line than the free safety does, and assists in stopping the run.

Defensive Positions (4 - 3)

The 4-3 is a more conservative defense, but that's not always a bad thing. In the 4-3 the linebackers play more behind the line, and the team will rely on its four defensive linemen to get the job done up front. This means stopping the run can potentially be more effective than with a 3-4 defense, as a 4-3 team utilizes two defensive tackles that shift and stunt to confuse the offensive linemen's blocking.

The 3-4 in a flexible defense, and provides some great advantages when it comes to rushing the quarterback and defending against the pass. Because there are only three linemen, the outside linebackers may play the role of the defensive end at some times, essentially giving a 4-3 look. The 3-4 can be confusing for opposing quarterbacks, who may find it tough to keep track of these roving linebackers who line up all over the place.

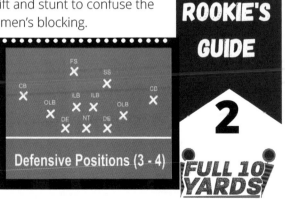

Defensive Positions (3 - 4)

ROOKIE'S GUIDE TO THE NFL
PENALTIES

5 Yard Penalty

Encroachment

When a defensive player crosses the line of scrimmage and makes contact with an opponent before the ball is snapped

When an interior lineman on the offensive team moves prior to the snap of the ball, or when any offensive player makes a quick, abrupt movement prior to the snap of the ball

False Start

Offside

When any part of a player's body is beyond the line of scrimmage or free kick line when the ball is put into play.

When a defensive player tackles or holds an offensive player other than the ball carrier. Results in a 1st down for offence.

Holding (defence)

Delay of Game

An action which delays the game; for example, if the offence allows the play clock to run out before the ball is snapped

Fewer than 7 players line up on the line of scrimmage; eligible receivers fail to line up as the leftmost and rightmost players on the line; or when five properly numbered ineligible players fail to line up on the line.

Illegal Formation

ROOKIE'S GUIDE

3

FULL 10 YARDS

10 Yard Penalty

Holding (offence)

When an offensive player uses his hands, arms, or other parts of his body to prevent a defensive player from tackling the ball carrier.

A blocker contacting a non-ball carrying member of the opposing team from behind and above the waist

Block in the Back

Tripping

When a player, usually close to the line of scrimmage, sees someone running past him and sticks out his leg or foot, tripping the player.

When a forward pass is thrown and an offensive player physically restricts or impedes a defender in a manner that's visually evident and materially affects the opponent's opportunity to gain position to catch the ball.

Pass Interference (offence)

Illegal use of Hands

This is usually called when players get hands in to the faces of their opponent usually when blocking or trying to get free of their opponent.

A violation of the rules where the passer throws a forward pass without a realistic chance of completion. Also results in a loss of down.

Intentional Grounding

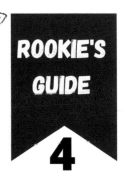

15 Yard Penalty

Personal Foul

Personal fouls encompass a few different infringements including "Roughing the Passer", "Unnecessary Roughness" and "Late Hit Out of Bounds". They are deemed an illegal, flagrant foul considered risky to the health of another player.

Roughing the Passer

When a defensive player makes direct contact with the quarterback after the quarterback has released the ball.

Unsportsmanlike Conduct

Any person that acts or speaks in a manner deemed to be intentionally harmful or especially objectionable by the game officials, or by rule. Unsportsmanlike conduct is a noncontact foul; if contact is involved it becomes a personal foul.

Roughing the Kicker

When a defensive player makes any contact with the punter, provided the defensive player hasn't touched the kicked ball before contact

Face Mask

When a player grabs the face mask of another player while attempting to block or tackle.

 ## Spot Foul

Pass Interference (defence)

A judgment call made by an official who sees a defensive player make contact with the intended receiver before the ball arrives, thus restricting his opportunity to catch the forward pass, resulting in an automatic 1st down at the spot of the foul.

ROOKIE'S GUIDE

5

FULL 10 YARDS

ROOKIE'S GUIDE TO THE NFL
NFL LINGO

AUDIBLE: When the quarterback changes the play at the line of scrimmage by calling out prescribed signals to his teammates.

BACKFIELD: The group of offensive players who line up behind the line of scrimmage.

BLITZ: A tactic used by the defense to disrupt pass attempts by the offence. During a blitz, a higher than usual number of defensive players will rush the opposing QB, to try to tackle him or force him to hurry his pass attempt.

COFFIN CORNER: The area between the opponent's end zone and five-yard line. Punters try to kick the ball into the coffin corner so that the offence takes over the ball deep in its own territory

COUNT/ SNAP COUNT: The numbers or words that a QB shouts loudly while waiting for the ball to be snapped. The QB usually informs his teammates in the huddle that the ball will be snapped on a certain count.

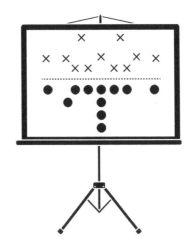

DRAW: A disguised run that initially looks like a pass play. The offensive linemen retreat like they're going to pass protect for the quarterback. The quarterback drops back and, instead of setting up to pass, he turns and hands the ball to a running back.

DOWN: A period of action that starts when the ball is put into play and ends when the ball is ruled dead (meaning the play is completed). The offence gets four downs to advance the ball 10 yards or surrender possession

DRIVE: The series of plays when the offence has the football, until it punts or scores and the other team gets possession of the ball.

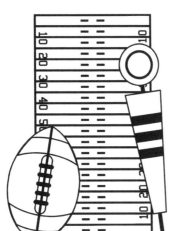

ROOKIE'S GUIDE

6

FULL 10 YARDS

END ZONE: A 10-yard-long area at each end of the field. You score a touchdown when you enter the end zone in control of the football. If you're tackled in your own end zone while in possession of the football, the other team gets a safety (right, red).

EXTRA POINT: A kick, worth one point, that's typically attempted after every touchdown (it's also known as the point after touchdown, or PAT). The ball is snapped from the 15-yard line. It must sail between the uprights and above the crossbar of the goalpost to be considered good.

FAIR CATCH: When the player returning a punt waves his extended arm from side to side over his head. After signaling for a fair catch, a player can't run with the ball, and those attempting to tackle him can't touch him.

FIELD GOAL: A kick, worth three points, that can be attempted from anywhere on the field. Like an extra point, a kick must sail above the crossbar and between the uprights of the goalpost to be ruled good.

FUMBLE: The act of losing possession of the ball while running with it or being tackled. Members of the offence and defense can recover a fumble. If the defense recovers the fumble, the fumble is called a turnover.

HAIL MARY: When the quarterback, usually in desperation at the end of a game, throws a long pass without targeting a receiver with the hope that a receiver will catch the ball and score a touchdown.

HANDOFF: The act of giving the ball to another player. Handoffs usually occur between the quarterback and a running back.

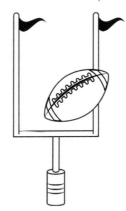

ROOKIE'S GUIDE

7

FULL 10 YARDS

HASH MARKS: The lines on the center of the field that signify 1 yard on the field. Before every play, the ball is spotted between the hash marks or on the hash marks, depending on where the ball carrier was tackled on the preceding play.

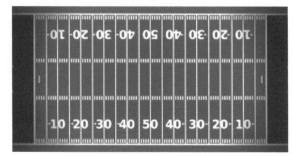

HUDDLE: When the 11 players on the field come together to discuss strategy between plays. On offence, the quarterback relays the plays in the huddle

INCOMPLETION: A forward pass that falls to the ground because no receiver could catch it, or a pass that a receiver dropped or caught out of bounds.

INTERCEPTION: A pass that's caught by a defensive player, ending the offence's possession of the ball.

KICKOFF: A free kick, that puts the ball into play. A kickoff is used at the start of the first and third quarters and after every touchdown and successful field goal.

LINE OF SCRIMMAGE: An imaginary line that extends from where the football is placed at the end of a play to both sides of the field. Neither the offence nor the defense can cross the line until the football is put in play again.

MAN COVERAGE: When any defensive back, or maybe even a linebacker, is assigned to cover a specific offensive player. The defender must track this player all over the field until the play ends.

NEUTRAL ZONE: The area in football between the two lines of scrimmage, stretching from sideline to sideline. The width of this area is defined by the length of the football. Other than the center, no player can be in the neutral zone prior to the snap; otherwise, the official calls an encroachment or violation of the neutral zone (offside) penalty.

ROOKIE'S GUIDE

8

FULL 10 YARDS

OFFENSIVE LINE: The human wall of five men who block for and protect the quarterback and ball carriers. Every line has a Center (who snaps the ball), two Guards, and two Tackles.

OPTION: When a quarterback has the choice — the option — to either pass or run. Usually decided even after the ball is snapped, reacting to the defenders.

PICK-SIX When a defender intercepts, or picks off, a pass in football and runs it back for a touchdown, thereby scoring six points.

PIGSKIN: The slang term for a football. Also known as the "rock".

POCKET: The area where the quarterback stands when he drops back to throw the ball. This area extends from a point two yards outside of either offensive tackle & includes the tight end if he drops off the line of scrimmage to pass-protect. The pocket extends longitudinally behind the line back to the offensive team's own end line.

PUNT: A kick made when a player drops the ball and kicks it while it falls toward his foot. A punt is usually made on a 4th down when the offence must surrender possession of the ball to the defense.

REDZONE: In football, the term "red zone" refers to the unofficial area from inside the 20-yard line to the opponent's goal line. Holding an opponent to a field goal in this area is considered a victory by the defense.

ROLLOUT/ BOOTLEG: When the quarterback runs left or right away from the pocket before throwing the ball.

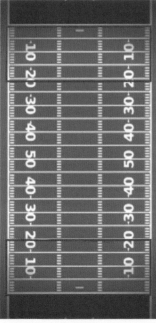

ROOKIE'S GUIDE

9

FULL 10 YARDS

SACK: When a defensive player tackles the quarterback behind the line of scrimmage for a loss of yardage.

SAFETY: A score, worth two points, that the defense earns by tackling an offensive player in possession of the ball in his own end zone.

SECONDARY: The defensive players who defend against the pass and line up behind the linebackers and wide on the corners of the field opposite the receivers.

SCRAMBLE: When the quarterback, to gain time for receivers to get open, moves behind the line of scrimmage, dodging the defense.

SNAP: The action in which the ball is hiked (tossed between the legs) by the center to the QB, to the holder on a kick attempt, or to the punter. When the snap occurs, the ball is officially in play and action begins

SPECIAL TEAMS: The 22 players who are on the field during kicks and punts. These units have special players who return punts and kicks, as well as players who are experts at covering kicks and punts.

SPIRAL: The tight spin on the football in flight after the quarterback releases it. The term "tight spiral" is often used to describe a solidly thrown football.

TAKEAWAY: How a defense describes any possession in which it forces a fumble & recovers the ball or registers an interception. In football, any turnover that the defense collects is called a takeaway.

TOUCHDOWN: A score, worth six points, that occurs when a player in possession of the ball crosses the plane of the opponent's goal line, when a player catches the ball while in the opponent's end zone, or when a defensive player recovers a loose ball in the opponent's end zone.

TURNOVER ON DOWNS: The offence failing to convert on its 4th down attempt (when not punting) leads to the opposition receiving the ball back for its own offence.

WEAK SIDE: The side of the offence opposite the side on which the tight end lines up.

ZERO DEFENCE: A defensive coverage scheme that leaves no defenders deep in the middle of the field.

ZONE COVERAGE: A type of defense that assigns each defender to a particular area in which he is responsible for marking any offensive player that enters

ROOKIE'S GUIDE

10

FULL 10 YARDS

ROOKIE'S GUIDE TO THE NFL
2019 SEASON

AFC

EAST
	W	L	T	W-L%	PF	PA	PD
New England Patriots	12	4	0	0.75	420	225	195
Buffalo Bills	10	6	0	0.625	314	259	55
New York Jets	7	9	0	0.438	276	359	-83
Miami Dolphins	5	11	0	0.313	306	494	-188

NORTH
	W	L	T	W-L%	PF	PA	PD
Baltimore Ravens	14	2	0	0.875	531	282	249
Pittsburgh Steelers	8	8	0	0.5	289	303	-14
Cleveland Browns	6	10	0	0.375	335	393	-58
Cincinnati Bengals	2	14	0	0.125	279	420	-141

SOUTH
	W	L	T	W-L%	PF	PA	PD
Houston Texans	10	6	0	0.625	378	385	-7
Tennessee Titans	9	7	0	0.563	402	331	71
Indianapolis Colts	7	9	0	0.438	361	373	-12
Jacksonville Jaguars	6	10	0	0.375	300	397	-97

WEST
	W	L	T	W-L%	PF	PA	PD
Kansas City Chiefs	12	4	0	0.75	451	308	143
Denver Broncos	7	9	0	0.438	282	316	-34
Oakland Raiders	7	9	0	0.438	313	419	-106
Los Angeles Chargers	5	11	0	0.313	337	345	-8

NFC

EAST
	W	L	T	W-L%	PF	PA	PD
Philadelphia Eagles	9	7	0	0.563	385	354	31
Dallas Cowboys	8	8	0	0.5	434	321	113
New York Giants	4	12	0	0.25	341	451	-110
Washington Redskins	3	13	0	0.188	266	435	-169

NORTH
	W	L	T	W-L%	PF	PA	PD
Green Bay Packers	13	3	0	0.813	376	313	63
Minnesota Vikings	10	6	0	0.625	407	303	104
Chicago Bears	8	8	0	0.5	280	298	-18
Detroit Lions	3	12	1	0.219	341	423	-82

SOUTH
	W	L	T	W-L%	PF	PA	PD
New Orleans Saints	13	3	0	0.813	458	341	117
Atlanta Falcons	7	9	0	0.438	381	399	-18
Tampa Bay Buccaneers	7	9	0	0.438	458	449	9
Carolina Panthers	5	11	0	0.313	340	470	-130

WEST
	W	L	T	W-L%	PF	PA	PD
San Francisco 49ers	13	3	0	0.813	479	310	169
Seattle Seahawks	11	5	0	0.688	405	398	7
Los Angeles Rams	9	7	0	0.563	394	364	30
Arizona Cardinals	5	10	1	0.344	361	442	-81

PLAYOFFS

				Score	
WildCard	Buffalo Bills	@	Houston Texans	19	22
WildCard	Tennessee Titans	@	New England Patriots	20	13
WildCard	Minnesota Vikings	@	New Orleans Saints	26	20
WildCard	Seattle Seahawks	@	Philadelphia Eagles	17	9
Division	Minnesota Vikings	@	San Francisco 49ers	10	27
Division	Tennessee Titans	@	Baltimore Ravens	28	12
Division	Seattle Seahawks	@	Green Bay Packers	23	28
Division	Houston Texans	@	Kansas City Chiefs	31	51
ConfChamp	Tennessee Titans	@	Kansas City Chiefs	24	35
ConfChamp	Green Bay Packers	@	San Francisco 49ers	20	37
Super Bowl	Kansas City Chiefs	v	San Francisco 49ers	31	20

ROOKIE'S GUIDE

11

BUFFALO BILLS

THE LOWDOWN:

Led by their youthful up and coming Quarterback Josh Allen, the Buffalo Bills are a few pieces away from being contenders in the AFC. With the departure of Tom Brady from the New England Patriots, many believe the AFC East now belongs to the Bills. They finished last season with the third overall defense and will aim to replicate that form again this season. The addition of Stefon Diggs to the offence will be a huge bonus for Josh Allen as he now has a solidified number one receiver he can target.

SCHEDULE

Week 1: Vs. Jets
Week 2: @ Dolphins
Week 3: Vs. Rams
Week 4: @ Raiders
Week 5: @ Titans
Week 6: Vs. Chiefs *(TNF)*
Week 7: @ Jets
Week 8: Vs. Patriots
Week 9: Vs. Seahawks
Week 10: @ Cardinals
Week 11: BYE
Week 12: Vs. Chargers
Week 13: @ 49ers *(MNF)*
Week 14: Vs. Steelers *(SNF)*
Week 15: @ Broncos
Week 16: @ Patriots *(MNF)*
Week 17: Vs. Dolphins

2020 NFL DRAFT CLASS

Round 2
A.J. Epenesa, EDGE,
Iowa
Round 3
Zack Moss, RB,
Utah
Round 4
Gabriel Davis, WR,
UCF
Round 5
Jake Fromm, QB,
Georgia
Round 6
Tyler Bass, K,
Georgia Southern
Isaiah Hodgins, WR,
Oregon State
Round 7
Dane Jackson, CB,
Pittsburgh

SIGNINGS

Mario Addison, DE
Vernon Butler, DT
Daryl Williams, OL
Quinton Jefferson, DE
Josh Norman, CB
E.J. Gaines, CB
Quinton Spain, OG

STAR SIGNING

Stefon Diggs, WR

NO LONGER ON TEAM

Frank Gore, RB
Corey Liuget, DT
Jordan Phillips, DT
Shaq Lawson, DE
Lorenzo Alexander, LB

TEAM DETAILS:

Owner: Terry & Kim Pegula
General Manager: Brandon Beane
Stadium: To be named for 2020
Location: Orchard Park, NY
Head Coach: Sean McDermott
Offensive Coordinator: Brian Daboll
Defensive Coordinator: Leslie Frazier
Coaching Staff:
Leslie Frazier (Assistant HC)
Ken Dorsey (QB Coach)
Kelly Skipper (RB Coach)
Chad Hall (WR Coach)
Rob Boras (TE Coach)
Heath Farwell (ST Coordinator)
Super Bowl Wins: 0
Conference Wins: 4 (AFC, 1990, 1991, 1992, 1993)
Divisional Wins: 7 (AFC East, 1980, 1988, 1989, 1990, 1991, 1993, 1995)

-2019-
Record: 10-6 (Lost Wild Card Rd)
Offence Rank: Passing (26th), Rushing (8th),Overall (23rd)
Defence Rank: Passing (4th), Rushing (10th), Overall (2nd)

KEY PLAYER

Tremaine Edmunds: The Bills defense ranked 2nd in pts allowed last season, providing the platform for a postseason appearance in which they nearly upset the Texans. Middle Linebacker Edmunds played a key role in the heart of that defense. At just 22, Edmunds is already a leader, with Defensive Coordinator, Leslie Frazier, saying he is the 'epitome of what you want your star players to be'.

A.J Epenesa: Epenesa will play on as a big defensive end in Buffalo's system, which should play to his strengths against the run, allowing him to maintain the edge as DT Ed Oliver collapses the pocket from the middle. Watch out for him lining up inside next to Ed Oliver too!

ROOKIE SPOTLIGHT

DEPTH CHART

Quarterback	Wide Receiver	Center	Edge	Line Backer	Cornerback
Josh Allen	Stefon Diggs	Mitch Morse	Mario Addison	Tremaine Edmunds	Tre-Davious White
Matt Barkley	John Brown	Evan Boehm	Jerry Hughes	Matt Milano	Josh Norman
Jake Fromm	Cole Beasley	Tackle	Trent Murphy	AJ Klein	EJ Gaines
Fullback	Isaiah McKenzie	Dion Dawkins	AJ Epenesa [R]	Tyler Matakevich	Levi Wallace
Patrick Dimarco	Duke Williams	Cody Ford	Defensive Tackle	Tyrel Dodson	Taron Johnson
Running Back	Robert Foster	Ty Nsekhe	Ed Oliver	Free Safety	Strong Safety
Devin Singletary	Tight End	Guard	Star Lotuleilei	Micah Hyde	Jordan Poyer
Zach Moss	Dawson Knox	Quinton Spain	Quinton Jefferson	Dean Marlowe	Jacquan Johnson
TJ Yeldon	Tyler Kroft	Jon Feliciano	Kicker	Punter	Long Snapper
Christian Wade	Lee Smith	Spencer Long	Stephen Hauschka	Corey Bojorquez	Reid Ferguson

NFL

1

FULL 10 YARDS

2019 RANKINGS

Player	Pos	Standard			0.5PPR			PPR		
		Pts	Avg	Rank	Pts	Avg	Rank	Pts	Avg	Rank
Josh Allen	QB	297.3	19.8	QB6						
Devin Singletary	RB	118.9	9.9	RB30	133.4	11	RB28	147.9	12	RB29
Frank Gore	RB	77.7	5.2	RB44	82.7	5.5	RB46	87.7	5.9	RB50
John Brown	WR	147.8	9.9	WR14	183.8	12	WR15	219.8	15	WR15
Cole Beasley	WR	117.8	7.9	WR29	151.3	10	WR28	184.8	12	WR27
Isaiah McKenzie	WR	32.6	2.3	WR102	45.1	3.2	WR98	57.6	4.1	WR96
Dawson Knox	TE	51.7	3.5	TE26	65.7	4.4	TE29	79.7	5.3	TE30
Tyler Kroft	TE	12.6	1.2	TE68	15.1	1.4	TE69	17.6	1.6	TE71
Buffalo Bills	DST	122.0	8.1	DST10						
Stephen Hauschka	K	101.0	6.7	K21						

JOSH ALLEN

2019's fantasy QB6 looks set for another big year. The big arm will rake in points with splash plays to a new look deep threat WR core, but it's Allen's ability to get out the pocket and run which makes him such a fantasy asset, 509 yards and TDs last season attest to that.

ADP 9.04

DEVIN SINGLETARY

ADP 4.07

Seemingly a lock to have a big year before the draft, Singletary's stock seems to have fallen slightly with the addition of Zack Moss. Still with the loss of Frank Gore, Singletary should operate as the lead back and is a good redraft RB3 option as he looks to build on a 969 total yard season in 2019.

ZACK MOSS

A violent downhill runner that will look to profit in short yardage situations. Moss doesn't have the vision of Singletary, but he does have the potential to add a pass catching option to the Bills backfield. Potential TD vulture but best picked as a handcuff to his 2nd year teammate.

ADP 9.05

STEFON DIGGS

ADP 6.05

PPR WR18 last season, Diggs moves to an out and out lead receiver role in Buffalo. An exceptional route runner who offers deep threat potential, he figures to benefit from the huge arm of Josh Allen. A great WR2 option in fantasy, Diggs could even function as WR1 for team drafting RBs early.

JOHN BROWN

A career best 1060 yards made Brown a great sleeper pick in 2019. The arrival of Diggs will undoubtedly eat into his target share but Brown's big play threat (he's never averaged less than 13.3 yards a catch) make him a great pick up in best ball and deep bench leagues.

ADP 13.05

2020 Projections

Position	Player	Standard		0.5PPR		Full PPR	
		Pts	Rank	Pts	Rank	Pts	Rank
QB	Josh Allen	324.0	7				
RB	Devin Singletary	163.5	25	186.5	22	209.5	21
RB	Zack Moss	149.1	30	157.6	32	166.1	39
WR	John Brown	112.0	43	138.0	45	164.0	45
WR	Stefon Diggs	131.8	30	167.3	28	202.8	26
WR	Cole Beasley	55.2	88	72.7	87	90.2	85
TE	Dawson Knox	89.8	13	114.3	15	138.8	15
TE	Tyler Kroft	11.9	66	17.9	65	23.9	66

ADP taken from Ultimate Draft Kit (PPR)

Projections by Rob Grimwood @FFBritballer

FANTASY FOOTBALL

2

BUFFALO BILLS

DO SAY..

We do the best tailgates...

DON'T SAY..

Josh Allen is an accurate passer

BETTING ODDS BY ADAM WALFORD (@TOUCHDOWNTIPS)

SUPER BOWL	30/1	
AFC CONFERENCE	14/1	
AFC EAST	6/4	

TO MAKE PLAYOFFS
10/19
TEAM TOTAL WINS
8.5

ADAM'S BEST BET
WIN THE AFC EAST
6/4

PLEASE GAMBLE RESPONSIBLY

VIEW FROM THE SIDELINES

By Matt Swain (@uk_bills)

The Bills return most of the roster from 2019 that took massive strides in becoming a real playoff contender. The biggest off-season addition was the trade for WR Stefon Diggs, who should help Josh Allen with his progression in year 3. The AFC East has lost Tom Brady & the Bills are primed to take over with coach of the year candidate Sean McDermott who is ready to take the Bills to the next level. The defence has added key pieces in AJ Epenesa, Mario Addison, Quintin Jefferson & Mario Addison that should help top draft pick from 2019 Ed Oliver take the next step towards stardom. With key pieces John Brown, Cole Beasley & Devin Singletary already established, as well as a top flight secondary including Tre White & Micha Hyde, the Bills should be primed for an attention grabbing 2020 season.

►RETRO FOCUS◄

JIM KELLY – QB

The history of the NFL is not complete without mentioning Bills QB Jim Kelly. After reaching, and losing, four consecutive Super Bowls in the 1990s, Kelly became a winner after he hung his cleats up, by beating cancer twice. Kelly cut his teeth in the USFL before joining the Bills aged 26. Five Pro Bowls, over 35,000 yards passing and a Canton bust (2002) later, makes Kelly a living legend.

DID YOU KNOW

The Bills are the only NFL team that actually plays its home games in the state of New York (the Jets and Giants are based in New Jersey).

KEY STAT

"Bulldozer!"

Josh Allen led all QBs with 9 rushing TDs in 2019, taking his total to 17 in his first 27 starts. Only Cam Newton has more (20) in the same no. of games out of all QBs.

FULL10YARDS VERDICT

Sean McDermott is looking for his third playoff appearance in four years and, for a change, the AFC East title isn't a gimme for the Patriots. Buffalo's defence is in decent shape and the arrival of Stefon Diggs from Minnesota is only going to beef up their attack.
If Josh Allen continues to progress, and their running back committee of Zack Moss and Devin Singletary beds in, the Bills could match, or even surpass, last year's 10-6. Don't be shocked if they take the division for the first time in 25 years.

BETTING, STATS, FANS VIEW, RETRO

3

FULL 10 YARDS

MIAMI DOLPHINS

THE LOWDOWN:

Last year's "Tank for Tua" mission was a success. The Miami Dolphins got their Quarterback for the future at the fifth overall pick in this year's draft. Brian Flores is responsible for the teams rebuild and the patience required for it. The Dolphins hauled in three first round players in the draft this year. QB Tua Tagovailoa, OT Austin Jackson & CB Noah Igbinoghene. Covering a multitude of areas, the Dolphins are slowly building a roster that will be competing for the AFC East title in the coming years.

SCHEDULE

Week 1: @ Patriots
Week 2: Vs. Bills
Week 3: @ Jaguars *(TNF)*
Week 4: Vs. Seahawks
Week 5: @ 49ers
Week 6: @ Broncos
Week 7: Vs. Chargers
Week 8: Vs. Rams
Week 9: @ Cardinals
Week 10: Vs. Jets
Week 11: BYE
Week 12: @ Jets
Week 13: Vs. Bengals
Week 14: Vs. Chiefs
Week 15: Vs. Patriots
Week 16: @ Raiders
Week 17: @ Bills

2020 NFL DRAFT CLASS

Round 1
Tua Tagovailoa, QB,
Alabama
Austin Jackson, OT,
USC
Noah Igbinoghene, CB,
Auburn
Round 2
Robert Hunt, IOL,
Louisiana
Raekwon Davis, IDL,
Alabama
Round 3
Brandon Jones, S,
Texas
Round 4
Solomon Kindley, IOL,
Georgia
Round 5
Jason Strowbridge, EDGE,
North Carolina
Curtis Weaver, EDGE,
Boise State
Round 6
Blake Ferguson, LS,
LSU
Round 7
Malcolm Perry, WR,
Navy

SIGNINGS

Ereck Flowers, OT
Jordan Howard, RB
Shaq Lawson, DE
Emmanuel Ogbah, DE
Kyle Van Noy, LB
Adrian Colbert, S
Ted Karras, OL

STAR SIGNING

Byron Jones, CB

NO LONGER ON TEAM

Charles Harris, DE
Taco Charlton, DE
Aqib Talib, CB
Reshad Jones, S

TEAM DETAILS:

Owner: Stephen M. Ross
General Manager: Chris Grier
Stadium: Hard Rock Stadium
Location: Miami, Florida
Head Coach: Brian Flores
Offensive Coordinator:
Chan Gailey
Defensive Coordinator:
Josh Boyer
Coaching Staff:
Danny Crossman (ST Coordinator)
Robby Brown (QB Coach)
Eric Studesville (RB Coach)
Josh Grizzard (WR Coach)
George Godsey (TE Coach)
Super Bowl Wins: 2 (1972, 1973)
Conference Wins: 5 (AFC, 1971, 1972, 1973, 1982, 1984)
Divisional Wins: 13 (AFC East, 1971, 1972, 1973, 1974, 1979, 1981, 1983, 1984, 1985, 1992, 1994, 2000, 2008)
-2019-
Record: 5-11
Offence Rank: Passing (12th), Rushing (32nd), Overall (25th)
DefenceRank: Passing (26th), Rushing (27th),Overall (32nd)

Byron Jones: The Dolphins' defence was a shambles at times last season, only beginning to show promise as the season drew to a close. A free spending off-season and a defence heavy draft has seen nearly the whole unit overhauled. One of the main additions is former Cowboys' Cornerback, Byron Jones. He'll be key opposite Xavien Howard as the Dolphins seek to build a no fly zone over South Beach.

Tua Tagovailoa: Mission accomplished, Dolphins fans! Whether Tagovailoa plays this coming season or not remains to be seen but the talented former Alabama passer is a potential franchise QB who has drawn comparisons with 49ers legend, Steve Young. Super accurate and a big game player, Tua has all the makings of a franchise changer.

DEPTH CHART

Quarterback	Wide Receiver	Center	Edge	Line Backer	Cornerback
Ryan Fitzpatrick	DeVante Parker	Ted Karras	Shaq Lawson	Kyle van Noy	Xavien Howard
Tua Tagovailoa	Preston Williams	Keaton Sutherland	Christian Wilkins	Vince Biegel	Byron Jones
Josh Rosen	Jakeem Grant	**Tackle**	Emmanuel Ogbah	Raekwon McMillan	Noah Igbinoghene [R]
Fullback	Chester Rogers	Julie'n Davenport	Avery Moss	Elandon Roberts	Nick Needham
Chandler Cox	Ricardo Louis	Jesse Davis	**Defensive Tackle**	Kamu Grugier-Hill	Cordrea Tankersley
Running Back	Isaiah Ford	Austin Jackson [R]	Davon Godchaux	**Free Safety**	**Strong Safety**
Jordan Howard	**Tight End**	Guard	Raekwon Davis [R]	Bobby McCain	Eric Rowe
Matt Breida	Mike Gesicki	Ereck Flowers	Benito Jones [R]	Adrian Colbert	Clayton Fejedelem
Kalen Ballage	Durham Smythe	Michael Dieter	**Kicker**	**Punter**	**Long Snapper**
Myles Gaskin	Michael Roberts	Robert Hunt [R]	Jason Sanders	Matt Haack	Blake Ferguson [R]

NFL

1

MIAMI DOLPHINS

2019 RANKINGS

Player	Pos	Standard			0.5PPR			PPR		
		Pts	Avg	Rank	Pts	Avg	Rank	Pts	Avg	Rank
Ryan Fitzpatrick	QB	230.4	16.5	QB18						
Kenyan Drake*	RB	149.9	11.5	RB17	173.4	13	RB18	196.9	15	RB16
Patrick Laird	RB	38.3	2.7	RB70	47.8	3.4	RB68	57.3	4.1	RB66
Kalen Ballage	RB	37.8	3.2	RB73	44.8	3.7	RB71	51.8	4.3	RB69
DeVante Parker	WR	160.5	10.7	WR8	192.5	13	WR11	224.5	15	WR13
Preston Williams	WR	58.8	7.4	WR74	74.8	9.4	WR74	90.8	11	WR73
Allen Hurns	WR	51.6	3.7	WR80	67.6	4.8	WR81	83.6	6	WR82
Mike Gesicki	TE	75.6	5.0	TE12	99.1	6.6	TE12	122.6	8.2	TE12
Miami Dolphins	DST	33.0	2.2	DST32						
Jason Sanders	K	106.1	7.1	K17						

RYAN FITZPATRICK — ADP U/D

Between weeks 12 and 17 last year, Ryan Fitzpatrick was the QB3 in fantasy football. The veteran can be a rollercoaster on the pitch & as a fantasy option, with the ability to make huge plays & throw terrible interceptions on any play. However, not a safe fantasy option with the addition of Tua Tagovailoa.

JORDAN HOWARD — ADP 7.08

Perennially underrated and often maligned, Jordan Howard was a clever addition for the Dolphins in the offseason. Still only 25, Howard has three 1,000 yard seasons under his belt already. The addition of Matt Breida eats into his fantasy value, but he still has potential as a solid flex option.

DEVANTE PARKER — ADP 6.09

Fantasy players have been waiting for DeVante Parker's breakout season forever. It finally happened last year, with Parker finishing as WR11. Parker remains a value add at his current ADP and he looks set to thrive as the Dolphins WR1 with Fitzpatrick or Tua under centre.

PRESTON WILLIAMS — ADP 13.4

A promising start to 2019 has left fantasy football Twitter salivating at the thought of Williams in Chan Gailey's offense. However, caution is urged, the Dolphins have drastically improved their run game and defence, and with Parker as the clear WR1, targets for Williams could be limited.

MIKE GESICKI — ADP 13.4

The 2018 2nd rounder began to grow into his role as the Dolphins main pass catching TE last season. With more experience and no significant competition, Gesicki is trending upwards as a fantasy option, and with a bit more stability in Miami, he's worth a gamble as your TE1 in 2019.

2020 Projections

Position	Player	Standard		0.5PPR		Full PPR	
		Pts	Rank	Pts	Rank	Pts	Rank
QB	Ryan Fitzpatrick	274.2	23				
RB	Jordan Howard	145.9	31	156.9	34	167.9	38
RB	Matt Breida	130.6	37	147.1	40	163.6	41
RB	Kalen Ballage	34.1	82	41.6	84	49.1	84
WR	DeVante Parker	160.4	14	199.4	15	238.4	15
WR	Preston Williams	109.1	47	134.1	48	159.1	48
WR	Jakeem Grant	51.2	96	65.2	98	79.2	97
TE	Mike Gesicki	110.4	7	141.9	7	173.4	7

ADP taken from Ultimate Draft Kit (PPR)

Projections by Rob Grimwood @FFBritballer

FANTASY FOOTBALL

2

MIAMI DOLPHINS

DO SAY..
The 1972 season

DON'T SAY..
The 2007 Season

BETTING ODDS BY ADAM WALFORD (@TOUCHDOWNTIPS)

SUPER BOWL **100/1**

AFC CONFERENCE **50/1**

AFC EAST **10/1**

TO MAKE PLAYOFFS
9/2

TEAM TOTAL WINS
6.5

ADAM'S BEST BET
FINISH 3RD IN AFC EAST
15/8

PLEASE GAMBLE RESPONSIBLY

VIEW FROM THE SIDELINES
By Liam Connolly (@DolphinAbroad)

Year Two of 'Flores in Florida' comes with a lot of optimism in the air. Key free agency signings of Bryon Jones & Kyle Van Noy were joined in the draft by quarterback Tua Tagovailoa, which came to many of Fins fans delight.Another year for Flores to nurture plenty of young & hungry talent cannot be a bad thing, with talents like wide receiver Preston Williams expected to take a step up for this offense, with Fitzpatrick to lead the team initially.In a competitive division & with a tough schedule, my record prediction of 7-9 and 3rd in the AFC East is a realistic one & would show clear progress and one in which most would be happy with.

►RETRO FOCUS◄

MERCURY MORRIS – RB

One of the great player names, RB Mercury Morris pops up every year to open the Bolly when the final team in an NFL season loses their unbeaten record. Morris is part of the famous undefeated 1972 Dolphins team. Morris spent 7 seasons in Miami, winning two Super Bowl rings. He averaged an impressive 5.1 yards a carry during his career, and carried the ball 21 times in total over 3 Consecutive Super Bowl appearances (1971 to 1973).

DID YOU KNOW

The 1972 Dolphins are the only NFL team to record a perfect season, winning 14 regular season wins & all three postseason games, including Super Bowl VII.

KEY STAT

"What's the point?"
The Dolphins allowed the most amount of points in 2019, including conceding 102 points in the first 2 games.

FULL10YARDS VERDICT

After gutting their roster last year, Miami are in rebuild mode and the new pieces – Matt Breida, Jordan Howard, Byron Jones, Kyle van Noy and Shaq Lawson – are dropping into place. Brian Flores is a savvy coach who gets the best out of his guys, and QB prospect Tua Tagovailoa will be groomed to step in for Fitzmagic when the time is right. The Dolphins' spirited performances during the second half of 2019 give cause for optimism and while they probably won't make the playoffs, the new additions could help to secure a .500 season.

BETTING, STATS, FANS VIEW, RETRO

3

FULL 10 YARDS

NEW ENGLAND PATRIOTS

THE LOWDOWN:

An historic season awaits in New England. For the first time in two decades somebody other than Tom Brady will be starting at Quarterback for the Patriots. That somebody is former league MVP Cameron Newton who hasn't played in a year and has a point to prove. HC Bill Belichick masterminded the move for Newton and managed to secure him for the leagues minimum salary. The Patriots' defence was historic last season and helped them to many of their wins, but with some key figures opting out this season, it will be interesting to see if they can maintain their form. The AFC East has belonged to the Patriots for the last eleven seasons and for the first time in what feels like forever, it's open for competition again.

SCHEDULE

Week 1: Vs. Dolphins
Week 2: @ Seahawks *(SNF)*
Week 3: Vs. Raiders
Week 4: @ Chiefs
Week 5: Vs. Broncos
Week 6: BYE
Week 7: Vs. 49ers
Week 8: @ Bills
Week 9: @ Jets *(MNF)*
Week 10: Vs. Ravens *(SNF)*
Week 11: @ Texans
Week 12: Vs. Cardinals
Week 13: @ Chargers
Week 14: @ Rams *(TNF)*
Week 15: @ Dolphins
Week 16: Vs. Bills *(MNF)*
Week 17: Vs. Jets

2020 NFL DRAFT CLASS

Round 2
Kyle Dugger, S,
Lenoir-Rhyne
Josh Uche, LB,
Michigan
Round 3
Anfernee Jennings, LB,
Alabama
Devin Asiasi, TE,
UCLA
Dalton Keene, TE,
Virginia Tech
Round 5
Justin Rohrwasser, K,
Marshall
Round 6
Michael Onwenu, IOL,
Michigan
Justin Herron, OT,
Wake Forest
Cassh Maluia, LB,
Wyoming
Round 7
Dustin Woodard, IOL,
Memphis

SIGNINGS

Beau Allen, DT
Damiere Byrd, WR
Brian Hoyer, QB

FRANCHISE TAG

Joe Thuney, OG

NO LONGER ON TEAM

Tom Brady, QB
Phillip Dorsett, WR
Ben Watson, TE (Ret.)
Danny Shelton, DT
Jamie Collins, LB
Kyle van Noy, LB
Stephen Gostkowski, K

TEAM DETAILS:

Owner: Robert Kraft
General Manager: Bill Belichick
Stadium: Gillette Stadium
Head Coach: Bill Belichick
Offensive Coordinator:
Josh McDaniels
Defensive Coordinator:
Bill Belichick
Coaching Staff:
Cameron Achord (ST Coordinator)
Jedd Fisch (QB Coach)
Ivan Fears (RB Coach)
Mick Lombardi (WR Coach)
Nick Caley (TE Coach/FB Coach)
Super Bowl Wins: 6 (2001, 2003, 2004, 2014, 2016, 2018)
Conference Wins: 11 (AFC, 1985, 1996, 2001, 2003, 2004, 2007, 2011, 2014, 2016, 2017, 2018)
Divisional Wins: 21 (AFC East, 1978, 1986, 1996, 1997, 2001, 2003, 2004, 2005, 2006, 2007, 2009-2019)

-2019-
Record: 12-4 (Lost Wildcard Rd)
Offence Rank: Passing (8th), Rushing (18th), Overall (7th)
Defence Rank: Passing (2nd), Rushing (6th), Overall (1st)

KEY PLAYER

Cam Newton: New England's roster was looking a little depleted until they got the bargain of the decade (so far) and signed Cam to a prove it deal. The former MVP oozes star power and gives Bill Belichick a chance to win yet another AFC East Championship. Newton will have veteran Julian Edelman and second year pro, N'Keal Harry as his main targets, but it's the run game that will benefit most from his presence.

Kyle Dugger: Dugger is a fantastic athlete who can lay the boom on any receiver or running back who comes into his vicinity. Dugger will be excellent in run support and could develop into an all around safety as time goes on - However, don't expect this to happen immediately as Dugger is making a huge step up from Lenoir-Rhyne.

ROOKIE SPOTLIGHT

DEPTH CHART

Quarterback	Wide Receiver	Center	Edge	Line Backer	Cornerback
Cam Newton	Julian Edelman	David Andrews	Lawrence Guy	Don't'a Hightower	Stephon Gilmore
Jarrett Stidham	N'Keal Harry	Dustin Woodard [R]	John Simon	Brandon Copeland	Jason McCoutry
Brian Hoyer	Mohamed Sanu	**Tackle**	Deatrich Wise	Shilique Calhoun	Jonathan Jones
Fullback	Damiere Byrd	Isaiah Wynn	Chase Winovich	Ja'Whaun Bentley	JC Jackson
Brandon Bolden	Marquise Lee	Marcus Cannon	**Defensive Tackle**	Josh Uche [R]	Justin Bethel
Running Back	Matthew Slater	Yodny Cajuste	Beau Allen	**Free Safety**	**Strong Safety**
Sony Michel	**Tight End**	**Guard**	Adam Butler	Patrick Chung	Devin McCourty
James White	Matt LaCosse	Joe Thuney	Byron Cowart	Terence Brooks	Adrian Phillips
Damien Harris	Devin Asiasi [R]	Shaquille Mason	**Kicker**	**Punter**	**Long Snapper**
Rex Burkhead	Ryan Izzo	Jermaine Eluemunor	Justin Rohrwasser [R]	Jake Bailey	Joe Cardona

NFL

1

FULL 10 YARDS

NEW ENGLAND PATRIOTS

2019 RANKINGS

Player	Pos	Standard			0.5PPR			PPR		
		Pts	Avg	Rank	Pts	Avg	Rank	Pts	Avg	Rank
Tom Brady	QB	255.8	17.1	QB12						
Sony Michel	RB	127.2	8.5	RB25	133.2	8.9	RB29	139.2	9.3	RB36
James White	RB	120.5	8.6	RB29	155.0	11	RB21	189.5	14	RB20
Julian Edelman	WR	153.7	10.3	WR10	202.2	14	WR7	250.7	17	WR5
N'Keal Harry	WR	23.6	3.9	WR123	28.1	4.7	WR130	32.6	5.4	WR133
Phillip Dorsett	WR	66.8	5.1	WR66	80.8	6.2	WR68	94.8	7.3	WR68
Josh Gordon	WR	47.7	4.3	WR84	61.2	5.6	WR85	74.7	6.8	WR86
Matt LaCosse	TE	19.1	1.7	TE54	25.6	2.3	TE54	32.1	2.9	TE56
New England Patriots	DST	234.0	15.6	DST1						
Stephen Gostkowski	K	33.0	8.3	K36						

CAM NEWTON
ADP 10.10

A fully healthy Cam Newton has the potential to be a fantasy monster, in 2015 he finished as QB1, averaging 24.32ppg. Clearly he hasn't reached those heights again since, but he's a worthy mid round pick up now he's on a team that likes to pound the rock and features play action packages regularly.

SONY MICHEL
ADP 9.11

Michel has struggled to make much of an impact in the Pats' running back committee. With Rex Burkhead, James White and Damien Harris all still on the roster and the addition of a running QB, it's hard to see that changing. Potentially worth a punt as a RB3 in standard format.

JAMES WHITE
ADP 6.12

In standard formats, White is very much in the same boat as Michel. However, in PPR formats White does have value. It's not hard to imagine the Patriots installing several of Newton's Carolina plays and putting White in the Christian McCaffrey role, he's well worth a pick up at his current ADP.

JULIAN EDELMAN
ADP 7.02

It's difficult to see Edelman repeating his PPR WR7 status in 2020. So much of his game in previous years has relied on a good connection with Brady and his dink and dunk approach. However, the Squirrel is by no means an 'avoid', instead he becomes a solid fantasy option with a potentially high weekly floor.

N'KEAL HARRY
ADP 13.11

Harry is still an unknown quantity in New England, an injury drastically curtailed his rookie season and there was little fantasy production there at all. However, history tells us that Newton likes his big bodied outside receivers, Harry fits that bill and is an upside pick at his current ADP.

2020 Projections

Position	Player	Standard		0.5PPR		Full PPR	
		Pts	Rank	Pts	Rank	Pts	Rank
QB	Cam Newton	288.9	16				
RB	Sony Michel	130.3	38	139.3	42	148.3	43
RB	Damien Harris	87.7	58	95.2	59	102.7	60
RB	James White	121.5	43	157.5	33	193.5	25
RB	Rex Burkhead	46.4	76	56.9	75	67.4	74
WR	Julian Edelman	129.7	31	164.2	30	198.7	30
WR	N'Keal Harry	76.9	70	98.9	69	120.9	68
WR	Mohamed Sanu	53.1	93	70.1	90	87.1	90
WR	Jakobi Meyers	32.2	115	42.2	114	52.2	113
TE	Devin Asiasi	66.1	25	86.6	25	107.1	25

ADP taken from Ultimate Draft Kit (PPR)

Projections by Rob Grimwood @FFBritballer

FANTASY FOOTBALL

2

FULL 10 YARDS

NEW ENGLAND PATRIOTS

LAST 5 YEARS

	W	L	T	Div	P/Offs
2019	12	4	0	1st	Lost WC
2018	11	5	0	1st	Won SB
2017	13	3	0	1st	Lost SB
2016	14	2	0	1st	Won SB
2015	12	4	0	1st	Lost Conf

DO SAY..
Bill Belichick is the reason we have 6 rings

DON'T SAY..
Cheat! Cheat! Cheat!

BETTING ODDS BY ADAM WALFORD (@TOUCHDOWNTIPS)

SUPER BOWL **22/1**

AFC CONFERENCE **12/1**

AFC EAST **5/4**

TO MAKE PLAYOFFS
11/20
TEAM TOTAL WINS
8

ADAM'S BEST BET
FINISH 2ND IN AFC EAST
12/5

PLEASE GAMBLE RESPONSIBLY

VIEW FROM THE SIDELINES
By Matt Inkster (@MattInkster)

So many questions to be answered! Cam/Stidham? The O-Line/Run Game? What about our receivers? With the signing of Cam Newton, the Patriots have suddenly gone from being written off to a playoff team almost overnight. I like Jarrett Stidham & he has the potential to be the face of the franchise, just like Jimmy Garappolo is now in the Bay Area but when the chance of a former MVP arises on the cheap, you have to take it. Cam Newton helps but he's unfortunately not the be all and end all. The Patriots still have to find ways to curb running backs from gaining 100 plus yards in a game. Isaiah Wynn hopefully has a clean bill of health and produces what is expected of him. Sony Michel has to become more dynamic & needs a bounce back year that improves running game. Bill & Josh may still be there but this is the dawn of a new era and I for one will be sitting waiting in the dark for the sun to rise.

▶RETRO FOCUS◀
MOSES TATUPU – FB

When you reach a Super Bowl for the first time there are often some unsung heroes on the roster, and that is the case with FB Moses Tatupu. He helped the Patriots reach their first ever Super Bowl by blocking for Tony Collins & taking a fair few handoffs himself. Tatupu spent 14 seasons in New England, grinding out over 2,400 yards on the ground, earning a Pro Bowl berth (1986) in an underrated career. His son, Lofa, played LB for the Seahawks.

DID YOU KNOW

Allegedly, Vladimir Putin pocketed a Super Bowl ring that Pats owner Robert Kraft let him look at. Kraft later said it was a gift and Putin cannot recall the event.

KEY STAT

"Brick Wall"
In 2019, the Patriots defense allowed a stingy 14.1 points per game on average.

FULL10YARDS VERDICT

You should never under-estimate Bill Belichick's Patriots but without Brady & Gronk, there are doubts about their offence in particular. Will new QB Cam Newton cut the mustard, and do the WR trio of Edelman, Harry & Sanu give him enough to work with? After 3 successive Super Bowl appearances in 2016–18, you write the ever-reliable Pats off at your peril, even though they've been weakened by several COVID-19 opt-outs, including Patrick Chung & Dont'a Hightower. The division may go down to the wire but if they don't pip the Bills, the Patriots make the playoffs as usual.

BETTING, STATS, FANS VIEW, RETRO

3

FULL 10 YARDS

NEW YORK JETS

THE LOWDOWN:

The New York Jets suffered perhaps the most disappointing off season of any. With the trade of Jamal Adams to the Seahawks and C.J Mosely opting out for the season, the Jets defense has been left with little to no star power or true leadership. Offensively, this will be a big year for Sam Darnold as he enters his third year. He will benefit from a bit more protection on his offensive line after the addition of Mekhi Becton in the draft. Head Coach Adam Gase will definitely be on the hot seat all season as results need to start improving.

SCHEDULE

Week 1: @ Bills
Week 2: Vs. 49ers
Week 3: @ Colts
Week 4: Vs. Broncos (TNF)
Week 5: Vs. Cardinals
Week 6: @ Chargers
Week 7: Vs. Bills
Week 8: @ Chiefs
Week 9: Vs. Patriots (MNF)
Week 10: @ Dolphins
Week 11: BYE
Week 12: Vs. Dolphins
Week 13: Vs. Raiders
Week 14: @ Seahawks
Week 15: @ Rams
Week 16: Vs. Browns
Week 17: @ Patriots

2020 NFL DRAFT CLASS

Round 1
Mekhi Becton, OT,
Louisville
Round 2
Denzel Mims, WR,
Baylor
Round 3
Ashtyn Davis, S,
California
Jabari Zuniga, EDGE,
Florida
Round 4
Lamichal Perine, RB,
Florida
James Morgan, QB,
Florida International
Cameron Clark, OT,
Charlotte
Round 5
Bryce Hall, CB,
Virginia
Round 6
Braden Mann, P,
Texas A&M

SIGNINGS

Pierre Desir, CB:
Joe Flacco, QB:
Frank Gore, RB:
Jordan Jenkins, DE
Connor McGovern, C
Breshad Perriman, WR

STAR SIGNING

George Fant, T

NO LONGER ON TEAM

Trevor Siemian, QB
Robby Anderson, WR
Demaryius Thomas, WR
Ryan Kalil, OL
Kelvin Beachum, OL
Brandon Copeland, LB
Darryl Roberts, CB
Maurice Canady, CB

TEAM DETAILS:

Owner: Woody & Chris Johnson
General Manager: Joe Douglas
Stadium: MetLife Stadium
Head Coach: Adam Gase
Location: East Rutherford, NJ
Offensive Coordinator:
Dowell Loggains
Defensive Coordinator:
Gregg Williams
Coaching Staff:
Dowell Loggains (QB Coach)
Brant Boyer (ST Coordinator)
Shawn Jefferson (Assistant HC/WR Coach)
Frank Bush (Assistant HC/LB Coach),
Jim Bob Cooter (RB Coach)
John Dunn (TE Coach)
Super Bowl Wins: 1 (1968)
Conference Wins: 0 (1 AFL Championship in 1968)
Divisional Wins: 4 (AFL East, 1968, 1969; AFC East, 1998, 2002)

-2019-
Record: 7-9
Offence Rank: Passing (29th), Rushing (31st), Overall (31st)
Defence Rank: Passing (17th), Rushing (2nd), Overall (16th)

KEY PLAYER

Sam Darnold: With Jamal Adams now in Seattle and CJ Mosley sitting out for the season, it falls to 3rd year QB, Sam Darnold, to take on an even bigger leadership role. Darnold has had his struggles so far, but for all of Adam Gase's faults, he clearly has faith that the former first rounder can fulfil his potential. An improved offensive line could make all the difference this season.

Mekhi Becton: This athletic ability that Mekhi Becton has for a man of his size is outrageous. A man of his dimensions should not be as quick and light on his feet and it goes without saying that he is an unbelievably powerful young man. If he develops and hits his ceiling, he could be one of the best tackles in the NFL in a few years.

ROOKIE SPOTLIGHT

DEPTH CHART

Quarterback	Wide Receiver	Center	Edge	Line Backer	Cornerback
Sam Darnold	Jamison Crowder	Connor McGovern	Quinnen Williams	CJ Mosley	Pierre Desir
Joe Flacco	Denzel Mims	Jonotthan Harrison	Henry Anderson	Blake Cashman	Arthur Maulet
David Fales	Breshad Perriman	**Tackle**	Harvi Langi	James Burgess	Brian Poole
Fullback	Josh Doctson	Mekhi Becton [R]	Frankie Luvu	Avery Williamson	Nate Hariston
Trevon Wesco	Josh Malone	Chuma Edoga	**Defensive Tackle**	Patrick Onwuasor	Quincy Wilson
Running Back	Brexton Berrios	George Fant	Steve McLendon	**Free Safety**	**Strong Safety**
Le'Veon Bell	**Tight End**	**Guard**	Folorunso Fatukasi	Marcus Maye	Jamal Adams
Frank Gore	Chris Herndon	Alex Lewis	Dominique Davis [R]	Ashtyn Davis	Matthias Farley
Trenton Cannon	Ryan Griffin	Brian Winters	**Kicker**	**Punter**	**Long Snapper**
Lamical Perine	Daniel Brown	Cameron Clark [R]	Sam Ficken	Braden Mann [R]	Thomas Hennessey

NFL

1

FULL 10 YARDS

NEW YORK JETS

2019 RANKINGS

Player	Pos	Standard			0.5PPR			PPR		
		Pts	Avg	Rank	Pts	Avg	Rank	Pts	Avg	Rank
Sam Darnold	QB	191.3	15.9	QB27						
Le'Veon Bell	RB	141.3	10.1	RB21	171.8	12	RB19	202.3	15	RB15
Bilal Powell	RB	23.5	1.8	RB85	27.0	2.1	RB86	30.5	2.4	RB87
Ty Montgomery	WR	19.3	1.3	RB91	25.8	1.7	RB88	32.3	2.2	RB84
Jamison Crowder	WR	107.1	7.1	WR38	142.1	9.5	WR33	177.1	12	WR32
Robby Anderson	WR	108.5	7.2	WR36	133.0	8.9	WR38	157.5	11	WR38
Demaryius Thomas	WR	49.3	4.5	WR83	67.3	6.1	WR83	85.3	7.8	WR79
Ryan Griffin	TE	64.0	4.9	TE20	81.0	6.2	TE20	98.0	7.5	TE21
New York Jets	DST	123.0	8.2	DST9						
Sam Ficken	K	85.0	6.1	K26						

SAM DARNOLD

Darnold has had some up weeks and a lot of down weeks since coming into the league, and that's reflected in his fantasy value. He averaged 15.5ppg last season, and whilst that isn't terrible for superflex leagues, you don't want to be relying on him as your QB1 this season.

ADP 19.1

ADP 3.04

Bell's fantasy value has fallen off a cliff since leaving the Steelers. Not a lot is set to change this year as the Jets look like a team that is collecting draft capital for 2021. That's not to say Bell isn't worth a pick up as your RB2, we know he has immense talent and his pass catching is valuable for PPR leagues.

LEVEON BELL

JAMISON CROWDER

Possibly the best fantasy pickup from the Jets in redraft leagues, Crowder is shaping up to be a target hog and PPR steal. Last season saw him rack up 122 targets from which he contributed 833 yards and 6 TDs. When you come to mid-round fliers, Crowder is well worth a pick up.

ADP 10.1

ADP 16.9

Mims enters the league as an intriguing prospect, a quick and powerful player who could be the long term solution at WR for the Jets. Fantasy-wise it's possible Mims has a Terry McLaurin style impact this year, but it's more likely that he is a bit part player whilst others take the targets of Robby Anderson.

DENZEL MIMS

BRESHAD PERRIMAN

There has been a lot of positivity around Brashad Perriman following a 2019 season in which he was fantasy relevant for more than a few weeks. In 2020 he figures to step in Robby Anderson's shoes and is a sneaky upside pick in rounds 10+ of your redraft leagues.

ADP 14.4

2020 Projections

Position	Player	Standard		0.5PPR		Full PPR	
		Pts	Rank	Pts	Rank	Pts	Rank
QB	Sam Darnold	223.8	32				
RB	Le'Veon Bell	199.0	13	233.5	9	268.0	9
RB	Frank Gore	45.2	77	49.2	79	53.2	82
RB	Lamical Perine	30.4	89	35.9	86	41.4	87
WR	Denzel Mims	76.6	72	96.6	73	116.6	72
WR	Breshad Perriman	92.2	57	110.2	60	128.2	63
WR	Jamison Crowder	115.3	40	151.3	38	187.3	34
TE	Chris Herndon	80.5	18	103.5	18	126.5	18
TE	Ryan Griffin	46.7	37	62.2	35	77.7	35

ADP taken from Ultimate Draft Kit (PPR)

Projections by Rob Grimwood @FFBritballer

FANTASY FOOTBALL

2

FULL 10 YARDS

NEW YORK JETS

LAST 5 YEARS

	W	L	T	Div	P/Offs
2019	7	9	0	3rd	
2018	4	12	0	4th	
2017	5	11	0	4th	
2016	5	11	0	4th	
2015	10	6	0	2nd	

DO SAY..
The 2020 draft isn't that far away...

DON'T SAY..
Butt-Fumble

BETTING ODDS
BY ADAM WALFORD (@TOUCHDOWNTIPS)

SUPER BOWL **80/1**

AFC CONFERENCE **50/1**

AFC EAST **12/1**

TO MAKE PLAYOFFS
9/2
TEAM TOTAL WINS
6.5

ADAM'S BEST BET
FINISH 4TH IN AFC EAST
11/8

PLEASE GAMBLE RESPONSIBLY

VIEW FROM THE SIDELINES
By Thomas Winrow (@downthemannyrd)

2020 looks set to be the beginning of another rebuilding project for the Jets. The expected departure of All-Pro safety Jamal Adams came in July. GM Joe Douglas amassed a haul of draft capital in return & has 4 first round picks in the 2021 & 2022 drafts. He aced the last one, addressing some glaring needs. Mekhi Becton has the potential to become a fearsome left tackle, and Denzel Mims was a Day Two steal. Le'Veon Bell and C.J. Mosley will provide some much needed leadership in Adams' absence. There's one remaining problem for Gang Green: Adam Gase. Combine one of the toughest schedules in the NFL with Gase's turgid play-calling & the Jets are on course for a 5th consecutive losing season.

>RETRO FOCUS<
WAYNE CHREBET – WR
Sometimes players become cult heroes in their NFL city, and the diminutive WR Wayne Chrebet was one such example. 580 catches, in an 11 year career in the Big Apple, puts Chrebet in the top 100 all-time pass catchers in NFL history. The 5ft 10inch WR only had one 1,000 yard season (1998), but he was a fan favourite, running kamikaze routes as a slot receiver and 3rd down favourite for quarterbacks such as Vinny Testaverde.

DID YOU KNOW
When Bill Parcells resigned in 2000, Bill Belichick was promoted to the Jets' HC job but quit after just one day. He's done OK since.

KEY STAT
"Rotten to the score"
The Jets ranked dead last in % of drives that ended with points, with only 23% drives leading to the scoreboard changing in 2019.

FULL10YARDS VERDICT
Under HC Adam Gase, it's hard to see New York matching last year's 7-9. Despite winning six of their last eight and young QB Sam Darnold making steady, if not stellar, progress, the Jets still had the league's worst offence. In response, Gang Green revamped their O-line, top draft pick Mekhi Becton included, while fellow rookie Denzel Mims comes in for Robby Anderson at wide receiver. At the end of July, safety Jamal Adams also shipped out of their already-suspect secondary while linebacker CJ Mosley has now opted out. Don't hold your breath, Jets fans.

BETTING, STATS, FANS VIEW, RETRO

3

FULL 10 YARDS

FULL10YARDS INTERVIEW
NAT COOMBS

With the lack of preseason, do you feel that the build-up of excitement to the new season will be a bit different this year?

It's an interesting point, and one that's accentuated right now by listening and watching the US coverage in August. I've never been a huge fan of pre-season games in terms of the game time action, but I do love the narratives that spin off from them: how did Rookie QB "X" look? How's the QB battle progressing? Who's this fringe player blowing up and winning a roster spot etc.
None of that is happening in the way that it normally does this year, although I wonder if that's specifically blunting any excitement, or rather that it's the unorthodox pre-season in totality, the spectre of Covid-19 looming large in so many parts of the US, and the doubt that the season will start on time.

Do you think the rookies coming into the league are at a bigger disadvantage because of the global pandemic?

Absolutely. I was talking with J-Bell on my ESPN podcast about this and he was explaining that there are plenty of players who are smart, football literate and attentive in team meetings/looking at film, but no amount of theory can prepare them, and they need to be experiencing things on the field in real time.
There's also the underestimated environmental aspect, for rookies and indeed for those vets new to a franchise. Settling in, building bonds with team-mates, getting bearings. NFL is a league of habit, of routine, and that's been turned on its head.

How do you think the veterans will be affected by the Coronavirus, especially those that have switched teams?

Logic suggests going to be a significant disadvantage, or to look at it another way, those teams bringing back majority of starters with continuity in coaching roles clearly have an edge. Although am not sure the adjustment will be as acute for veterans' rookies. Tom Brady is one of the more fascinating examples. A new offense to learn, new receivers to be on the same page with – a simpatico that Brady places particular significance on. Will the most successful QB to ever play the game – one of the most driven players of all time, who reacts with fire when faced with a challenge – acclimatise, adjust and adapt? It'll be so interesting to see.

Do you think that the teams with bigger home-field advantages will struggle a bit more to get going and will it be a bit more of a level playing field?

You talk to players and there's no doubt that many feed off the energy of the crowd – and in a place like Seattle, or New Orleans, the absence of noise will benefit the road team's offense for sure. That said, homefield advantage extends beyond the game itself – travel for example is still going to disadvantage the road team, particularly a coast to coast trip.

Do you think that this season's playoff teams will be dictated by those that have had more or less disruption due to the pandemic? Could we see a few teams that are less talented in the playoffs purely because some teams stayed more "Covid-free" than those that are perhaps more talented but affected more by the virus?

Almost certainly yes. We're seeing this already in other sports that have (re) started since Covid-19 appeared. Strength in depth of the roster, always of fundamental importance, will increase in significance. Luck always plays a part in a season with regards to injury/illness and even more so this year. In terms of opt outs, no team has been hit more than the Patriots, particularly with Chung and Hightower, leaders in the locker room, choosing to miss the season.

FULL10YARDS INTERVIEW
NAT COOMBS

At what point do you think we'll see fans in stadiums and how will the NFL transition back into having spectators?

I'd be amazed if any games this year carried spectators, and I wonder if it'll be an all or nothing approach, rather than phased. The expanse of America does allow variability here, but does if one team is able to welcome fans because of the Covid situation in that particular, does that load the deck unfairly?

Do you think it was the right decision to cancel the International Series this year? Is there any lasting affect it will leave on games in the UK/rest of the world?

Absolutely the right decision, disappointing as it is. We can't tell at this stage the short-term effect beyond the 2020 season until the pandemic is under control, but even if the 2021 games have to be cancelled, it doesn't affect the long-term prognosis. The NFL is set on international expansion, it's working, so this is a delay, a roadblock, not anything more.

You are of course an avid Dolphins fan, what do you think are the expectations from the coaching staff this year?

Anything that's a tangible improvement on last year collectively, certainly an advancement on record, even if ultimately the team still goes under .500, will be deemed enough progress. Talk of the East being easier than in many years is probably fair given the Pats decline, although I think that's being overstated, and the Jets are perhaps not as shambolic as people suggest. The Bills, tougher record, but they're stronger year on year so will contend. The way that Flores and his staff kept the team competitive most of the time was the most encouraging aspect, and so a regression in that respect would be a concern.

How do you see the Quarterback battle between Ryan Fitzpatrick and Tua Tagovailoa working out?

I think Tua's got a perfect environment to come into. Not expected to start week one, could conceivably sit for much of the season, learning from a seasoned pro who knows the succession plan is written. Not dissimilar to Mahomes and Alex Smith in Kansas City.

Are there any particular new faces that you've brought in this offseason you are looking forward to seeing in a Dolphins' jersey?

I like the upside of Matt Breida & Jordan Howard, given how anaemic the run game was last year. Byron Jones is a proven top-level player and adding vets with a winning mentality like Kyle Van Noy is needed in a young roster at a team that hasn't succeeded for a long time

BALTIMORE RAVENS

THE LOWDOWN:

Lamar magic swept through the NFL last season as the Ravens put up all time offensive records. With his ground-breaking style of play and Houdini-like escape ability, the Ravens star QB was the unanimous League MVP at the age of just 23. Baltimore have a strong defense and having added Calais Campbell and Derek Wolfe to the defensive line, along with the addition of a couple of play-makers on offense through the draft, Baltimore will no doubt be contenders again this season. The AFC North has some great defenses & fans are in for a treat this season.

SCHEDULE

Week 1: Vs. Browns
Week 2: @ Texans
Week 3: Vs. Chiefs *(MNF)*
Week 4: @ Washington
Week 5: Vs. Bengals
Week 6: @ Eagles
Week 7: Vs. Steelers
Week 8: BYE
Week 9: @ Colts
Week 10: @ Patriots (SNF)
Week 11: Vs. Titans
Week 12: @ Steelers (Thanksgiving)
Week 13: Vs. Cowboys (TNF)
Week 14: @ Browns (MNF)
Week 15: Vs. Jaguars
Week 16: Vs. Giants
Week 17: @ Bengals

2020 NFL DRAFT CLASS

Round 1
Patrick Queen, LB,
LSU
Round 2
J.K. Dobbins, RB,
Ohio State
Round 3
Justin Madubuike, IDL,
Texas A&M
Devin Duvernay, WR,
Texas
Malik Harrison, LB,
Ohio State
Tyre Phillips, IOL,
Mississippi State
Round 4
Ben Bredeson, IOL,
Michigan
Round 5
Broderick Washington Jr., IDL,
Texas Tech
Round 6
James Proche, WR,
SMU
Round 7
Geno Stone, S,
Iowa

SIGNINGS

Calais Campbell, DE
D.J. Fluker, OG
Derek Wolfe, DL
Jimmy Smith, CB

FRANCHISE TAG

Matt Judon, DE

NO LONGER ON TEAM

Hayden Hurst, TE
Marshal Yanda, OL (Ret.)
Chris Wormley, DT
Michael Pierce, DT
Brandon Carr, CB
Tony Jefferson, S

TEAM DETAILS:

Owner: Steve Bisciotti
General Manager: Eric DeCosta
Stadium: M&T Bank Stadium
Location: Baltimore, Maryland
Head Coach: John Harbaugh
Offensive Coordinator: Greg Roman
Defensive Coordinator: Don Martindale
Coaching Staff:
David Culley (Assistant HC, also Pass Coordinator & WR Coach)
James Urban (QB Coach);
Matt Weiss (RB Coach);
Bobby Engram (TE Coach)
Chris Horton (ST Coordinator)
Super Bowl Wins:
2 (AFC, 2000, 2012)
Conference Wins:
2 (AFC, 2000, 2012)
Divisional Wins:
6 (AFC North 2003, 2006, 2011, 2012, 2018, 2019)
-2019-
Record: 14-2 (Lost Divisional Rd)
Offence Rank: Passing (27th), Rushing (1st), Overall (1st)
Defence Rank: Passing (6th), Rushing (5th),Overall (3rd)

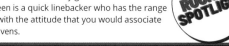

KEY PLAYER

Lamar Jackson: The Ravens have a stacked roster, but it's hard to look past their MVP Quarterback as their key player. Jackson was electric last year, both in the passing and rushing game, driving Baltimore to 14 regular season wins. The Ravens only lost backup Tight End Hayden Hurst in the off-season, meaning there's no reason to suspect Jackson can't repeat his heroics in 2020.

Patrick Queen: There are some players who just fit the team they get drafted to - Patrick Queen does that with the Baltimore Ravens. Queen is a quick linebacker who has the range to clean up from sideline to sideline and plays with the attitude that you would associate with the Ravens.

ROOKIE SPOTLIGHT

DEPTH CHART

Quarterback	Wide Receiver	Center	Edge	Line Backer	Cornerback
Lamar Jackson	Marquise Brown	Matt Skura	Calais Campbell	Matt Judon	Marcus Peters
Robert Griffin III	Miles Boykin	Patrick Mekari	Pernell McPhee	Patrick Queen [R]	Marlon Humphrey
Trace McSorley	Willie Snead	**Tackle**	Patrick Ricard	Malik Harrison [R]	Jimmy Smith
Fullback	Chris Moore	Ronnie Stanley	Jaylon Ferguson	Tyus Bowser	Tavon Young
Patrick Ricard	Devin Duvernay [R]	Orlando Brown	**Defensive Tackle**	Chris Board	Anthony Averett
Running Back	Jaleel Scott	Andre Smith	Derek Wolfe	**Free Safety**	**Strong Safety**
Mark Ingram	**Tight End**	**Guard**	Brandon Williams		Chuck Clark
JK Dobbins	Mark Andrews	Ben Powers	Justin Madubuike [R]	DeShon Elliott	Jordan Richards
Gus Edwards	Nick Boyle	Bradley Bozeman	**Kicker**	**Punter**	**Long Snapper**
Justice Hill	Charles Scarff	DJ Fluker	Justin Tucker	Sam Koch	Morgan Cox

NFL

1

FULL 10 YARDS

2019 RANKINGS

Player	Pos	Standard			0.5PPR			PPR		
		Pts	Avg	Rank	Pts	Avg	Rank	Pts	Avg	Rank
Lamar Jackson	QB	421.7	28.1	QB1						
Mark Ingram II	RB	216.5	14.4	RB6	229.5	15	RB8	242.5	16	RB9
Gus Edwards	RB	74.4	5.0	RB45	77.4	5.2	RB50	80.4	5.4	RB54
Marquise Brown	WR	98.9	7.6	WR41	120.9	9.3	WR44	142.9	11	WR44
Willie Snead	WR	61.9	4.1	WR69	75.9	5.1	WR72	89.9	6	WR75
Miles Boykin	WR	37.8	2.5	WR95	44.3	3	WR99	50.8	3.4	WR106
Mark Andrews	TE	143.2	9.6	TE2	175.2	12	TE2	207.2	14	TE3
Hayden Hurst	TE	43.4	2.9	TE37	57.4	3.8	TE37	71.4	4.8	TE36
Baltimore Ravens	DST	136.0	9.1	DST5						
Justin Tucker	K	136.0	9.1	K4						

LAMAR JACKSON

Many will have rose tinted glasses from 2019 when Lamar Jackson was a late round darling, helping you storm to your Fantasy title wins. He'll be vying for your selections as the QB1 off the boards with Mahomes in the early rounds of your drafts. With his rushing floor & a strong arm he's versatile & can be the top point scorer this season.

ADP 2.09

MARK INGRAM

ADP 4.11

Ingram remains as the lead back but he will have to watch out as the RB room is getting more crowded with talent. You get the sense it's a transition season to allow the new wave to take over but last season the Ravens struggled when Ingram was out of the lineup so he will hope to have another run before the wheels start falling off.

J.K DOBBINS

That new wave coming through is headed by Dobbins who is the clear heir apparent for Ingram. For this season it's easy to envisage them being a solid 1-2 punch tandem operation but if either goes down injured the other can pick up the slack. Long term, Dobbins is in a fantastic place with huge prospects, but if you're in a redraft league, don't go too early while Ingram is still there.

ADP 6.12

MARQUISE BROWN

ADP 6.05

"Hollywood" played a starring role in the Ravens run last season and is the clear WR1 for the team. With an average of 12.7 yards per catch and 7 Touchdowns, the cousin of Antonio Brown was one of the focal points. With Miles Boykin, Willie Snead and rookie Devin Duvernay providing backup a lot of attention will be on Brown and Mark Andrews in the passing game.

MARK ANDREWS

Andrews had a monster 2019 season. The 2nd of 2 Tight Ends drafted in that 2018 draft (after Hayden Hurst) he's turned into a top tier Tight End and a top 2 receiving option for the Ravens. With 852 yards and 10TDs last season, he's progressed as a receiving threat and red zone target and will be in many peoples top 5 Tight Ends which puts a premium on his draft price.

ADP 4.08

2020 Projections

Position	Player	Standard		0.5PPR		Full PPR	
		Pts	Rank	Pts	Rank	Pts	Rank
QB	Lamar Jackson	402.3	1				
RB	Mark Ingram	151.6	27	161.6	30	171.6	35
RB	J.K Dobbins	159.9	26	175.9	25	191.9	27
RB	Justice Hill	56.0	68	61.5	71	67.0	75
RB	Gus Edwards	50.8	73	52.8	78	54.8	80
WR	Marquise Brown	134.2	27	166.7	29	199.2	29
WR	Willie Snead	40.4	109	53.4	107	66.4	107
WR	Miles Boykin	90.9	59	110.9	58	130.9	60
WR	Devin Duvernay	59.2	83	74.2	84	89.2	87
TE	Mark Andrews	129.8	3	163.3	4	196.8	4
TE	Nick Boyle	18.4	54	29.4	53	40.4	53

ADP taken from Ultimate Draft Kit (PPR)

Projections by Rob Grimwood @FFBritballer

FANTASY FOOTBALL

2

FULL 10 YARDS

BALTIMORE RAVENS

LAST 5 YEARS

	W	L	T	Div	P/Offs
2019	14	2	0	1st	Lost Div
2018	10	6	0	1st	Lost WC
2017	9	7	0	2nd	
2016	8	8	0	2nd	
2015	5	11	0	3rd	

DO SAY..
Lamar Jackson is the future of the game

DON'T SAY..
Lamar Jackson's playoff record

BETTING ODDS BY ADAM WALFORD (@TOUCHDOWNTIPS)

SUPER BOWL **8/1**

AFC CONFERENCE **7/2**

AFC NORTH **1/2**

TO MAKE PLAYOFFS **1/9**

TEAM TOTAL WINS **11**

ADAM'S BEST BET
TO WIN AFC NORTH **1/2**

PLEASE GAMBLE RESPONSIBLY

VIEW FROM THE SIDELINES
By Louis Hobbs (@ReportRavens)

I think that the Ravens undoubtedly had one of the best off seasons in the NFL, including yet another excellent draft. Our main area of concern that term was our defensive line, which has been beefed up with the additions of Calais Campbell and Derek Wolfe, who will both improve our pass rush. Moreover, I really like the look of rookie WR's Devin Duvernay and James Proche, and think they will take a lot of pressure of Lamar Jackson with their fantastic hands. Not to mention, J.K Dobbins is going to make our rushing game even more terrifying. I'd be very disappointed if we didn't at least win the AFC North& see Lamar get his first playoff win. But, building on such an impressive regular season last term, my eyes are firmly set on that Lombardi Trophy.

▶RETRO FOCUS◀
JERMAINE LEWIS – WR

A fifth round pick in 1996, Jermaine Lewis was an outstanding returner in his six seasons with the Ravens. A first team All-Pro in 1998, it was an 84 yard kickoff return in the 2nd half of Super Bowl XXXV against the Giants that was the game breaker. Lewis ranks 8th all-time for punt return yardage (3,282) & his six punt returns touchdowns rank 6th in NFL history. Lewis was selected 6th overall by the Texans in the 2002 expansion draft.

DID YOU KNOW

The team name was inspired by Edgar Allan Poe's poem "The Raven", and their mascot is a raven called Poe.

KEY STAT

"Not Bad for a Running Back"

Last season Lamar Jackson set the NFL record for QBs with 1,206 yards on the ground. That accounted for 15.6 percent of the 7,698 yards quarterbacks rushed for in 2019.

FULL10YARDS VERDICT

With MVP Lamar Jackson, who's gone 19-3 in his regular season starts, a(nother) 1,000-yard running back, a revamped defensive line & a top-class secondary, it's hard to see the Ravens not retaining the AFC North title. They've made the playoffs in back-to-back years but have only one postseason win since their 2012 championship triumph. Ultimately, for Baltimore to wrestle the Lombardi trophy out of Kansas's hands, Jackson will need to improve on his 0-2 postseason record. I'll stick my neck out and say they'll reach the end game this time.

BETTING, STATS, FANS VIEW, RETRO

3

FULL 10 YARDS

CINCINNATI BENGALS

THE LOWDOWN:

After a 2-14 finish last season, the Bengals were awarded the 1st overall pick in the 2020 draft. With this selection they selected Heisman Trophy winner & College Football National Champion Joe Burrow from LSU. Securing their future franchise QB was essential after the departure of their long-time servant Andy Dalton. The Bengals also spent some cash in free agency which was an unusual move for the team. They bolstered their defence with additions such as D.J Reader, Mackensie Alexander & Vonn Bell while also beefing up their offensive line with the signing of Xavier Su'a–Filo. With a Rookie QB & a rebuilt roster, The Bengals and Zac Taylor need to hit the ground running.

SCHEDULE

Week 1: Vs LAC
Week 2: @ CLE (TNF)
Week 3: @ PHI
Week 4: Vs. JAX
Week 5: @ BAL
Week 6: @ IND
Week 7: Vs CLE
Week 8: Vs. TEN
Week 9: BYE
Week 10: @ PIT
Week 11: @ WAS
Week 12: Vs. NYG
Week 13: @ MIA
Week 14: Vs. DAL
Week 15: Vs. PIT (MNF)
Week 16: @ HOU
Week 17: Vs BAL

2020 NFL DRAFT CLASS

Round 1
Joe Burrow, QB,
LSU
Round 2
Tee Higgins, WR,
Clemson
Round 3
Logan Wilson, LB,
Wyoming
Round 4
Akeem Davis-Gaither, LB,
Appalachian State
Round 5
Khalid Kareem, EDGE,
Notre Dame
Round 6
Hakeem Adeniji, OT,
Kansas
Round 7
Markus Bailey, LB,
Purdue

SIGNINGS

Mackensie Alexander, CB
Vonn Bell, S
D.J. Reader, DT
Trae Waynes, CB
Xavier Su'a-Filo, OG

FRANCHISE TAG

A.J. Green, WR

NO LONGER ON TEAM

Andy Dalton, QB
Tyler Eifert, TE
Cordy Glenn, OL
Andrew Billings, DT
Darqueze Dennard, CB
Dre Kirkpatrick, CB

TEAM DETAILS:

Owner: Mike Brown
General Manager: Mike Brown
Play at: Paul Brown Stadium
Location: Cincinnati, OH
Head Coach: Zac Taylor
Offensive Coordinator: Brian Callahan
Defensive Coordinator: Lou Anarumo
Coaching Staff:
Darrin Simmons (Assistant HC, ST Coordinator);
Dan Pitcher (QB Coach);
Jemal Singleton (RB Coach);
Bob Bicknell (WR Coach);
James Casey (TE Coach)
Super Bowl Wins: 0
Conference Wins: 2 (AFC, 1981, 1988)
Divisional Wins: 9 (AFC Central, 1970, 1973, 1981, 1988, 1990; AFC North, 2005, 2009, 2013, 2015)

-2019-
Record: : 2-14
Offence Rank: Passing (19th), Rushing (25th), Overall (30th)
Defence Rank: Passing (21st), Rushing (32nd), Overall (25th)

KEY PLAYER

Joe Mixon: In addition to "Smokin' Joe" with the 1st overall pick, there's already an elite player named Joe on the Bengals roster - running back, Joe Mixon. Despite the Bengals' woeful record last season, Mixon still rushed for 1137 yards & 5 TDs. With an improved offensive line, and a rookie under center, it makes sense that Mixon will be the focal point of Zac Taylor's plans.

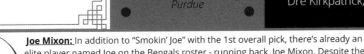

Joe Burrow: As a QB who just went 1st overall, the spotlight is going to be on Joe Burrow more than any other rookie in the class. Fortunately for Joe Burrow, everything just seems to be under control and he's just authored one of the all time college football seasons (5,671 passing yards, 60 TDs with a 76.3 completion %. Be excited Bengals fans!

ROOKIE SPOTLIGHT

DEPTH CHART

Quarterback	Wide Receiver	Center	Edge Rusher	Line Backer	Cornerback
Joe Burrow [R]	AJ Green	Trey Hopkins	Carlos Dunlap	Jordan Evans	William Jackson III
Ryan Finley	Tyler Boyd	Billy Price	Sam Hubbard	Germaine Pratt	Mackensie Alexander
Jacob Dolegala	Tee Higgins [R]	**Tackle**	Andrew Brown	Josh Bynes	Trae Waynes
Fullback	John Ross III	Jonah Williams	Carl Lawson	Logan Wilson [R]	Greg Mabin
N/A	Auden Tate	Bobby Hart	**Defensive Tackle**	Akeem Davis-Gaither [R]	Torry McTyer
Running Back	Alex Erickson	Fred Johnson	Geno Atkins	**Free Safety**	**Strong Safety**
Joe Mixon	**Tight End**	**Guard**	DJ Reader	Jessie Bates	Shawn Williams
Gio Bernard	CJ Uzomah	Michael Jordan	Josh Tupou	Vonn Bell	Trayvon Henderson
Trayveon Williams	Drew Sample	Xavier Su'a-Filo	**Kicker**	**Punter**	**Long Snapper**
Rodney Anderson	Cethan Carter	O'Shea Dugas	Randy Bullock	Kevin Huber	Clark Harris

NFL

1

FULL 10 YARDS

CINCINNATI BENGALS

2019 RANKINGS

Player	Pos	Standard			0.5PPR			PPR		
		Pts	Avg	Rank	Pts	Avg	Rank	Pts	Avg	Rank
Andy Dalton	QB	198.9	16.6	QB26						
Joe Mixon	RB	160.8	10.7	RB15	177.8	11.9	RB16	194.8	13	RB17
Giovani Bernard	RB	38	2.5	RB72	53	3.5	RB64	68	4.5	RB60
Tyler Boyd	WR	127	8.5	WR25	169.5	11.3	WR22	212	14.1	WR21
Auden Tate	WR	61.5	4.7	WR71	81.5	6.3	WR67	101.5	7.8	WR66
Alex Erickson	WR	51.1	3.4	WR81	72.1	4.8	WR76	93.1	6.2	WR70
John Ross	WR	63	9	WR67	76	10.9	WR70	89	12.7	WR76
C.J. Uzomah	TE	27.7	1.9	TE45	38.7	2.6	TE45	49.7	3.3	TE44
Cincinnati Bengals	DST	49	3.3	DST31	49	3.3	DST31	49	3.3	DST31
Randy Bullock	K	106	7.1	K18	106	7.1	K18	106	7.1	K18

JOE BURROW
ADP 13.1

After breaking records left, right & centre with LSU in his final collegiate year, Burrow finds himself in a decent offence with arguably one of the best sets of weapons in the NFL. Because of this, he'll be a fairly hot commodity & you should see him finish as a high QB2 right off the bat.

JOE MIXON
ADP 1.12

Joe Mixon has put together stellar fantasy years (though has missed games) & been decent value. It may be hard to find the same value but you'll get a running back in the late 1st round with the potential to be THE top RB overall. He's hoping for the best O-line he's ever had & a step forward in year 2 of Zac Taylor's scheme.

A.J. GREEN
ADP 6.03

Many people will question AJ Green's health, whilst some will point to motivation. But when on the field, AJ Green is an elite WR. His current ADP of the 6th round is a good spot for those that have taken RBs with their first 2 picks. But as recent history will suggest, you shouldn't be relying on him too heavily.

TYLER BOYD
ADP 8.01

Boyd stepped up for fantasy owners when AJ Green went down with injury and has been rewarded with a decent contract. Can Boyd return value with his 4th round ADP? There are a few mouths to feed and you have a rookie QB throwing the ball so there are risks in taking Boyd, but should return a WR2 season.

C.J. UZOMAH
ADP U/D

There are a few whispers in the fantasy community that like Uzomah for a breakout/uptick in production this year. He'll likely be close to free so you could do a lot worse for a bye week fill in or if your TE goes down but don't expect many TE1 finishes each week. Definitely a piece for depth if bench size allows it.

2020 Projections

Position	Player	Standard		0.5PPR		Full PPR	
		Pts	Rank	Pts	Rank	Pts	Rank
QB	Joe Burrow	283.3	19				
RB	Joe Mixon	247.7	4	268.2	6	288.7	6
RB	Giovani Bernard	43.1	78	56.6	76	70.1	72
WR	A.J Green	124.8	36	154.8	37	184.8	37
WR	Tee Higgins	34.9	110	43.4	112	51.9	114
WR	Tyler Boyd	113.2	41	143.2	42	173.2	40
WR	John Ross	92.7	55	112.7	57	132.7	58
TE	C.J Uzomah	62.1	29	82.6	28	103.1	27
TE	Drew Sample	8.9	71	14.4	70	19.9	70

ADP taken from Ultimate Draft Kit (PPR)

Projections by Rob Grimwood @FFBritballer

FANTASY FOOTBALL

2

CINCINNATI BENGALS

DO SAY..
Who Dey?

DON'T SAY..
Postseason Record

BETTING ODDS BY ADAM WALFORD (@TOUCHDOWNTIPS)

SUPER BOWL **150/1**

AFC CONFERENCE **100/1**

AFC NORTH **33/1**

TO MAKE PLAYOFFS
13/2

TEAM TOTAL WINS
5.5

ADAM'S BEST BET

BURROW OVER 21.5 PASS TDS
10/11

PLEASE GAMBLE RESPONSIBLY

VIEW FROM THE SIDELINES

By Adam Walford (@Touchdowntips)

A 2019 for the Bengals meant they finished with just 2 wins, but the 1st overall pick in the draft which they used to bring in their QB of the future Joe Burrow who put up one of the greatest college season of all time. He should be the man in Cincy for the next decade or so & makes the future just that little bit brighter. They were terrible on defense last year & invested heavily there. Unfortunately the schedule is tough as is the division, with the all teams projected to have non-losing seasons. Even for positive Bengals fans, an 8 win season seems very ambitious.

▶RETRO FOCUS◀

ANTHONY MUNOZ – OT

Anthony Munoz can arguably be crowned the greatest offensive tackle in NFL history. Munoz played in 11 consecutive Pro Bowls, a 9 time All-Pro and named to the 75th & 100th Anniversary all-time teams. He was drafted 3rd overall in 1980, after spending time at USC, where he won a National Championship (1978). What you may not know is that in his time with the Trojans he also won a College World Series ring as a pitcher. Munoz was inducted into the Hall of Fame in 1998, aged just 40.

DID YOU KNOW

When Paul Brown was fired by the Browns, he took the orange kit and used it for his new team, just slapping a Bengals logo on the helmets

KEY STAT

"Postseason Traumatic Stress Disorder"
The Bengals have not won a playoff game since 1990.

FULL10YARDS VERDICT

The Bengals' fortunes rest largely on the shoulders of rookie QB Joe Burrow. If he gels quickly with his receivers, AJ Green stays healthy and the O-line protects him long enough to do his thing, Cincy will improve on last year's pitiful 2-14. The defence has also improved across the board through free agency and the draft. Cincinnati won't be troubling the playoffs but just playing well and winning a few games should be enough to give their long-suffering supporters something they've not had in a while: hope.

BETTING, STATS, FANS VIEW, RETRO

3

FULL 10 YARDS

CLEVELAND BROWNS

THE LOWDOWN:

The hype surrounding the 2019 Cleveland Browns was palpable. The team created an energy & buzz that the city hadn't experienced with their team in many years. The star studded offence & youthful, quick defense had many predicting the Browns would go all the way to the Superbowl. Unfortunately, that wasn't the case. Undisciplined, poorly coached & unproductive play left many supporters devastated. This off-season, it has been much quieter & the hype isn't nearly as much as it was a year ago. Mayfield is entering his third year and is now playing under his third HC but many believe Kevin Stefanski's tougher regime will be a positive for the former Heisman winner. The AFC North is now one of the tougher divisions in football & the Browns once again have no hiding place.

SCHEDULE

Week 1: @ Ravens
Week 2: Vs. Bengals *(TNF)*
Week 3: Vs. Washington
Week 4: @ Cowboys
Week 5: Vs. Colts
Week 6: @ Steelers
Week 7: @ Bengals
Week 8: Vs. Raiders
Week 9: BYE
Week 10: Vs. Texans
Week 11: Vs. Eagles
Week 12: @ Jaguars
Week 13: @ Titans
Week 14: Vs. Ravens *(MNF)*
Week 15: @ Giants
Week 16: @ Jets
Week 17: Vs. Steelers

2020 NFL DRAFT CLASS

Round 1
Jedrick Wills, OT, *Alabama*
Round 2
Grant Delpit, S, *LSU*
Round 3
Jordan Elliott, IDL, *Missouri*
Jacob Phillips, LB, *LSU*
Round 4
Harrison Bryant, TE, *Florida Atlantic*
Round 5
Nick Harris, IOL, *Washington*
Round 6
Donovan Peoples-Jones, WR, *Michigan*

SIGNINGS

Andy Janovich, FB
Andrew Billings, DT
Adrian Clayborn, DE
Jack Conklin, OT
B.J. Goodson, LB
Austin Hooper, TE
Case Keenum, QB
Andrew Sendejo, S

RFA TENDERED

Kareem Hunt, RB
(2nd Round)

NO LONGER ON TEAM

Drew Stanton, QB
Demetrius Harris, TE
Christian Kirksey, LB
Joe Schobert, LB
T.J. Carrie, CB
Eric Murray, S
Damarious Randall, S

TEAM DETAILS:

Owner: Jimmy Haslam
General Manager: Andrew Berry
Stadium: FirstEnergy Stadium
Location: Cleveland, Ohio
Head Coach: Kevin Stefanski
Offensive Coordinator: Alex Van Pelt
Defensive Coordinator: Joe Woods
Coaching Staff:
Stump Mitchell (Running Game Coordinator, RB Coach);
Chad O'Shea (Passing Game Coordinator, WR Coach)
Drew Petzing (TE Coach)
Mike Priefer (ST Coordinator)
Super Bowl Wins: 0
Conference Wins: 0
Divisional Wins: 6 (AFC Central, 1971, 1980, 1985, 1986, 1987, 1989)

-2019-
Record: 6-10
Offence Rank: Passing (22nd), Rushing (12th),Overall (22nd)
Defence Rank: Passing (7th), Rushing (30th), Overall (20th)

KEY PLAYER

Jarvis Landry: Is there a more underrated wide receiver in the NFL than Jarvis Landry? Since his rookie season, Landry has averaged at least 61 yards a game, at least 131 targets per season and has led both the Dolphins and Browns in receiving yardage every year. Alongside college teammate OBJ, Landry will be crucial as Kevin Stefanski looks to get the most out of a stacked Browns roster.

Jedrick Wills: The best present that the Browns front office staff could have given to Baker Mayfield this offseason was a pair of tackles. Jedrick Wills is an agile and aggressive tackle who loves burying defenders both in pass protection and in the run game. Cleveland loves Joe Thomas... Jedrick Wills could be the next Joe Thomas.

ROOKIE SPOTLIGHT

DEPTH CHART

Quarterback	Wide Receiver	Center	Edge Rusher	Line Backer	Cornerback
Baker Mayfield	Odell Beckham Jr	JC Tretter	Myles Garrett	Sione Takitaki	Denzel Ward
Case Keenum	Jarvis Landry	Nick Harris [R]	Olivier Vernon	Mack Wilson	Greedy Williams
Garrett Gilbert	Rashard Higgins	**Tackle**	Chad Thomas	Jacob Phillips [R]	Mack Wilson
Fullback	KhaDarel Hodge	Jack Conklin	Adrian Clayborn	BJ Goodson	Donnie Lewis Kr
Andy Janovich	Damion Ratley	Jedrick Wills [R]	**Defensive Tackle**	Jermaine Grace	Terrance Mitchell
Running Back	Taywan Taylor	Chris Hubbard	Larry Ogunjobi	**Free Safety**	**Strong Safety**
Nick Chubb	**Tight End**	**Guard**	Sheldon Richardson	Grant Delpit [R]	Karl Joseph
Kareem Hunt	Austin Hooper	Joel Bitonio	Andrew Billings	Andrew Sendejo	JT Hassell
Dontrell Hillard	David Njoku	Wyatt Teller	**Kicker**	**Punter**	**Long Snapper**
D'Ernest Johnson	Harrison Bryant [R]	Drew Forbes	Austin Seibert	Jamie Gillan (GB)	Charley Hughlett

NFL

1

FULL 10 YARDS

2019 RANKINGS

Player	Pos	Standard Pts	Standard Avg	Standard Rank	0.5PPR Pts	0.5PPR Avg	0.5PPR Rank	PPR Pts	PPR Avg	PPR Rank
Baker Mayfield	QB	227.2	15.2	QB19						
Nick Chubb	RB	215.0	14.3	RB7	232.5	16	RB7	250.0	17	RB8
Kareem Hunt	RB	60.8	7.6	RB53	77.8	9.7	RB49	94.8	12	RB47
Odell Beckham Jr.	WR	113.2	7.6	WR34	148.7	9.9	WR31	184.2	12	WR29
Jarvis Landry	WR	140.2	9.4	WR20	180.7	12	WR16	221.2	15	WR14
Damion Ratley	WR	13.6	1.1	WR141	18.6	1.6	WR141	23.6	2	WR140
Ricky Seals-Jones	TE	44.9	3.5	TE34	51.9	4	TE38	58.9	4.5	TE39
Demetrius Harris	TE	34.9	2.5	TE41	42.4	3	TE42	49.9	3.6	TE43
Cleveland Browns	DST	85.0	5.7	DST24						
Austin Seibert	K	110.0	7.3	K14						

BAKER MAYFIELD
ADP 12.5

It's not quite gone Mayfield's way so far but he's exceeded 3700 yards & 25TDs in both his seasons but saw regression in 2019. Interceptions have blotted his copybook but he will be hoping a healthy OBJ and stronger O-Line will give him a chance to prove his worth.

NICK CHUBB
ADP 2.04

Nick Chubb exploded last season with almost 1500 rushing yards and adding 278 receiving yards on top of that. 8 Touchdowns shows he has the power to be a bell cow for the team with an O-Line that should improve tenfold. The main issue is whether Kareem hunt comes in and absorbs some of his workload.

ODELL BECKHAM JR.
ADP 3.11

There's only one stat you need to know about OBJ. The higher the % of blonde in his hair, the better he performs on the field. Please note: OBJ's hair is the blondest it's ever been. After core muscle surgery in the off season he will be looking to bounce back after only notching 1035 yards & 4TDs last season. He'll need some improved QB play to achieve this but this makes him a decent value in drafts.

JARVIS LANDRY
ADP 7.10

In 2019 Landry put up his highest yardage total in a year with 1174yds on a relatively low 83 receptions (he had 6 TDs to make it a useful season). Like Beckham, Landry had off season surgery (for a hip issue which was bothering him) so with some fresh health he could be in line for an improved season.

AUSTIN HOOPER
ADP 12.4

Hooper was TE6 last year but leaves a team who had the highest pass % in 2019 & joins a team intent on running the ball. I can't condone Rob Gronkowski & Jared Cook being drafted ahead of him but, equally, players such as T.J. Hockenson & Dallas Goedert that should be. Plus who knows what Njoku does this year.

2020 Projections

Position	Player	Standard Pts	Standard Rank	0.5PPR Pts	0.5PPR Rank	Full PPR Pts	Full PPR Rank
QB	Baker Mayfield	286.3	17				
RB	Nick Chubb	214.3	10	227.8	13	241.3	14
RB	Kareem Hunt	145.1	33	175.6	26	206.1	23
WR	Odell Beckham Jr	170.7	9	215.7	6	260.7	6
WR	Jarvis Landry	132.9	28	168.4	26	203.9	25
WR	D.Peoples-Jones	24.3	0	32.8	124	41.3	123
TE	Austin Hooper	93.5	11	124.5	10	155.5	10
TE	David Njoku	39.7	41	51.7	41	63.7	41
TE	Harrison Bryant	29.8	48	37.8	48	45.8	50

ADP taken from Ultimate Draft Kit (PPR)

Projections by Rob Grimwood @FFBritballer

FANTASY FOOTBALL

2

FULL 10 YARDS

CLEVELAND BROWNS

LAST 5 YEARS

	W	L	T	Div	P/Offs
2019	6	10	0	3rd	
2018	7	8	0	3rd	
2017	0	16	0	4th	
2016	1	15	1	4th	
2015	3	13	0	4th	

DO SAY..

This might finally be the season we reach the playoffs

DON'T SAY..

This might finally be the season we reach the playoffs

BETTING ODDS BY ADAM WALFORD (@TOUCHDOWNTIPS)

SUPER BOWL **40/1**

AFC CONFERENCE **20/1**

AFC NORTH **7/1**

TO MAKE PLAYOFFS
27/20
TEAM TOTAL WINS
8.5

ADAM'S BEST BET

J.LANDRY U 950.5 RECEIVING YARDS
10/11

PLEASE GAMBLE RESPONSIBLY

 # VIEW FROM THE SIDELINES

By Jack Duffin (@JackDuffin)

The Browns are in a very promising position moving forward. We have a Head Coach whose wide zone scheme elevates the play of their QB and managed to get the best out of Kirk Cousins. The issue the Browns face is a disrupted offseason where they would have liked to been working on chemistry and learning the scheme, instead it has been replaced by Zoom meetings. Their big weakness last offseason was a lack of talent at offensive tackle and right guard. They spent big this offseason on a RT and drafted one in the first round. Expect Baker to have more time in the pocked with improved results. 9-10 wins and a steady improvement across the season is what should be expected.

 # RETRO FOCUS

FRANK MINNIFIELD & HANFORD DIXON – CB

You cannot separate Minnifield and Dixon, arguably the greatest CB pairing of the 1980s. The Browns duo combined for 46 interceptions in 253 career games – all for Cleveland. Their status is legendary in the Dawg Pound, the Browns rabid fan section, and was it not for that pesky John Elway they would have helped the Browns reach two Super Bowl's in the 1986 and 1987 seasons. Both combined for 7 Pro Bowls & 3 All Pro nods.

DID YOU KNOW

The Browns scored the NFL's first two-point conversion, when punter Tom Tupa ran in a fake extra point attempt against the Bengals in 1994

KEY STAT

"Strike it Lucky"

In the strike-hit 1982 season, the Browns reached the playoffs with only four wins

FULL10YARDS VERDICT

Last year, many tipped the Browns for the Super Bowl but under the inexperienced Freddie Kitchens, they flopped to 6-10. Mayfield, Landry, Beckham Jr., Chubb, Hunt, Garrett and co have now been joined by Jack Conklin and rookie Jedrick Wills so, on paper, they could finally live up to last year's hype. In new HC Kevin Stefanski, Cleveland have a steady hand on the tiller and, with a relatively easy schedule, could be this year's most improved team. They'll battle it out with Pittsburgh in the AFC North for a Wild Card spot.

BETTING, STATS, FANS VIEW, RETRO

3

PITTSBURGH STEELERS

THE LOWDOWN:

HC Mike Tomlin was touted for Coach of the Year Honours last season as he took a depleted Steelers roster to an 8-8 finish. Without starting QB Ben Roethlisberger, and having lost star wide receiver Antonio Brown, the Steelers offence was a fraction of what it once was. Mason Rudolph took up starting duties but failed to impress on many fronts as a viable back up option. Defensively, the Steelers performed at a high level all season. With the acquisition of Minkah Fitzpatrick helping to sure up the secondary and the dominant play of T.J Watt, the Steelers will be hopeful of a return to form for their defensive unit in a division where they play the reigning MVP Lamar Jackson twice a season.

SCHEDULE

Week 1: @ Giants *(MNF)*
Week 2: Vs. Broncos
Week 3: Vs. Texans
Week 4: @ Titans
Week 5: Vs. Eagles
Week 6: Vs. Browns
Week 7: @ Ravens
Week 8: BYE
Week 9: @ Cowboys
Week 10: Vs. Bengals
Week 11: @ Jaguars
Week 12: Vs. Ravens *(SNF)*
Week 13: Vs. Washington
Week 14: @ Bills *(SNF)*
Week 15: @ Bengals *(MNF)*
Week 16: Vs. Colts
Week 17: @ Browns

2020 NFL DRAFT CLASS

Round 2
Chase Claypool, WR,
Notre Dame
Round 3
Alex Highsmith, EDGE,
Charlotte
Round 4
Anthony McFarland Jr., RB,
Maryland
Kevin Dotson, IOL,
Louisiana
Round 6
Antoine Brooks Jr., S,
Maryland
Round 7
Carlos Davis, IDL,
Nebraska

SIGNINGS

Chris Wormley, DT:
Eric Ebron, TE:
Derek Watt, FB:
Stefen Wisniewski, OL

FRANCHISE TAG

Bud Dupree, DE

NO LONGER ON TEAM

Nick Vannett, TE
B.J. Finney, OL
Javon Hargrave, DT
Anthony Chickillo, LB
Artie Burns, CB

TEAM DETAILS:

Owner: Art Rooney II
General Manager: Kevin Colbert
Stadium: Heinz Field
Head Coach: Mike Tomlin
Offensive Coordinator:
Randy Fichtner
Defensive Coordinator:
Keith Butler
Coaching Staff:
Danny Smith (ST Coordinator)
Matt Canada (QB Coach)
Eddie Faulkner (RB Coach)
Ike Hilliard (WR Coach)
James Daniel (TE Coach)
Super Bowl Wins: 6 (1974, 1975, 1978, 1979, 2005, 2008)
Conference Wins: 8 (AFC, 1974, 1975, 1978, 1979, 1995, 2005, 2008, 2010)
Divisional Wins: 23 (AFC Central, 1972, 1974, 1975, 1976, 1977, 1978, 1979, 1983, 1984, 1992, 1994, 1995, 1996, 1997, 2001; AFC North, 2002, 2004, 2007, 2008, 2010, 2014, 2016, 2017)
-2019-
Record: 8-8
Offence Rank: Passing (31st), Rushing (29th), Overall (27th)
Defence Rank: Passing (3rd), Rushing (14th), Overall (6th)

KEY PLAYER

Minkah Fitzpatrick: When the Steelers sent a 1st round pick to Miami for Minkah Fitzpatrick, they must have known they were onto a winner. Not everyone else did, however. He was monumental for the Steelers after the trade, racking up 5 interceptions & holding opposition QBs to a passer rating of 46.3 when targeting him. Steelers' fans are convinced they've got a defensive leader for years to come in the 'Bama product.

Chase Claypool: Claypool is a little bit of a great athlete rather than a great receiver at the moment. He has a great blend of height/weight/speed but needs to work on the nuances of playing wide receiver, such as route running and his release off the line. Pittsburgh is the best team at developing receivers in the NFL so he's in the right place.

ROOKIE SPOTLIGHT

DEPTH CHART

Quarterback	Wide Receiver	Center	Edge	Line Backer	Cornerback
Ben Roethlisberger	Juju Smith-Schuster	Maurkice Pouncey	TJ Watt	Devin Bush	Joe Haden
Mason Rudolph	Dionte Johnson	JC Hassenauer	Bud Dupree	Vince Williams	Steven Nelson
Devlin (Duck) Hodges	James Washington	Tackle	Stephon Tuitt	Ulysees Gilbert III	Mike Hilton
Fullback	Chase Claypool [R]	Alejandro Villanueva	Tyson Alualu	Alex Highsmith [R]	Justin Layne
Derek Watt	Ryan Smitzer	Matt Feiler	Defensive Tackle	Christian Kuntz	Alexander Myres
Running Back	Deon Cain	Chukwuma Okorafor	Cameron Heyward	Free Safety	Strong Safety
James Conner	Tight End	Guard	Isaiah Buggs	Minkah Fitzpatrick	Terrell Edmunds
Jaylen Samuels	Eric Ebron	Stefen Wisniewski	Chris Wormley	Marcus Allen	Jordan Dangerfield
Benny Snell	Vance McDonald	David DeCastro	Kicker	Punter	Long Snapper
Anthony McFarland [R]	Zach Gentry	Zach Banner	Chris Boswell	Jordan Berry	Kameron Canaday

NFL

1

FULL 10 YARDS

PITTSBURGH STEELERS

2019 RANKINGS

Player	Pos	Standard			0.5PPR			PPR		
		Pts	Avg	Rank	Pts	Avg	Rank	Pts	Avg	Rank
Mason Rudolph	QB	117.8	11.8	QB30						
James Conner	RB	111.5	11.2	RB33	128.5	13	RB32	145.5	15	RB31
Jaylen Samuels	RB	56.8	4.4	RB55	79.8	6.1	RB48	102.8	7.9	RB44
Benny Snell Jr.	RB	39.8	3.3	RB69	41.3	3.4	RB74	42.8	3.6	RB75
Juju Smith-Schuster	WR	70.6	6.4	WR62	90.6	8.2	WR62	110.6	10	WR62
Diontae Johnson	WR	98.7	6.6	WR42	126.2	8.4	WR41	153.7	10	WR41
James Washington	WR	89.5	6.4	WR48	111.5	8	WR48	133.5	9.5	WR50
Vance McDonald	TE	43.6	3.4	TE35	61.6	4.7	TE33	79.6	6.1	TE31
Pittsburgh Steelers	DST	166.0	11.1	DST2						
Chris Boswell	K	122.0	8.1	K8						

BEN ROETHLISBERGER

When Big Ben plays full seasons, he's usually a decent asset in the later rounds for your teams. The decision this year is whether you want to take that risk of him playing 16 games. With the way QBs are treated in fantasy, Big Ben is a great later round pick for upside in redraft, but you may get your fingers burned in Superflex leagues where you'll be leaning on him more heavily.

ADP 11.10

ADP 3.01

For a running back being taken in the early rounds, Conner is a high risk/high reward player in 2020. For dynasty owners, this season is probably his last chance to prove he is talented & durable enough to be the teams premier running back. He started 10 games last season & exited 3 with injuries. 2018 stats suggest he's a 1000+ yard rusher & get double digit TDs, will his body let him?

JAMES CONNER

JUJU SMITH-SCHUSTER

After a 2019 to forget JuJu will be looking to bounce back with a vengeance & hopefully a full bill of health. A year removed from a 1426yd, 7TD season he only clocked up 553yrds & 3TDs in 12 games with a QB carousel. His production is tied to having Ben fit & with a stronger group of WR running with him, it gives him a chance to fulfill his fantasy draft price, but not a guarantee.

ADP 3.12

ADP 8.03

The new kid on the block for the Steelers is Diontae Johnson. 680 yards and 5TDs last season as well as his strong return game, he was one of the few positives for the team in 2019. It'll be interesting to see how he does with Ben at QB and whether the likes of James Washington and rookie Chase Claypool stunt his potential growth.

DIONTAE JOHNSON

ERIC EBRON

Ebron joins the Steelers from the Colts and looks set to be a major Redzone threat. Another player who missed a chunk of last season with injury (ankle), his 2018 was spectacular with 13TDs & 750 yards. In a tandem with Vance McDonald there are a lot of mouths to feed but he has a clear role and as a later round tight end, any week he finds paydirt will give fantasy owners a good feeling.

ADP 13.6

2020 Projections

Position	Player	Standard		0.5PPR		Full PPR	
		Pts	Rank	Pts	Rank	Pts	Rank
QB	Ben Roethlisberger	272.2	25				
RB	James Conner	173.3	22	182.3	23	191.3	28
RB	Jaylen Samuels	32.9	83	37.4	85	41.9	86
RB	Anthony McFarland	122.0	42	140.5	41	159.0	42
WR	JuJu Smith-Schuster	146.5	19	184.0	18	221.5	19
WR	James Washington	54.3	90	68.8	92	83.3	92
WR	Diontae Johnson	107.5	49	139.0	43	170.5	43
WR	Chase Claypool	54.3	91	74.8	83	95.3	82
TE	Eric Ebron	54.8	33	72.3	33	89.8	32
TE	Vance McDonald	75.2	23	98.2	21	121.2	22

ADP taken from Ultimate Draft Kit (PPR)

Projections by Rob Grimwood @FFBritballer

FANTASY FOOTBALL

2

FULL 10 YARDS

PITTSBURGH STEELERS

DO SAY..
Santonio Holmes Super Bowl 43 catch

DON'T SAY..
Myles Garrett's helmet

BETTING ODDS BY ADAM WALFORD (@TOUCHDOWNTIPS)

SUPER BOWL **28/1**

AFC CONFERENCE **14/1**

AFC NORTH **4/1**

TO MAKE PLAYOFFS **4/5**

TEAM TOTAL WINS **9**

ADAM'S BEST BET
TJ WATT DEFENSIVE PLAYER OF THE YEAR **12/1**

PLEASE GAMBLE RESPONSIBLY

VIEW FROM THE SIDELINES

By Freddie Hall (@freddiegth9)

Aging Big Ben hasn't got time left to mess about, so he needs to really push this offence this year if he has any hope of reaching a Super Bowl. The defence we already know is incredibly talented & dangerous. They may even be the best defence coming into this season. The huge question mark is the offence. Reinforcements have arrived in newly drafted WR Chase Claypool & FA signing TE Eric Ebron which may be able get this offence to jump to the next level. JuJu Smith-Schuster also needs to prove he is an elite number one wide receiver.

► RETRO FOCUS ◄

MEL BLOUNT – CB

It's not very often that the performance of an individual athlete forces an entire league to change a rule, but that was the case with CB Mel Blount. Blount played so aggressively at the line of scrimmage that receivers were unable to get in stride. Blount won four Super Bowl rings with the 1970s Steelers, picking off 57 passes & returning them for a grand total of 736 yards. Now in the Hall of Fame, Blount was a game changer & a rule changer who helped make his Steelers team a dynasty.

DID YOU KNOW

With World War II creating a player shortage, the Steelers – down to six players – merged with the Eagles and completed the 1943 season as the "Steagles".

KEY STAT

"Drives me Mad!"
The Steelers ranked dead last in average plays per drive in 2019, averaging only 5.1.

FULL10YARDS VERDICT

Losing Big Ben, JuJu and James Conner for much of last year's 8-8 campaign, the Steelers' medical room needs to be less busy in 2020. Their season rides on whether Roethlisberger bounces back from a serious elbow injury to his 5,000-yard best; if he does, we'll also see the receivers and new TE Eric Ebron excel. The Pittsburgh D is an obvious strength, leading the league in sacks for the last three years, and Mike Tomlin is pulling the strings, so they'll be competitive for sure. But will they be competitive enough?

BETTING, STATS, FANS VIEW, RETRO

3

FULL 10 YARDS

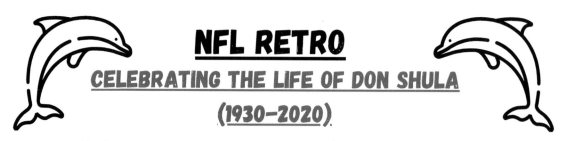

NFL RETRO
CELEBRATING THE LIFE OF DON SHULA
(1930-2020)

By Lawrence Vos (@NFLFanInEngland/@F10YRetro)

I happened to be flicking through a 2000 NFL Record and Fact Book the other day, and as the league looked forward to a new century of statistical achievements I stumbled upon a table that listed head coaches with over 100 career wins.

Atop the table was the former Baltimore Colts and Miami Dolphins head coach Don Shula with an all-time leading 328 regular season victories and 347 overall, including playoffs. As the league headed into a new millennium Patriots head coach Bill Belichick had just 36 wins, just over 10% of Shula's total wins.

Fast forward 20 years, and as we hopefully enter the 2020 NFL season in September, I took another look at the all-time wins for an NFL head coach. Whilst Bill Belichick has now moved into third all-time with 273 wins, the man he still trails by 55 games remains Don Shula.

If Belichick wins 11 games a season for the next five years, which is going to be a fascinating watch without Tom Brady at the helm, then he will tie Shula's record at the end of the 2024 regular season. That's how impressive Shula's coaching record is in NFL history.

Shula sadly passed away in May 2020, aged 90, with a résumé that may be light in Super Bowl trophies, but is undeniably outstanding;

- Two Super Bowl wins with the Miami Dolphins (VII and VIII)
- An NFL Championship in 1968 with the Baltimore Colts (prior to the NFL/AFL merger)
- Four time NFL Coach of the Year (1964, 67, 68 and 72)
- Sports Illustrated Sportsman of the Year 1993
- A place on the NFL 100th Anniversary all-time team
- The only coach to go an entire season (plus playoffs) undefeated (1972)
- 33 seasons coaching in the NFL – 31 of those ending as winning seasons
- And most importantly the most wins by a coach in NFL history

The raw numbers say one thing, but it was the man behind the victories that made Don Shula such a remarkable person.

Shula was roaming the Dolphins side-line in 1988 when I attended my first ever NFL game at Wembley Stadium. The Shula led Dolphins won the game against the 49ers thanks in huge part to a single coaching call, a David Woodley bootleg touchdown run in the final period sealing the win. By the late 80s Shula had been coaching the Miami Dolphins for 18 full seasons, after moving from the Baltimore Colts in 1970.

NFL RETRO
DON SHULA
TRIBUTE

1

FULL 10
YARDS

NFL RETRO
CELEBRATING THE LIFE OF DON SHULA
(1930-2020)

AS A PLAYER...

You have to go back almost a further 20 years to 1951 to mark the occasion that Shula and the NFL first came together.

Following a successful college career as a running-back at John Carroll University, a private Jesuit school in Cleveland, Shula got the attention of NFL scouts. Shula was drafted by the Browns in the 9th round of the 1951 draft, joining a Cleveland team that was the reigning NFL champion and featured Hall of Fame players Otto Graham and Marion Motley.

Shula was one of only two rookies the Browns drafted that year to make the Week 1 roster. In the NFL Shula was moved to the position of defensive back, and as a rookie had four picks in 12 games. The Browns lost the NFL championship in Shula's first season, giving him a very early taste for finals.

Despite some military service time in 1952 Shula returned to the Browns and lost in a second NFL championship game. The following season Shula got traded as part of a behemoth 15-player trade with the Baltimore Colts. 1953 also saw Shula complete a Master's Degree in PE. Shula suffered four consecutive losing seasons with the Colts, from 1953-56, which included an eventful 1955 season when Shula had five interceptions and one broken jaw.

After being released before the start of the 1957 season by the Colts Shula was picked up by the Washington Redskins where he played his final season as a DB.

AS A COACH...

Shula began his coaching career between 1958 and 1959 with two one-year stints at college teams. He was DB coach at the University of Virginia and then the same job at the University of Kentucky.

His college career saw him on teams that won just five games in two seasons. In 1960 Detroit Lions head coach George Wilson welcomed Shula back into the NFL family, recruiting him as a defensive backs coach. In three seasons with the Lions (1960-62) Shula was part of a Detroit team that had winning records, somewhat aided by a legendary defensive line called the 'Fearsome Foursome'.

1963 saw Shula return to the Baltimore Colts, but this time in his first role as an NFL head coach. Colts owner at the time Carroll Rosenbloom made the bold move to hire Shula, who was aged just 33, and the youngest head coach ever. The 1963 Colts went 8-6 under Shula's leadership on the side-line and Johnny Unitas on the field. The Colts followed with a four game improvement to finish 12-2 in 1964, but they suffered a heart-breaking 27-0 loss to the underdog Cleveland Browns in the NFL championship game. Shula did gain some redemption as he was given the Coach of the Year moniker.

In 1965 the Colts again did well, finishing 10-3-1 but again failed to cap off the season with any silverware after a defeat to the Packers in a playoff contest prior to the NFL Championship.

In 1966 the Colts went 9-5, and improved to 11-1-2 in 1967 but failed to gain a playoff berth. Shula won a second Coach of the Year award although he did not reach the final.

Finally the Colts managed to gain revenge on the Browns and in 1968 they dismantled them in the NFL Championship game before reaching the third ever Super Bowl. Shula's Colts, a heavy favourite against the upstart New York Jets from the AFL, again failed to pick up all the marbles as Joe 'Willy' Namath 'guaranteed' victory and delivered on his proclamation with a 16-7 win that shook the professional sports world to its core.

Shula saw out the 1960s with the Colts, with 8 wins in 1969, and a total of 71 wins in seven seasons, averaging over 10 wins a year.

NFL RETRO
DON SHULA
TRIBUTE

2

FULL 10 YARDS

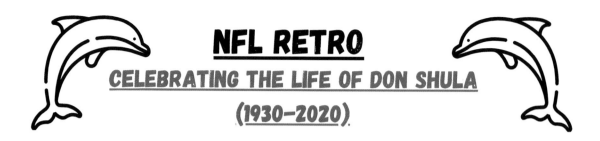

NFL RETRO
CELEBRATING THE LIFE OF DON SHULA
(1930-2020)

WITH THE DOLPHINS...

As the 60s faded into the sunset and the 70s rose, like a crocus in the dawning of a new spring, Shula got snapped up by the Miami Dolphins, to become just their second ever head coach.

What you may not know was the decision by Dolphins owner Joe Robbie to recruit Shula cost his team a first round draft pick. As negotiations occurred before and after the NFLs merger with the AFL it was seen as tampering.

Shula valued a dominant running game and an intimidating defensive line as the foundations of his winning recipe and those ingredients helped him and the Dolphins to nine winning seasons in the 1970s, along with five AFC East division titles.

In 1970 Shula led the Dolphins to 10 wins but Miami got dumped out of the playoffs in the divisional round by the Oakland Raiders.

For you history buffs the first touchdown scored in the Shula Dolphins era was a 5-yard scramble by QB Bob Griese Miami repeated 10 wins in 1971 and won two playoff games before Shula suffered a fifth finals defeat as a player and coach in a loss to the Dallas Cowboys in Super Bowl VI.

Having accrued enough bridesmaid dresses to start a small boutique in a leafy part of Surrey, Shula finally lifted a Super Bowl trophy at the end of the 1972 season, with a team that remains the only one to ever complete an entire NFL season and playoffs without a loss. The 14-7 win in Super Bowl VII cemented Shula's legacy as a great head coach.

Not to rest on his laurels Shula showed the rest of the NFL that his Dolphins were not in any way lucky, as Miami went 12-2 and won their second Vince Lombardi Trophy with a 24-7 win against the Minnesota Vikings. Looking to three-peat in 1974 the Raiders again proved to be the Dolphins nemesis in the playoffs, and to somewhat of a surprise the Dolphins failed to win a playoff game for the rest of the decade, despite four of their last five seasons of the 1970s culminating in 10 or more regular season wins.

In the 21st century it's doubtful Shula would have kept his job going into the next decade, but back in the 80s Shula was seen as untouchable in Miami. An inauspicious start to the decade, an 8-8 dud, was followed by five consecutive division wins, and 11 playoff games between 1981 and 1985. More heartbreak followed for Shula as his Dolphins lost not one, but two Super Bowls (XVII to the Redskins in 1982 and XIX to the 49ers in 1984).

It's not often that you lose a Super Bowl and then the following Spring draft your starting quarterback for the next 17 seasons, but canny Shula snagged Dan Marino at pick 27 in the first round of the 1983 NFL draft.

Much like the 70s Shula only had one losing season in the entire 1980s, reaching three AFC Championship games. Between 1986 and 1989 the Dolphins ownership stuck with Shula despite no playoffs and no more than eight wins.

The 1990s saw Shula game-planning in his fourth decade as an NFL head coach, and in his final six seasons Don won two more division titles, three more playoff games and had one trip to a Conference championship in 1992, where they were outclassed by Jim Kelly and the Buffalo Bills.

Shula's final NFL game was another playoff loss to the Bills, this time in the wild-card round. The Dolphins were 27-0 down after three quarters before scoring 22 in the final period. The final points scored in the Shula era was a Dan Marino two-point conversion to Wide Receiver O.J. McDuffie.

NFL RETRO
DON SHULA
TRIBUTE

3

FULL 10
YARDS

NFL RETRO
CELEBRATING THE LIFE OF DON SHULA
(1930-2020)

THE DON SHULA LEGACY...

Shula's 328 regular season victories stand as a record that at the start of the 21st century seemed impossible to ever be beaten, but Patriots Dark Lord Belichick has a chance to eclipse this by the end of the 2020s, but it will be one almighty challenge.

For me I spent over 20 seasons watching Don Shula on tv, adding to his leather faced tan in the Florida sunshine, and I even went to one of his steak houses on a trip to Miami around 10 years ago. I was simply not brave enough to try his 48oz steak challenge, but I clearly recall the menu being painted on an authentic NFL ball. I also remember being served the best French onion soup I have ever eaten.

The history of the NFL cannot be written without including a jam-packed chapter about Donald Francis Shula, son of Hungarian immigrants, who had to fake his parents signature to play High-School football.

I would normally say rest in peace when an NFL legend passes away, but I hope Shula has a headset on up in heaven and is barking out orders as his team drives down into the red-zone to get good field position for the game-winning field-goal.

NFL RETRO
DON SHULA
TRIBUTE

4

FULL 10
YARDS

HOUSTON TEXANS

THE LOWDOWN:

Many Texans fans became infuriated with GM / HC Bill O'Brien when he seemingly went into self-destruct mode when he traded the team's all-star wide receiver DeAndre Hopkins to Arizona for little to nothing in return. Despite making it to the divisional round last season the team seems to have gone backwards compared to where they were a year ago. Their season ended in horrible fashion after their playoff meltdown when they blew a 24-0 lead at Arrowhead against the Chiefs. On a positive note, David Johnson, the RB received in the Hopkins trade is back from injury & hopes to return to previous performance levels. Also in are WR Randall Cobb & Brandin Cooks to help fill the Nuk void.

SCHEDULE

Week 1: @ Chiefs *(TNF)*
Week 2: Vs. Ravens
Week 3: @ Steelers
Week 4: Vs. Vikings
Week 5: Vs. Jaguars
Week 6: @ Titans
Week 7: Vs. Packers
Week 8: BYE
Week 9: @ Jaguars
Week 10: @ Browns
Week 11: Vs. Patriots
Week 12: @ Lions
(Thanksgiving)
Week 13: Vs. Colts
Week 14: @ Bears
Week 15: @ Colts
Week 16: Vs. Bengals
Week 17: Vs. Titans

2020 NFL DRAFT CLASS

Round 2
Ross Blacklock, IDL,
TCU
Round 3
Jonathan Greenard, EDGE,
Florida
Round 4
Charlie Heck, OT,
North Carolina
John Reid, CB,
Penn State
Round 5
Isaiah Coulter, WR,
Rhode Island

SIGNINGS

Brandin Cooks, WR
Randall Cobb, WR
Jaylen Watkins, DB

STAR SIGNING

David Johnson, RB

NO LONGER ON TEAM

Carlos Hyde, RB
Lamar Miller, RB
DeAndre Hopkins, WR
D.J. Reader, DT
Barkevious Mingo, LB
Johnathan Joseph, CB
Jahleel Addae, S
Mike Adams, S (Ret.)
Tashaun Gipson, S

TEAM DETAILS:

Owner: Janice McNair
General Manager: Bill O'Brien
Stadium: NRG Stadium
Location: Houston, Texas
Head Coach: Bill O'Brien
Offensive Coordinator:
Tim Kelly
Defensive Coordinator:
Anthony Weaver
Coaching Staff:
Carl Smith (QB Coach)
Danny Barrett (RB Coach)
John Perry (WR Coach)
Will Lawing (TE Coach)
Tracy Smith (ST Co-ordinator)
Super Bowl Wins: 0
Conference Wins: 0
Divisional Wins: 2011, 2012, 2015, 2016, 2018, 2019
-2019-
Record: 10-6 (Lost Divisional Rd)
Offence Rank: Passing (15th), Rushing (9th), Overall (14th)
Defence Rank: Passing (29th), Rushing (25th), Overall (19th)

KEY PLAYER

Deshaun Watson: With the loss of DeAndre Hopkins in the offseason, the Texans offense has got notably worse. This will inevitably heap more pressure on the shoulders of Quarterback, Deshaun Watson. In last season's Wildcard game against the Bills we saw the Clemson product's incredible ability to step up and be a gamechanger. Texans' fans will be hoping he can keep their team relevant this season.

ROOKIE SPOTLIGHT

Ross Blacklock: Houston let D.J. Reader walk in free agency and sign with the Bengals and immediately drafted his replacement in Ross Blacklock. Blacklock is a technically gifted tackle whose motor always runs hot, he's not as big as Reader but will get after the QB more often.

DEPTH CHART

Quarterback	Wide Receiver	Center	Edge	Line Backer	Cornerback
Deshaun Watson	Brandin Cooks	Nick Martin	JJ Watt	Whitney Mercilus	Gareon Conley
AJ McCarron	Will Fuller	Greg Mancz	Duke Ejiofor	Zach Cunningham	Bradley Roby
Alex McGough	Randall Cobb	Tackle	Charles Omenihu	Benardrick McKinney	Vernon Hargreaves
Fullback	Kenny Stills	Laremy Tunsil	Angelo Blackson	Brennan Scarlett	Lonnie Johnson
Cullen Gillaspia	Keke Coutee	Tytus Howard	Defensive Tackle	Dylan Cole	Keion Crossen
Running Back	Steven Mitchell	Roderick Johnson	Eddie Vanderdoes	Free Safety	Strong Safety
David Johnson	Tight End	Guard	Ross Blacklock [R]	Justin Reid	Eric Murray
Duke Johnson	Darren Fells	Max Scharping	Brandon Dunn	Eric Murray	Michael Thomas
Buddy Howell	Jordan Thomas	Zach Fulton	Kicker	Punter	Long Snapper
Karan Higdon	Jordan Akins	Senio Kelemete	Ka'imi Fairbairn	Bryan Anger	Jon Weeks

NFL

1

FULL 10 YARDS

2019 RANKINGS

Player	Pos	Standard			0.5PPR			PPR		
		Pts	Avg	Rank	Pts	Avg	Rank	Pts	Avg	Rank
Deshaun Watson	QB	332.0	22.1	QB2						
Carlos Hyde	RB	141.9	9.5	RB20	146.9	9.8	RB23	151.9	10	RB26
Duke Johnson	RB	98.3	6.6	RB38	117.8	7.9	RB37	137.3	9.2	RB37
DeAndre Hopkins	WR	165.5	11.0	WR6	217.5	15	WR3	269.5	18	WR3
Will Fuller	WR	85.0	7.7	WR50	109.5	10	WR50	134.0	12	WR49
Kenny Stills	WR	80.1	6.2	WR55	100.1	7.7	WR56	120.1	9.2	WR56
Darren Fells	TE	76.1	5.1	TE11	93.1	6.2	TE15	110.1	7.3	TE16
Jordan Akins	TE	48.4	3.2	TE32	63.9	4.3	TE31	79.4	5.3	TE32
Houston Texans	DST	94.0	6.3	DST17						
Ka'imi Fairbairn	K	108.0	7.2	K15						

DESHAUN WATSON

Watson has been, or on pace to be, a top 5 fantasy QB every year he's been in the league. Despite losing his main weapon this off-season, there will still be plenty of opportunity to throw. The rushing upside is strong too, with having a 32.4 rush yards per game career average & has had 12 rushing TD's over the last 2 years.

ADP 6.08

ADP 3.08

Hasn't been himself since injuring his wrist 3 seasons ago, but has every opportunity to bounce back with a fresh start & new team in 2020. Carlos Hyde produced well behind this unchanged o-line last year seeing over 1,000 rush yards. If DJ can find just a glimmer of his former self this season, he could turn the tide of recent disappointment to fantasy owners

DAVID JOHNSON

WILL FULLER

If Fuller can stay healthy he's got top 10 potential. He's rapid, possesses good hands and has a fantastic ability to create separation. But staying healthy is the issue. Fuller is the most likely to take over as the WR1 now Hopkins is a Cardinal. He should be the go to guy but this might not be quite the field-stretching offence we are used to.

ADP 7.03

ADP 7.06

The speedster journeyman finds himself on his 4th team in 5 years but could have found his home at last. Until last season, Cooks was coming off 4 back to back 1,000+ receiving yard seasons but found himself out of favour in 2019 with the Rams. With a glaring Nuk sized hole in this offense, Cooks could well find himself back in fantasy relevance, especially with another talented QB throwing him the ball. Brees, Brady, Goff and now Watson.

BRANDIN COOKS

RANDALL COBB

Cobb could be great value at the back end of drafts, especially in PPE leagues. The Houston Texans gave him a massive contract and Bill O' Brien and co. may look to employ a shorter passsing style compared to previous years. Cobb showed flashes in Dallas and was fantasy relevant with Aaron Rodgers in Green Bay. Deshaun Watson can keep Cobb relevant.

ADP 16.3

2020 Projections

Position	Player	Standard		0.5PPR		Full PPR	
		Pts	Rank	Pts	Rank	Pts	Rank
QB	Deshaun Watson	354.0	3				
RB	David Johnson	183.1	17	203.1	17	223.1	16
RB	Duke Johnson	103.0	46	122.0	46	141.0	46
WR	Brandin Cooks	96.1	52	121.1	52	146.1	52
WR	Will Fuller	124.7	37	155.7	35	186.7	35
WR	Kenny Stills	66.8	80	91.3	75	115.8	73
WR	Randall Cobb	68.8	78	86.3	80	103.8	80
WR	Isaiah Coulter	28.4	119	37.9	119	47.4	119
TE	Jordan Akins	64.1	27	85.1	26	106.1	26

ADP taken from Ultimate Draft Kit (PPR)

Projections by Rob Grimwood @FFBritballer

FANTASY FOOTBALL

2

HOUSTON TEXANS

LAST 5 YEARS

	W	L	T	Div	P/Offs
2019	10	6	0	1st	Lost Div
2018	11	5	0	1st	Lost WC
2017	4	12	0	3rd	
2016	9	7	0	1st	Lost Div
2015	9	7	0	1st	Lost WC

DO SAY..

Best team in Texas

DON'T SAY..

"The DeAndre Hopkins trade was great value for us"

BETTING ODDS BY ADAM WALFORD (@TOUCHDOWNTIPS)

Super Bowl	66/1
AFC Conference	40/1
AFC South	7/2

To make Playoffs
6/4
Team Total Wins
7.5

ADAM'S BEST BET

To lose first 4 games

11/4

PLEASE GAMBLE RESPONSIBLY

VIEW FROM THE SIDELINES

By Euan De Ste Croix (@dissy89)

The Texans will require an increase in offensive output to remain atop of the AFC South. Having their first choice, starting offensive line, coupled with his most diverse skill position talent to date should help Deshaun Watson's development in year four. First year play-caller, Tim Kelly, will have extensive weapons to shape his passing attack but effectiveness in running the ball will be the acid test of offensive legitimacy. Defensively, the team will be reliant on Anthony Weaver getting more out of arguably less talent than a year ago. Finding late season from will determine their post season success.

▶RETRO FOCUS◀

BRIAN CUSHING – ILB

As a relatively new franchise the Texans do not have a rich history, but they do have some players that have made a huge impact, ILB Brian Cushing being one of them. Cushing's career was marred by injury, but when he was fit he was an absolute tackling machine, racking up 664 hits in 9 seasons. Unfortunately for Cushing he never quite matched his first pro season when he was awarded AP Defensive Rookie of the Year (2009).

DID YOU KNOW

The Texans are the NFL's newest franchise, joining as an expansion team in 2002.

KEY STAT

"Endzone available to rent"

The Texans ranked dead last In allowing TDs when opposing offences reached the redzone in 2019

FULL10YARDS VERDICT

The Texans have had a trying time of late, shipping more than 50 points against Kansas in last season's AFC Divisional Game, and swapping perennial Pro Bowler DeAndre Hopkins for David Johnson in a perplexing trade. Despite their experience, replacements Brandin Cooks and Randall Cobb are no Hopkins so, if Deshaun Watson et al have playoff aspirations, their defence will need JJ Watt to stay healthy. A tough first few weeks could mean a slow start and while they should bounce back, it might not be soon enough for Houston to make the playoffs.

BETTING, STATS, FANS VIEW, RETRO

3

FULL 10 YARDS

INDIANAPOLIS COLTS

THE LOWDOWN:

Philip Rivers will suit up as Colts' Quarterback this season as he prepares to play for somebody other than the Chargers for the first time in his career. Rivers is in on a 1-year deal as the Colts continue to build a championship roster, whilst also seemingly being in "win now" mode. Indianapolis traded away their 1st round pick in the draft to the San Francisco 49ers in return for defensive lineman DeForest Buckner. Their first selection in the draft was WR Michael Pittman Jr. who will be a welcomed addition to the Colts offense & will line up on the opposite side of the field to veteran receiver T.Y Hilton. Their 2nd pick, Jonathon Taylor is expected to have a big year in his rookie season.

SCHEDULE

Week 1: @ Jaguars
Week 2: Vs. Vikings
Week 3: Vs. Jets
Week 4: @ Bears
Week 5: @ Browns
Week 6: Vs. Bengals
Week 7: BYE
Week 8: @ Lions
Week 9: Vs. Ravens
Week 10: @ Titans *(MNF)*
Week 11: Vs. Packers
Week 12: Vs. Titans
Week 13: @ Texans
Week 14: @ Raiders
Week 15: Vs. Texans
Week 16: @ Steelers
Week 17: Vs. Jaguars

2020 NFL DRAFT CLASS

Round 2
Michael Pittman Jr., WR,
USC
Jonathan Taylor, RB,
Wisconsin
Round 3
Julian Blackmon, S,
Utah
Round 4
Jacob Eason, QB,
Washington
Round 5
Danny Pinter, IOL,
Ball State
Round 6
Robert Windsor, IDL,
Penn State
Isaiah Rodgers, CB,
UMass
Dezmon Patmon, WR,
Washington State
Jordan Glasgow, LB,
Michigan

SIGNINGS
Philip Rivers, QB:
Trey Burton, TE
Xavier Rhodes, CB

STAR SIGNING
DeForest Buckner, DT

NO LONGER ON TEAM
Brian Hoyer, QB
Devin Funchess, WR
Dontrelle Inman, WR
Eric Ebron, TE
Margus Hunt, DE
Jabaal Sheard, DE
Pierre Desir, CB

TEAM DETAILS:
Owner: Jim Irsay
General Manager: Chris Ballard
Stadium: Lucas Oil Stadium
Location: Indianapolis, Indiana
Head Coach: Frank Reich
Offensive Coordinator:
Nick Siranni
Defensive Coordinator:
Matt Eberflus
Coaching Staff:
Raymond Ventrone (ST Coordinator)
Marcus Brady (QB Coach)
Tom Rathman (RB Coach)
Mike Groh (WR Coach)
Jason Michael (TE Coach)
Super Bowl Wins: 2 (1970, 2006)
Conference Wins: 3 (AFC, 1970, 2006, 2009)
Divisional Wins: 15 (AFC East, 1970, 1975, 1976, 1977, 1987, 1999; AFC South, 2003, 2004, 2005, 2006, 2007, 2009, 2010, 2013, 2014)
-2019-
Record: 7-9
Offence Rank: Passing (30th), Rushing (7th), Overall (17th)
Defence Rank: Passing (23rd), Rushing (7th), Overall (18th)

KEY PLAYER

DeForest Buckner: The Colts may have gotten the steal of the draft this year, flipping their first round pick for proven defensive lineman DeForest Buckner. With 28 sacks and 263 tackles in his four years in the league, Buckner could be just the piece the Colts needed to shut down opposition defenses and give Philip Rivers the time he needs to get the offense firing.

Michael Pittman Jr.: If we look back at Philip Rivers' career and look at some receivers that he's had success with; Vincent Jackson, Malcolm Floyd, Mike Williams - The former Charger certainly has a type. Michael Pittman Jr. is a Philip Rivers receiver to a tee. If they strike up chemistry early on, watch out!

ROOKIE SPOTLIGHT

DEPTH CHART

Quarterback	Wide Receiver	Center	Edge	Line Backer	Cornerback
Philip Rivers	TY Hilton	Ryan Kelly	Kemoko Turay	Darius Leonard	Xavier Rhodes
Jacoby Brissett	Michael Pittman	Javon Pattersson	Justin Houston	Anthony Walker	TJ Carrie
Jacob Eason	Parris Campbell	**Tackle**	Ben Banogu	Bobby Okereke	Rock Ya-Sin
Fullback	Zach Pascal	Anthony Castonzo	Al-Quadin Muhammed	Matthew Adams	Marvell Tell III
Roosevelt Nix	Marcus Johnson	Braden Smith	**Defensive Tackle**	CJ Speed	Kenny Moore II
Running Back	Artavias Scott	Le'Raven Clark	DeForest Buckner	**Free Safety**	**Strong Safety**
Marlon Mack	**Tight End**	**Guard**	Grover Stewart	Malik Hooker	Khari Willis
Jonathan Taylor	Jack Doyle	Quenton Nelson	Denico Autry	Julian Blackmon [R]	Rolan Milligan
Nyheim Hines	Trey Burton	Mark Glowinski	**Kicker**	**Punter**	**Long Snapper**
Jordan Wilkins	Mo Alie-Cox	Jake Eldrenkamp	Chase McLaughlin	Rigoberto Sanchez	Luke Rhodes

NFL

1

FULL 10 YARDS

INDIANAPOLIS COLTS

2019 RANKINGS

Player	Pos	Standard			0.5PPR			PPR		
		Pts	Avg	Rank	Pts	Avg	Rank	Pts	Avg	Rank
Jacoby Brissett	QB	218.5	15.6	QB20						
Marlon Mack	RB	147.6	11.4	RB19	154.6	12	RB22	161.6	12	RB22
Nyheim Hines	RB	68.3	4.6	RB49	88.8	5.9	RB44	109.3	7.3	RB43
Jordan Wilkins	RB	47.0	3.4	RB62	50.5	3.6	RB66	54.0	3.9	RB67
T.Y. Hilton	WR	72.9	8.1	WR59	93.9	10	WR60	114.9	13	WR58
Zach Pascal	WR	92.9	6.2	WR45	112.9	7.5	WR46	132.9	8.9	WR51
Jack Doyle	TE	68.2	4.6	TE18	89.2	6	TE17	110.2	7.4	TE15
Eric Ebron	TE	55.5	5.1	TE23	71.0	6.5	TE24	86.5	7.9	TE25
Indianapolis Colts	DST	110.0	7.3	DST14						
Adam Vinatieri	K	80.0	6.7	K28						

PHILIP RIVERS — ADP 14.6

Rivers has an o-line that should be able to protect him a lot better than what he had in L.A. He's got young, talented receivers to throw to & a plethora of good talent to catch passes out of the backfield. Limited rushing upside hampers fantasy value, but he should be able to continue throwing north of 4,000 yards.

ADP 4.03 — JONATHAN TAYLOR

This tantalising rookie set all sorts of records in college. He has a lot of mileage on his young legs, but his ability rivals that of Zeke & Saquon coming out of college. He'll have to compete with Marlon Mack to start the season & Nyheim Hines will likely see the bulk of the passing work. However, Taylor is an elite weapon & Frank Reich will rely on him around the goaline

T.Y. HILTON — ADP 5.09

Now has a QB not afraid to throw the ball downfield and will want to keep his place atop the depth chart with exciting prospects Parris Campbell and Michael Pittman Jr biting at his heels. Hilton should still be the target hog in this offense though and Rivers will likely want the veteran as his "Keenan Allen"

ADP 13.12 — MICHAEL PITTMAN

The exciting rookie out of USC has been compared to the likes of Mike Williams (Chargers) which is fitting considering Rivers is the new signal caller in Indy. Expect Pittman to play opposite Hilton using his 6'4 223lb frame to demand red-zone work.

JACK DOYLE — ADP 14.4

Has had, or at least been on pace for 70 targets every season for the last 4. Should be the TE1 for the Colts in 2020 and has a QB that has a good history of utilizing tight ends. Rivers has thrown 128 TD's to TEs in his career, a 1 TD every other game pace.

2020 Projections

Position	Player	Standard		0.5PPR		Full PPR	
		Pts	Rank	Pts	Rank	Pts	Rank
QB	Philip Rivers	299.1	14				
RB	Jonathan Taylor	168.5	23	175.5	27	182.5	31
RB	Marlon Mack	128.7	40	135.7	43	142.7	44
RB	Nyheim Hines	125.8	41	160.3	31	194.8	24
WR	T.Y Hilton	138.5	24	179.0	21	219.5	20
WR	Michael Pittman Jr.	128.8	32	162.8	32	196.8	31
WR	Parris Campbell	76.2	73	98.2	70	120.2	69
WR	Zach Pascal	46.9	104	60.9	102	74.9	101
TE	Jack Doyle	75.8	22	102.8	19	129.8	17
TE	Trey Burton	58.8	31	75.8	31	92.8	31

ADP taken from Ultimate Draft Kit (PPR)

Projections by Rob Grimwood @FFBritballer

FANTASY FOOTBALL

2

INDIANAPOLIS COLTS

LAST 5 YEARS

	W	L	T	Div	P/Offs
2019	7	9	0	3rd	
2018	10	6	0	2nd	Lost Div
2017	4	12	0	3rd	
2016	8	8	0	3rd	
2015	8	8	0	2nd	

DO SAY..
Peyton Manning

DON'T SAY..
The New England Patriots, Deflategate or Andrew Luck

BETTING ODDS BY ADAM WALFORD (@TOUCHDOWNTIPS)

SUPER BOWL	28/1
AFC CONFERENCE	14/1
AFC SOUTH	7/5

TO MAKE PLAYOFFS
5/8
TEAM TOTAL WINS
9

ADAM'S BEST BET
TO WIN AFC SOUTH
7/5

PLEASE GAMBLE RESPONSIBLY

VIEW FROM THE SIDELINES
By Chris Carpenter (Carpy85)

A season where so much relies on newly-acquired signal-caller Philip Rivers. He's got something in Indy that he's never had: Protection. With some of the best in the business looking after him (a big nod to Quenton Nelson, here) he's gonna have a lot of time in the pocket & it's all about whether his arm is still there. TY Hilton must stay healthy & it's a big one for Parris Campbell in his 2nd year. Watch out for TE Jack Doyle to really come into his own now Eric Ebron has left & there's a lot of excitement about rookie WR Michael Pittman who walks into a starting role from the off. The defense has been slowly improving in recent years... it's very middle-of-the-road but good enough to challenge. DeForest Buckner / Xavier Rhodes could be very shrewd acquisitions and Darius Leonard / Anthony Walker were both sensational last year and should be so again in 2020. It should be a fun year.

▶RETRO FOCUS◀
RAYMOND BERRY – WR

Johnny Unitas may be the name that springs to mind when you think of Colts legends, but the man catching a large volume of his passes was WR Raymond Berry. Between 1955 and 1967 Berry averaged 60 yards receiving a game and caught 631 balls and 68 touchdowns. Now in the Hall of Fame, Berry was one of the toughest wideouts in NFL history, gaining 6 Pro Bowl berths and won two NFL Championships in the 50s (1958 & 1959).

DID YOU KNOW
All three of the Colts' Super Bowl appearances have been in Miami.

KEY STAT
"Give kicking the boot"
The Colts missed 9 Field Goal attempts and 6 Extra point tries in 2019.

FULL10YARDS VERDICT
This time last year, the wheels fell off the wagon when Andrew Luck announced his retirement during preseason. They limped to 7-9 but with Philip Rivers now installed at QB, new offensive playmakers in place and incoming DeForest Buckner boosting the defence, the Colts could bolt out of the gate. It'll be nip and tuck with Tennessee in the playoff race but winning the AFC South is certainly within reach. Rivers could be rejuvenated behind a better offensive line than LA's and Indy could well be a surprise package, much like divisional foes the Titans were last year.

BETTING, STATS, FANS VIEW, RETRO
3

FULL 10 YARDS

JACKSONVILLE JAGUARS

THE LOWDOWN:

The Jacksonville Jaguars have had a troublesome couple of seasons. After reaching the heights of the AFC Championship game in 2017, the team has struggled to have any success since then. Last year fans were delighted with the injection of excitement and life provided by Quarterback Gardner Minshew. Finishing with a disappointing 6-10 record, Jaguars fans will be hoping to see an improvement this season as the rest of the AFC South look to be on the up. As rumours continue to circulate of a potential relocation in the near future, fans will be wanting to see a positive season from their hometown Jaguars.

SCHEDULE

Week 1: Vs. Colts
Week 2: @ Titans
Week 3: Vs. Dolphins *(TNF)*
Week 4: @ Bengals
Week 5: @ Texans
Week 6: Vs. Lions
Week 7: BYE
Week 8: @ Chargers
Week 9: Vs. Texans
Week 10: @ Packers
Week 11: Vs. Steelers
Week 12: Vs. Browns
Week 13: @ Vikings
Week 14: Vs. Titans
Week 15: @ Ravens
Week 16: Vs. Bears
Week 17: @ Colts

2020 NFL DRAFT CLASS

Round 1
C.J. Henderson, CB,
Florida
K'Lavon Chaisson, EDGE,
LSU
Round 2
Laviska Shenault, WR,
Colorado
Round 3
Davon Hamilton, IDL,
Ohio State
Round 4
Ben Bartch, OT,
St. Johns
Josiah Scott, CB,
Michigan State
Shaquille Quarterman, LB,
Miami
Round 5
Daniel Thomas, S,
Auburn
Collin Johnson, WR,
Texas
Round 6
Jake Luton, QB,
Oregon State
Tyler Davis, TE,
Georgia Tech
Round 7
Chris Claybrooks, CB,
Memphis

SIGNINGS

Joe Schobert, LB
Tyler Eifert, TE
Rashaan Melvin, CB
Chris Thompson, RB
Al Woods, DT

FRANCHISE TAG

Yannick Ngakoue, DE

NO LONGER ON TEAM

Nick Foles, QB
Marqise Lee, WR
Geoff Swaim, TE
Calais Campbell, DE
Marcell Dareus, DT
A.J. Bouye, CB

TEAM DETAILS:

Owner: Shahid Khan
General Manager: David Caldwell
Stadium: TIAA Bank Field
Location: Jacksonville, Florida
Head Coach: Doug Marrone
Offensive Coordinator:
Jay Gruden
Defensive Coordinator:
Todd Wash
Coaching Staff:
Joe DeCamillis (ST Coordinator)
Ben McAdoo (QB Coach)
Terry Robiskie (RB Coach)
Keenan McCardell (WR Coach)
Ron Middleton (TE Coach)
Super Bowl Wins: 0
Conference Wins: 0
Divisional Wins: 3 (AFC Central, 1998, 1999; AFC South, 2017)
-2019-
Record: 6-10
Offence Rank: Passing (16th), Rushing (17th), Overall (26th)
Defence Rank: Passing (16th), Rushing (28th), Overall (21st)

Josh Allen: The players that made up the core of the 'Sacksonville' defense in 2017 are mostly out the door, and there's an air of a rebuild in Jacksonville this offseason. One player who the Jags will be looking to centre that rebuild is Defensive End, Josh Allen. The second year pro stormed onto the scene last year with 10.5 sacks. He'll be key again this season and for many more to come.

C.J. Henderson: With lightning quick footwork and the ability to be lockdown in coverage, C.J Henderson is one of the most exciting cornerbacks to come out of the draft this year. Jags fans will be hoping that Henderson will be the long term, and hopefully less troublesome, replacement for Jalen Ramsey.

DEPTH CHART

Quarterback	Wide Receiver	Center	Edge	Line Backer	Cornerback
Gardner Minshew	DJ Chark	Brandon Linder	Josh Allen	Myles Jack	Rashaan Melvin
Mike Glennon	Dede Westbrook	Tyler Gauthier	Yannick Ngakoue	Joe Schobert	DJ Hayden
Josh Dobbs	Chris Conley	**Tackle**	Dawuane Smoot	K'Lavon Chiasson [R]	CJ Henderson [R]
Fullback	Laviska Shenault [R]	Cam Robinson	Al Woods	Quincy Williams	Parry Nickerson
Connor Slonka	Keelan Cole	Jawaan Taylor	**Defensive Tackle**	Shaquille Quarterman [R]	Tre Herndon
Running Back	CJ Board	Ryan Pope	Abry Jones	Free Safety	Strong Safety
Leonard Fournette	**Tight End**	**Guard**	Taven Bryan	Jarrod Wilson	Ronnie Harrison
Chris Thompson	Tyler Eifert	Andrew Norwell	Rodney Gunter	Andrew Winguard	Doug Middleton
Ryquell Armstead	Josh Oliver	AJ Cann	**Kicker**	**Punter**	**Long Snapper**
Devine Ozigbo	James O'Shaghnessy	Tyler Shatley	Josh Lambo	Logan Cooke	Matt Orzech

NFL

1

JACKSONVILLE JAGUARS

2019 RANKINGS

Player	Pos	Standard			0.5PPR			PPR		
		Pts	Avg	Rank	Pts	Avg	Rank	Pts	Avg	Rank
Gardner Minshew II	QB	209.8	16.1	QB23						
Leonard Fournette	RB	183.4	12.2	RB10	221.4	15	RB9	259.4	17	RB6
Ryquell Armstead	RB	22.7	1.5	RB86	27.2	1.8	RB85	31.7	2.1	RB85
D.J. Chark	WR	149.4	10.7	WR12	183.9	13	WR14	218.4	16	WR16
Dede Westbrook	WR	75.5	5.4	WR57	105.0	7.5	WR52	134.5	9.6	WR47
Chris Conley	WR	105.7	7.1	WR39	127.7	8.5	WR40	149.7	10	WR42
Keelan Cole	WR	42.0	2.8	WR87	52.5	3.5	WR89	63.0	4.2	WR90
James O'Shaughnessy	TE	27.3	5.5	TE46	34.3	6.9	TE46	41.3	8.3	TE46
Jacksonville Jaguars	DST	85.0	5.7	DST22						
Josh Lambo	K	118.0	7.9	K11						

GARDNER MINSHEW

ADP 18.7

Respect the tash. Minshew is being incredibly undervalued by fantasy drafters this off-season. This is a guy that has got nothing to lose, wears his heart on his sleeve and is sneaky good with his legs (he was on a 400 yard rush pace last season). The Jags are likely going to be behind in games all season long so will be relying on the passing game to keep them in games. Minshew is a sleeper and could be a pivotal plus-matchup spot starter.

LEONARD FOURNETTE

ADP 3.09

Fournette can catch. 76 receptions for 552 yards last season proves that. The addition of Chris Thompson stealing a big portion of that work shouldn't faze you either, he's only played in 59% of games since entering the league in 2013. The Jags refused his 5th year option meaning Fournette is playing this season with a chip on his shoulder. There shouldn't be any regression from last seasons' RB9 finish providing he stays healthy.

D.J. CHARK

ADP 5.02

Last year's breakout of the year candidate comes at a top price this season. It's a gamble to be drafting him any earlier than his current ADP considering the small sample size. However, he's undoubtedly struck up a healthy camaraderie with Minshew and with the Jags seemingly needing all weapons firing on all cylinders this year of they're to get anything out of 2020, Chark will be that centerpiece again.

DEDE WESTBROOK

ADP 15.9

It's not all gone to plan for Westbrook really. Supposedly a breakout/sleeper/target monster last year when Nick Foles arrived through the door, but nothing manifested. The Jaguars will be playing from behind a lot meaning potential higher floor than you would think but he is not the primary target amongst fellow WR and he isn't going to score a lot of TDs.

LAVISKA SHENAULT

ADP 19.2

The highly rated 2nd round draft prospect out of Colorado is not getting the fantasy sleeper notice that he should be. This guy was lights out at college and came into the draft as one of the most talented receivers in the 2020 class. If he's able to make the number two role his opposite Chark this season, Shenault could prove a great flex option for fantasy owners, particularly if he can feast of the infamous Jaguars garbage time.

2020 Projections

Position	Player	Standard		0.5PPR		Full PPR	
		Pts	Rank	Pts	Rank	Pts	Rank
QB	Gardner Minshew	285.1	18				
RB	Leonard Fournette	198.3	15	228.3	12	258.3	11
RB	Chris Thompson	70.1	64	92.6	60	115.1	54
RB	Ryquell Armstead	23.1	98	29.6	98	36.1	94
WR	D.J Chark	128.1	33	159.1	33	190.1	33
WR	Laviska Shenault	126.5	35	156.0	34	185.5	36
WR	Dede Westbrook	55.8	87	73.8	85	91.8	84
WR	Chris Conley	53.2	92	70.2	89	87.2	89
TE	Tyler Eifert	48.8	35	66.3	34	83.8	34

ADP taken from Ultimate Draft Kit (PPR)

Projections by Rob Grimwood @FFBritballer

FANTASY FOOTBALL

2

FULL 10 YARDS

JACKSONVILLE JAGUARS

LAST 5 YEARS

	W	L	T	Div	P/Offs
2019	6	10	0	3rd	
2018	5	11	0	2nd	
2017	10	6	0	3rd	Lost Conf
2016	3	13	0	3rd	
2015	5	11	0	2nd	

DO SAY..
Minshew Mania is the future

DON'T SAY..
We're relocating to London

BETTING ODDS BY ADAM WALFORD (@TOUCHDOWNTIPS)

SUPER BOWL **200/1**

AFC CONFERENCE **100/1**

AFC SOUTH **28/1**

TO MAKE PLAYOFFS
8/1
TEAM TOTAL WINS
4.5

ADAM'S BEST BET
L.FOURNETTE UNDER 1200.5 TOTAL YARDS
10/11

PLEASE GAMBLE RESPONSIBLY

VIEW FROM THE SIDELINES

By Robson Kightley (@JaguarsGB)

Jacksonville Jaguars 2020 season is going to be interesting; We have Minshew leading the offence with Fournette hopefully completing another 1000+ yard season & our leading TD scorer of 2019 DJ Chark at WR. Notable offensive rookie to watch out for is Laviska Shenault, who'll fit in well with Minshew's strengths. I expect to see a few completions & TDs from this guy. Defence is going through a major rebuild this season; Having lost Campbell & Ngakoue holding out of practice we are looking at a completely different team but we have our franchise leading sack Edge rusher Josh Allen leading on the line with a new addition who calls himself 'Sack Guru" K'Lavon Chaisson. Our #9 pick CJ Henderson will be going straight into the important CB position. Myles Jack will be able to move back into his more natural Weak side Linebacker position as the Jaguars picked up Joe Schobert from the Browns on a 5 year deal. Our prediction - 7-9

▶RETRO FOCUS◀

MAURICE JONES-DREW - RB

MJD may be know to NFL fans in 2020 as a TV personality, but he was an outstanding running back in 9 NFL seasons (8 with the Jaguars). His finest season was 2011 when he led the entire NFL in rushing (1,606 yards), earning him an All Pro accolade. 81 career TDs ranks Jones-Drew in the top 75 all-time, and his 11,111 yards from scrimmage is 80th in NFL history. He only won one playoff game, but scored twice in it and had a 96 yard kick return.

DID YOU KNOW

Team owner Shahid Khan also owns London-based soccer team Fulham and tried to buy Wembley Stadium, the home of the England national team.

KEY STAT

"You make a valid point"
The Jaguars only scored 30+ points in one game throughout 2019, in their final game of the season in week 17 vs Indianapolis Colts.

FULL10YARDS VERDICT

The Jags are widely tipped to pick first in next year's draft, which suggests a regression from last year's 6-10. Second-year quarterback Gardner Minshew II held his own as a sixth-round rookie, but can he carry the team for a whole season? Running back Leonard Fournette needs to step up while the defence, depleted after several high-profile departures, will be leaning heavily on franchise-tagged DE Yannick Ngakoue and incoming linebacker Joe Schobert. Doug Marrone is on one of the hottest seats in the league and I can't see it cooling down any time soon.

BETTING, STATS, FANS VIEW, RETRO

3

FULL 10 YARDS

TENNESSEE TITANS

THE LOWDOWN:

The Titans went on an unpredictable run last season and made at all the way to the AFC title game were they were eventually beaten by the Chiefs. Under the direction of HC Mike Vrabel, the Titans went through a whirlwind of a season. Marcus Mariota began the season as the team's starter but was benched after a blowout defeat to the Broncos in week 6. Ryan Tannehill took over the starting role and injected a bit of life into the team. Derrick Henry continued to run rampant over the entire league as he earned the leagues rushing title for 2019. With both Henry and Tannehill resigned for 2020, Titans fans will be holding out hope for similar levels of success this season.

SCHEDULE

Week 1: @ Broncos *(MNF)*
Week 2: Vs. Jaguars
Week 3: @ Vikings
Week 4: Vs. Steelers
Week 5: Vs. Bills
Week 6: Vs. Texans
Week 7: BYE
Week 8: @ Bengals
Week 9: Vs. Bears
Week 10: Vs. Colts *(TNF)*
Week 11: @ Ravens
Week 12: @ Colts
Week 13: Vs. Browns
Week 14: @ Jaguars
Week 15: Vs. Lions
Week 16: @ Packers *(SNF)*
Week 17: @ Texans

2020 NFL DRAFT CLASS

Round 1
Isaiah Wilson, OT,
Georgia
Round 2
Kristian Fulton, CB,
LSU
Round 3
Darrynton Evans, RB,
Appalachian State
Round 5
Larrell Murchison, IDL,
N.C. State
Round 7
Cole McDonald, QB,
Hawaii
Chris Jackson, S,
Marshall

FREE AGENCY SIGNINGS

Vic Beasley, DE:
Johnathan Joseph, CB:

NEW DEAL

Derrick Henry, RB
Ryan Tannehill, QB

NO LONGER ON TEAM

Marcus Mariota, QB
Dion Lewis, RB
Tajae Sharpe, WR
Delanie Walker, TE
Jack Conklin, OL
Jurrell Casey, OL
Wesley Woodyard. LB
Kamalei Correa, LB
Cameron Wake, LB
Logan Ryan, CB

TEAM DETAILS:

Owner: KSA Industries
General Manager: Jon Robinson
Stadium: Nissan Stadium
Location: Nashville, Tennessee
Head Coach: Mike Vrabel
Offensive Coordinator:
Arthur Smith
Defensive Coordinator:
Terrell Williams
Coaching Staff:
Craig Aukerman (ST Coordinator)
Pat O'Hara (QB Coach)
Tony Dews (RB Coach)
Rob Moore (WR Coach)
Todd Downing (TE Coach)
Super Bowl Wins: 0
Conference Wins: 1
Divisional Wins: 6 (AFL Eastern, 1967; AFC Central, 1991, 1993, 2000; AFC South, 2002, 2008)
-2019-
Record: 9-7 (Lost AFC Championship)
Offence Rank: Passing (21st), Rushing (3rd), Overall (10th)
Defence Rank: Passing (24th), Rushing (12th), Overall (12th)

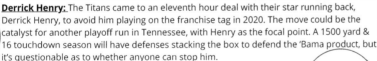

KEY PLAYER

Derrick Henry: The Titans came to an eleventh hour deal with their star running back, Derrick Henry, to avoid him playing on the franchise tag in 2020. The move could be the catalyst for another playoff run in Tennessee, with Henry as the focal point. A 1500 yard & 16 touchdown season will have defenses stacking the box to defend the 'Bama product, but it's questionable as to whether anyone can stop him.

Isaiah Wilson: Another giant offensive tackle who makes himself difficult to beat by just his sheer size. Despite his size, he carries his weight well and he has a nice blend of strength in his lower half in anchor and hand placement and hand fighting techniques; blending size and power with finesse really nicely.

ROOKIE SPOTLIGHT

DEPTH CHART

Quarterback	Wide Receiver	Center	Edge	Line Backer	Cornerback
Ryan Tannehill	AJ Brown	Ben Jones	Harold Landry	Rashaan Evans	Adoree Jackson
Logan Woodside	Corey Davis	Jamil Douglas	Vic Beasley	Jayon Brown	Malcolm Butler
Cole McDonald [R]	Adam Humphries	**Tackle**	Jeffrey Simmons	David Long	Jonathan Joseph
Fullback	Cody Hollister	Taylor Lewan	D'Andre Walker	Nick Dzunbar	Kristian Fulton [R]
Khari Blasingame	Kalif Raymond	Dennis Kelly	**Defensive Tackle**	Nigel Harris	Kenneth Durden
Running Back	Trevion Thomspon	David Quessenberry	Jack Crawford	**Free Safety**	**Strong Safety**
Derrick Henry	**Tight End**	**Guard**	DaQuan Jones	Kevin Byard	Kenny Vaccaro
Darrynton Evans [R]	Jonnu Smith	Rodger Saffold	Jordan Williams	Amani Hooker	Dane Cruikshank
Dalyn Dawkins	Anthony Firkser	Nate Davis	**Kicker**	**Punter**	**Long Snapper**
Senorise Perry	MyCole Pruitt	Daniel Munyer	Greg Joeph	Brett Kern	Beau Brinkley

NFL

1

FULL 10 YARDS

TENNESSEE TITANS

2019 RANKINGS

Player	Pos	Standard			0.5PPR			PPR		
		Pts	Avg	Rank	Pts	Avg	Rank	Pts	Avg	Rank
Ryan Tannehill	QB	212.3	19.3	QB21						
Derrick Henry	RB	237.5	17.0	RB4	246.5	18	RB6	255.5	18	RB7
Dion Lewis	RB	40.6	2.7	RB67	53.1	3.5	RB63	65.6	4.4	RB62
A.J. Brown	WR	146.7	9.8	WR15	170.7	11	WR21	194.7	13	WR23
Corey Davis	WR	67.7	4.8	WR65	87.2	6.2	WR65	106.7	7.6	WR65
Adam Humphries	WR	49.5	4.1	WR82	68.0	5.7	WR80	86.5	7.2	WR77
Tajae Sharpe	WR	55.6	4.0	WR76	67.6	4.8	WR82	79.6	5.7	WR84
Jonnu Smith	TE	69.0	4.6	TE17	86.5	5.8	TE19	104.0	6.9	TE19
Tennessee Titans	DST	124.0	8.3	DST8						
Ryan Succop	K	27.0	3.9	K39						

RYAN TANNEHILL

If Tannehill can continue where he's left off last season he's in for a career year. The former Dolphin doesn't get enough credit for being a QB that has multiple 4,000+ yard seasons. After being chased out of Miami, he's seemingly found his home in Tennessee and will look to produce similar numbers (he was on a 4,300 yard pace last season) in 2020. Could prove a nice matchup based starter for fantasy owners who adopt the late QB strategy.

ADP 13.12

DERRICK HENRY

ADP 1.08

He thundered his way to become the lead rusher in the NFL in 2019 with a solid 1,540 yards on the ground. The issue for fantasy owners is the lack of receiving work, but quite honestly, the guy is so productive on the ground it doesn't really matter. He still finished as the RB5 in full PPR leagues last year so don't worry yourself about it. The role shouldn't change for Henry, the offense is not the deepest on the depth chart so the offense will flow through his role. 300+ carries again in 2020? Sure, why not.

A.J. BROWN

The biggest beneficiary of Tannehill's success last season was the rookie out of Ole Miss. Brown took to the NFL like a duck to water and fired his way to 20.2 yards per reception, 2nd most in the league in 2019. I expect that number to regress slightly, but the production will still likely be there as he is the clear no.1 option for Tannehill in that offense. Another 1,000+ receiving yard season is very likely on the cards

ADP 4.08

COREY DAVIS

ADP 16.5

The man that hasn't yet delivered on his promise to be a fantasy relevant player. Well, if he's going to do it, this will be his best opportunity. The Titans are very thin on receiving talent behind Davis and Brown so he should get a good piece of the action providing Tannehill can repeat. Davis should be every fantasy players late round pickup as he could well be the DeVante Parker of 2020. He's a no lose pick.

JONNU SMITH

Jonnu Smith has the potential to be the late round dart throw that turns into a title winning decision much like George Kittle, Mark Andrews, Darren Waller have been the past few years. It isn't an offence where yards or TDs are easy to come by but there aren't a lot of mouths to feed and for those punting the position, make Smith a target.

ADP 13.9

2020 Projections

Position	Player	Standard		0.5PPR		Full PPR	
		Pts	Rank	Pts	Rank	Pts	Rank
QB	Ryan Tannehill	273.0	24				
RB	Derrick Henry	221.0	9	229.0	11	237.0	15
RB	Darrynton Evans	130.3	39	152.3	39	174.3	32
WR	A.J Brown	146.4	20	173.4	24	200.4	27
WR	Corey Davis	92.6	56	115.6	55	138.6	56
WR	Adam Humphries	48.1	100	65.6	96	83.1	93
TE	Jonnu Smith	113.8	6	144.3	6	174.8	6

ADP taken from Ultimate Draft Kit (PPR)

Projections by Rob Grimwood @FFBritballer

FANTASY FOOTBALL

2

TENNESSEE TITANS

LAST 5 YEARS

	W	L	T	Div	P/Offs
2019	9	7	0	3rd	Lost Conf
2018	9	7	0	2nd	
2017	9	7	0	3rd	Lost Div
2016	9	7	0	3rd	
2015	3	13	0	2nd	

DO SAY..
The Music City Miracle

DON'T SAY..
I think they'll finish 9-7 this year

BETTING ODDS BY ADAM WALFORD (@TOUCHDOWNTIPS)

SUPER BOWL **40/1**

AFC CONFERENCE **20/1**

AFC SOUTH **9/5**

TO MAKE PLAYOFFS
5/7
TEAM TOTAL WINS
8.5

ADAM'S BEST BET
D.HENRY UNDER 1325.5 RUSHING YARDS
10/11

PLEASE GAMBLE RESPONSIBLY

VIEW FROM THE SIDELINES
Adam Foxcroft (@ADFoxcroft)

After a 2-4 start & a shaky Marcus Mariota, few thought 2019 would end up how it did, but it showed just how far the Titans have come under Mike Vrabel. We have secured long term deals for both Tannehill & Henry, and oppositions have found them hard to stop. Tight Ends will continue to be a key part of the Titans' game plan, and Jonnu Smith just keeps getting better. On the other side of the ball, the retirement of DC Dean Pees is a loss, but Vrabel will take on these duties himself & bring just as much grit & steeliness. The Defence will need to keep oppositions in check, as the Titans still are not built to regularly come from behind. A 10-6 finish is the prediction, followed by a wild card playoff win seems likely. Sadly however, the Chiefs are still in the AFC.

▶RETRO FOCUS◀

CHRIS JOHNSON – RB
He may only have stopped playing 3 years ago, but RB Chris Johnson is already a Titans legend, with his own legendary nickname – CJ2K. The moniker was given to him after he rushed for over 2,000 yards in 2009 (along with making 50 catches). Johnson lasted six seasons in Tennessee, and in each and every one of them he rushed for over 1,000 yards. In a 10 year career CJ2K made only one playoff appearance, a loss to the Ravens as a 2008 rookie.

DID YOU KNOW
During their 60-year history as the Titans and the Houston Oilers, the team has had six different homes: three in Houston, one in Memphis and two in Nashville.

KEY STAT
"The Hot Hand"
Ryan Tannehill finished the 2019 season with a passer rating of 117.5 - This was the 4th best rating of all time for a single season.

FULL10YARDS VERDICT
Last year's surprise package reached the AFC Championship Game, thanks largely to Derrick Henry carrying the rock and the reborn Ryan Tannehill throwing it. Both are still in place so Tennessee stand a good chance to repeat their postseason achievements. A lot will rest on Tannehill staying fit – there's no quality back-up – and their defensive additions filling the gaps left by the likes of former team captain Jurrell Casey. The Colts will give them a run for their money but I'd expect the Titans to at least hit 9-7 (for a fifth successive time) and push on from there.

BETTING, STATS, FANS VIEW, RETRO

3

FULL 10 YARDS

BRITS FLYING THE FLAG IN 2020

By Sean Tyler (@SeanTylerUK)

JACK CRAWFORD (TENNESSEE TITANS – DE/DT)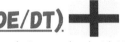

Raised in Kilburn, the early claim for this 6'5", 20-stone bald guy (due to alopecia) was being at school with Harry Potter actor Daniel Radcliffe. He then moved to the States as a teenager with dreams of becoming an NBA star but due to international transfer rules, that didn't pan out.

Undaunted, he took up football in high school and after four years at Penn State, was selected by the Oakland Raiders in the fifth round of the 2012 NFL Draft. Not a bad plan B...Crawford featured as a backup in his rookie season and appeared in 15 games the following year before being waived. He then enjoyed three-year spells with the Cowboys (you may have seen him at Wembley against the Jaguars in 2015) and the Falcons.

Arguably not a starting-calibre lineman, Crawford, who has played at both defensive end and defensive tackle, has registered 136 tackles and 16 sacks to date.A couple of months ago, Crawford signed a one-year deal with the Tennessee Titans. It's hard to say how it'll pan out for Jack as he enters his ninth year in the league, but he's certainly able to fill in should Mike Vrabel need him to.

With Austin Johnson signing with the Giants and five-time Pro-Bowler Jurrell Casey packing himself off to Denver during the off-season, there may even be a decent chance we might see him starting in 2020.

 EFE OBADA (CAROLINA PANTHERS – DE)

Obada had a tough start in life. Born in Nigeria before moving to the Netherlands, Obada and his sister got moved to London, where they slept rough and ended up in foster care. He fell into football when he saw how a college friend transformed himself playing for the London Warriors.

Looking for some cameraderie, Obada joined him and was taken under the wing of Aden Durde, who told his Dallas Cowboys contacts about Efe. Obada had only played five games for the Warriors when he was offered the chance to work out for Dallas, ahead of their Wembley game against the Jaguars. Despite his lack of experience, Efe was signed as an undrafted free agent a year later.

It didn't work out, nor did it with the Chiefs and Falcons, so his last hope was the NFL's inaugural International Player Pathway Program, which placed him with the Panthers' practice squad.The following year, Obada become the first player from the program to make a 53-man roster, and played his first regular season game in Week 3 against the Bengals, earning NFC Defensive Player of the Week honors for his performance.

Last October, Obada posted a career-best 24 tackles and played in all 16 of Carolina's games, including the Buccaneers game at the Tottenham Hotspur Stadium. Obada was named an honorary team captain for the 37-26 victory that day, a fitting tribute in front of a 'home' London crowd.

JAMIE GILLAN (CLEVELAND BROWNS – P)

Growing up in Inverness, Scotland, Jamie's all-consuming passion for rugby took him to Merchiston Castle, a boarding school in Edinburgh with a reputation for fast-tracking players into the Scottish national squad. As a promising fly-half, he developed a talent for kicking – one that would eventually stand him in good stead.

When his RAF dad was posted to Maryland, the Gillan family, including a 16-year-old Jamie, moved too. He had never watched football and initially, had no intention of playing it, but he asked to join the high school team, purely to keep fit during the rugby off-season.

With a few tweaks to his technique, Gillan soon became an accomplished kicker and offers began to trickle in. "All my mates were telling me you could get scholarships for kicking a ball and I didn't believe them at first," he told the BBC sport website last year, "but I thought I'd give it a try after I saw the guy missing field goals."Well, the punt – if you'll excuse the pun – was worth it. A year ago, the undrafted rookie was brought in by the Cleveland Browns as a back-up to Britton Colquitt. And whaddya know, after some impressive pre-season turnouts – including a 74-yard punt and some robust, rugby-style tackles on punt returners – he took the starting job from the 10-year veteran.

Known as "The Scottish Hammer" for his solid physique, the long-haired Scotsman soon got the fans and the pundits onside. Gillan was named the AFC Special Teams Player of the Month in September, and his debut campaign – 63 punts for 2913 yards, including a 71-yard season's best – earned him a place on the PFWA All-Rookie team.

As he enters his second season, the sky's the limit for Jamie. He's been working out and bulking up even more so he should be raring to go by the time the new season starts.

BRITS FLYING THE FLAG

1

FULL 10 YARDS

BRITS FLYING THE FLAG IN 2020

JERMAINE ELUEMUNOR (NEW ENGLAND PATRIOTS – G)

Now 25, Eluemunor was born in Chalk Farm, London, to a Nigerian/English family and grew up in Camden. He played rugby and cricket as a youngster – preferring the former – but got into football because of the other football, and in particular, his beloved Arsenal (check out @TheMainShow_ on Twitter).

The story goes that in 2007, he was skipping through the channels looking for the Arsenal match when he stumbled on the NFL International Series game between the Giants and Dolphins at Wembley. His interest piqued, he started down a path that would lead him to play high school football in New Jersey before attending Texas A&M. He and his father briefly came back to England but Eluemunor was allowed to return Stateside, as long as he graduated and put everything into pursuing a career in football.

On the eve of the 2017 Draft, in which he was picked by the Ravens in the fifth round, Jermaine told The Independent "Wherever I get picked, I'm gonna work as hard as I've ever worked to make this happen and my dream come true. This is just the start."

And that he did. Eluemunor made the Pro Football Writers Association (PFWA) All-Rookie Team in his first year, and played 27 regular-season games and one postseason contest in Baltimore before being traded to the Patriots. The 335-pound offensive lineman played 10 times in New England last year and has been retained for the 2020 campaign. Sitting behind left guard Joe Thuney in the depth charts, he isn't a starter but provides depth in the middle of the line and we should see him get a decent number of snaps this season.

JULIAN OKWARA (DETROIT LIONS – DE)

Okwara was born in London, when his mother was visiting family, but grew up near Lagos in Nigeria. He moved to North Carolina aged eight and eventually took up football, following his older brother Romeo through Ardrey Kell High School and Notre Dame on his way to the NFL. Romeo (also a defensive end) signed with the Giants as an undrafted free agent in 2016 and was claimed off waivers by the Lions in 2018.Julian was a standout at Notre Dame, making 19.5 tackles for loss and 13 sacks over his last two seasons.

And now, he finally catches up with Romeo, having been selected by Detroit in the third round of the 2020 Draft. According to Mike Renner of Pro Football Focus, Okwara could prove to be the steal of this year's class, after a broken leg toward the end of last season impacted his Combine and quelled any first-round chatter.Helping to address one of the Lions' biggest weaknesses last year, their pass rush (tied for second-last with just 28 sacks), Okwara – also considered an outside linebacker – may end up competing with Trey Flowers and Austin Bryant, as well as his big brother, for starting snaps.

Matt Patricia is getting a versatile player who can drop back into coverage or rush the passer.

On signing with the Lions, he told Detroit Free Press reporters "They're getting a pass rusher, great defensive end, someone who wreaks havoc in the backfield." So look out for Okwara to come out from his brother's shadow and make a name for himself in the NFC North next season.

CHRISTIAN WADE (BUFFALO BILLS – RB)

Christian Wade is currently on the Buffalo Bills practice squad, with hopes of another year of development ahead of him, but he's already had an impressive career in rugby.

The lad from High Wycombe, Buckinghamshire, played for Wasps since his school days and went on to score 82 tries for them, which puts him fourth on the Premiership's all-time list. He also represented England at all levels (alas, only the one national appearance though), and was also called up to the British and Irish Lions squad.

Frustrated with the lack of England opportunities, he decided to switch codes, clubs and countries and try out as an NFL running back, despite having zero experience. He came through the NFL's International Player Pathway Program, and spent last season in upstate New York on the Bills' practice squad.

Almost immediately, he made headlines, with a 65-yard TD run with his first-ever touch in a preseason game against the Colts, and a 48-yard run with his first catch.Despite his undoubted speed and athletic ability, Wade failed to make the active roster last year and is yet to appear in a regular-season game. But he's undaunted, telling The Telegraph "It has been a success to come across, learn the game, participate in practice at full speed and to play in preseason. I just want to keep improving. I'm going to give it the same energy as I did this year and see where that gets me."

BRITS FLYING THE FLAG

2

HONOURABLE MENTION: GRAHAM GANO (NEW YORK GIANTS – K)

DENVER BRONCOS

THE LOWDOWN:

The 2019 Denver Broncos finished their season with an unusual sense of optimism for a team that had just finished 7-9. Usually, when a team finishes below .500 on the season they come under fire from the media and fans alike wondering if it's time to hit the reset button. Well, not in Denver. After taking over the reins with just five games left to play, Quarterback Drew Lock provided both hope and confidence for the future. They added star wide receiver Jerry Jeudy through the draft and now have an exciting offensive line-up. The youthful defense will face challenges in a difficult AFC West but will be well drilled & excellently coached under the watchful eye of Head Coach Vic Fangio.

SCHEDULE

Week 1: Vs. Titans *(MNF)*
Week 2: @ Steelers
Week 3: Vs. Buccaneers
Week 4: @ Jets *(TNF)*
Week 5: @ Patriots
Week 6: Vs. Dolphins
Week 7: Vs. Chiefs
Week 8: BYE
Week 9: @ Falcons
Week 10: @ Raiders
Week 11: Vs. Chargers
Week 12: Vs. Saints
Week 13: @ Chiefs *(SNF)*
Week 14: @ Panthers
Week 15: Vs. Bills
Week 16: @ Chargers
Week 17: Vs. Raiders

2020 NFL DRAFT CLASS

Round 1
Jerry Jeudy, WR,
Alabama
Round 2
K.J. Hamler, WR,
Penn State
Round 3
Michael Ojemudia, CB,
Iowa
Lloyd Cushenberry, IOL,
LSU
McTelvin Agim, IDL,
Arkansas
Round 4
Albert Okwuegbunam, TE,
Missouri
Round 5
Justin Strnad, LB,
Wake Forest
Round 6
Netane Muti, IOL,
Fresno State
Round 7
Tyrie Cleveland, WR,
Florida
Derrek Tuszka, EDGE,
North Dakota State

SIGNINGS

A.J. Bouye, CB
Jurrell Casey, DL
Graham Glasgow, OG
Sam Martin, P
Nick Vannett, TE

STAR SIGNING

Melvin Gordon, RB

NO LONGER ON TEAM

Joe Flacco, QB
Ronald Leary, OL
Connor McGovern, C
Derek Wolfe, DE
Chris Harris Jr., CB
Will Parks, S

TEAM DETAILS:

Owner: Bowlen Family
General Manager: John Elway
Stadium: Empower Field
Location: Denver, Colorado
Head Coach: Vic Fangio
Offensive Coordinator: Pat Shurmur
Defensive Coordinator: Ed Donatell
Coaching Staff:
Mike Shula (QB Coach)
Curtis Modkins (RB Coach)
Zach Azzanni (WR Coach)
Wade Harman (TE Coach)
Tom McMahon (ST Coordinator)
Super Bowl Wins: 3 (1997, 1998, 2015)
Conference Wins: 8 (1977,1986, 1987,1989,1997,1998,2013, 2015)
Divisional Wins: 15 (AFC West, 1977,1978,1979,1983,1984,1986, 1987,1989,1991,1993,1996, 1997, 1998,2000,2003,2004,2005,2011, 2012,2013,2014,2015)
-2019-
Record: 7-9
Offence Rank: Passing (28th), Rushing (20th),Overall (28th)
Defence Rank: Passing (11th), Rushing (16th), Overall (10th)

KEY PLAYER

Bradley Chubb: With a young offense carrying a lot of expectation going into the 2020 season, it would seem that the defense is going under the radar. Additions of AJ Bouye & Jurrell Casey have certainly added strength & depth, but it's the star pass rush pairing of Von Miller & Bradley Chubb which will strike fear into opposition QBs. Chubb had an injury hit season but will be looking to take over from Miller as the main threat coming off the edge.

Jerry Jeudy: Denver feels like they have their guy at QB in Drew Lock & now they are putting weapons around him to encourage further growth. What makes life easy for young QB's? Players who create separation & are generally wide open. Jeudy's route running creates a lot of separation, he's already one of the best route runners in the NFL. Yes, we said it.

ROOKIE SPOTLIGHT

DEPTH CHART

Quarterback	Wide Receiver	Center	Edge	Line Backer	Cornerback
Drew Lock	Courtland Sutton	Lloyd Cushenberry [R]	Von Miller	Bradley Chubb	AJ Bouye
Jeff Driskel	Jerry Jeudy	Patrick Morris	Jeremiah Attachu	Alexander Johnson	Bryce Callahan
Brett Rypien	KJ Hamler	**Tackle**	Shelby Harris	Todd Davis	De'Vounte Dausby
Fullback	Tim Patrick	Garrett Bolles	Dre'Mont Jones	Joseph Jones	Isaac Yiadom
Andrew Beck	DaeSean Hamilton	Ju'Wuan James	**Defensive Tackle**	Josey Jewell	
Running Back	Diontae Spencer	Jake Rodgers	Jurrell Casey	**Free Safety**	**Strong Safety**
Melvin Gordon	**Tight End**	**Guard**	Mike Purcell	Justin Simmons	Kareem Jackson
Phillip Lindsey	Noah Fant	Dalton Risner	Jonathan Harris	Kahani Smith	Trey Marshall
Royce Freeman	Jeff Heuerman	Graham Glasgow	**Kicker**	**Punter**	**Long Snapper**
Khalifani Muhammed	Nick Vannett	Elijah Wilkinson	Brandon McManus	Sam Martin	Wes Farnsworth

NFL

1

FULL 10 YARDS

DENVER BRONCOS

2019 RANKINGS

Player	Pos	Standard			0.5PPR			PPR		
		Pts	Avg	Rank	Pts	Avg	Rank	Pts	Avg	Rank
Joe Flacco	QB	89.9	11.2	QB33						
Phillip Lindsay	RB	157.4	10.5	RB16	174.9	12	RB17	192.4	13	RB18
Royce Freeman	RB	98.8	6.6	RB37	119.8	8	RB36	140.8	9.4	RB34
Courtland Sutton	WR	145.2	9.7	WR16	179.2	12	WR19	213.2	14	WR18
Emmanuel Sanders*	WR	121.8	7.6	WR27	153.3	9.6	WR26	184.8	12	WR28
DaeSean Hamilton	WR	29.2	2.0	WR107	40.7	2.7	WR103	52.2	3.5	WR101
Tim Patrick	WR	20.4	2.9	WR133	27.9	4	WR131	35.4	5.1	WR125
Noah Fant	TE	70.6	4.7	TE15	90.1	6	TE16	109.6	7.3	TE17
Denver Broncos	DST	94.0	6.3	DST19						
Brandon McManus	K	117.0	7.8	K12						

* 9 games with San Francisco

DREW LOCK — ADP 14.4

Lock is now the starter in Denver after playing the final five weeks of the 2019 season. Lock is surrounded with some great offensive weapons in Courtland Sutton, Melvin Gordon and rookie Jerry Jeudy & the Broncos will surely look to improve upon their average of just 31.5 pass attempts per game that they offered in 2019. Lock could be a steal in the later rounds.

MELVIN GORDON — ADP 3.11

In 2019, Gordon returned his worst statistical season since his rookie year but that didn't stop the Broncos from offering him a 2-year contract. Gordon will have to compete for snaps with Phillip Lindsay & it's unclear how the two running backs will share the load. If Gordon is the lead back, he has plenty of potential especially towards the end of the 3rd Rd.

COURTLAND SUTTON — ADP 5.12

Sutton has shown the ability to make big plays and much of his production in 2020 will depend on how second year QB Drew Lock performs. In 2019 Sutton had over 1100 yards receiving on 124 targets. Sutton is a number 1 wide receiver and if his targets stay around that number then he should have great fantasy value in 2020.

JERRY JEUDY — ADP 10.06

Jerry Jeudy is pretty much tied to Drew Lock's success. If Lock takes a decent step forward, Jeudy could be a great PPR floor player in the mid to late rounds. His ADP is probably inflated due to the draft hype but he could quite easily become an early round player in 2021. There are other superstars on this team, but expect Jeudy to hold his own.

NOAH FANT — ADP 11.02

Fant has so much potential and athletic ability at the tight end position! He will have more competition for targets in 2020 due to the acquisition of Jerry Jeudy to play opposite Courtland Sutton at the wide receiver position but Fant could be one of the top fantasy tight ends in the upcoming season. Once again it depends on how Drew Lock performs.

2020 Projections

ADP taken from Ultimate Draft Kit (PPR)

Projections by Rob Grimwood @FFBritballer

FANTASY FOOTBALL

Position	Player	Standard		0.5PPR		Full PPR	
		Pts	Rank	Pts	Rank	Pts	Rank
QB	Drew Lock	310.8	11				
RB	Melvin Gordon	179.1	19	199.1	19	219.1	18
RB	Phillip Lindsay	139.3	35	154.3	38	169.3	37
RB	Royce Freeman	51.1	72	59.6	72	68.1	73
WR	Courtland Sutton	144.5	22	176.0	23	207.5	23
WR	Jerry Jeudy	135.8	25	167.8	27	199.8	28
WR	K.J Hamler	57.7	84	73.7	86	89.7	86
WR	DaeSean Hamilton	47.3	103	58.8	103	70.3	104
TE	Noah Fant	94.4	10	119.4	11	144.4	13
TE	A. Okwuegbunam	31.6	46	40.6	47	49.6	47

2

FULL 10 YARDS

DENVER BRONCOS

LAST 5 YEARS

	W	L	T	Div	P/Offs
2019	7	9	0	2nd	
2018	6	10	0	3rd	
2017	5	11	0	4th	
2016	9	7	0	3rd	
2015	12	4	0	1st	Won SB

DO SAY..
That Super Bowl 50 winning defence

DON'T SAY..
John Elway doesn't know how to draft a QB

BETTING ODDS BY ADAM WALFORD (@TOUCHDOWNTIPS)

SUPER BOWL **55/1**

AFC CONFERENCE **25/1**

AFC WEST **12/1**

TO MAKE PLAYOFFS
7/4
TEAM TOTAL WINS
7.5

ADAM'S BEST BET
UNDER 7.5 WINS
10/11

PLEASE GAMBLE RESPONSIBLY

VIEW FROM THE SIDELINES
By Chris Mitchell (@5yardrush)

So as the name states Mile High stadium, is, well, high. The altitude hurts opponents at the best of times. Now no practice for teams means it could become a fortress. The 'No Fly Zone' could once again be a thing with the addition of AJ Boye and rookie Michael Ojemudia. How do you protect a fortress? Arm the cannon. Drew Lock has got the arm and now he has all the weapons he could need. Courtland Sutton balled out last year and now the Broncos add top tier rookie wideout Jerry Jeudy, speedster KJ Hamler and beast mode Tight End Albert O. Oh and also strengthened the backfield by adding Melvin Gordon. The armoury is full in pursuit of the Chiefs. Playoffs should be the minimum aim this year.

▶RETRO FOCUS◀
ED MCCAFFREY – WR

If you pick 1.1 in a 2020 fantasy draft you are likely to pick the son of former Broncos WR Ed McCaffrey. A three-time Super Bowl winner, twice with the Broncos, Ed was a fantastic route runner who survived 13 NFL seasons. He had three 1,000 yard seasons, all with Denver, and his 565 regular season catches ranks exactly 100th in NFL history. McCaffrey caught 5 passes in Super Bowl XXXIII (1997 season) but never scored a TD in the big game.

DID YOU KNOW
Matt Stone and Trey Parker, creators of South Park, are Broncos fans and often mention the team on their show.

KEY STAT
"Rollin' in the deep"
Courtland Sutton had 42.93% of Denver's air yards, the largest share of any receiver in the league in 2019.

FULL10YARDS VERDICT
After a revolving cast of coaches and QBs, Denver are finally feeling more settled and, dare I say it, optimistic, having won four of their last five with new quarterback Drew Lock, The team have brought in weapons, with Melvin Gordon and draft picks Jerry Jeudy and KJ Hamler joining Courtland Sutton and Noah Fant, so there's a chance the Broncos won't have a mare in 2020. The AFC West is a toughie but they're locked and loaded on offence, so anything less than the playoffs would be a disappointment. Alas, they may fall just short.

BETTING, STATS, FANS VIEW, RETRO

3

FULL 10 YARDS

KANSAS CITY CHIEFS

THE LOWDOWN:

The Kansas City Chiefs really earned their Super Bowl last year. Losing Patrick Mahomes mid-season to a knee injury & several huge playoff comebacks showed the world how worthy they were of being champions. The core of the team has managed to stay together with no major losses to trades or free agency and will be a major help in terms of team chemistry & morale as we enter the season. The pre-built relationships will prove that keeping a team together year on year can be a big bonus. The obvious news over the off-season was the $503m extension that Patrick Mahomes signed keeping him in Kansas City until 2032 plus his star TE Kelce inking a long term deal too. Suffice to say it will take something special to dethrone the Champions this year.

SCHEDULE

Week 1: Vs. Texans *(TNF)*
Week 2: @ Chargers
Week 3: @ Ravens *(MNF)*
Week 4: Vs. Patriots
Week 5: Vs. Raiders
Week 6: @ Bills *(TNF)*
Week 7: @ Broncos
Week 8: Vs. Jets
Week 9: Vs. Panthers
Week 10: BYE
Week 11: @ Raiders *(SNF)*
Week 12: @ Buccaneers
Week 13: Vs.Broncos *(SNF)*
Week 14: @ Dolphins
Week 15: @ Saints
Week 16: Vs. Falcons
Week 17: Vs. Chargers

2020 NFL DRAFT CLASS

Round 1
Clyde Edwards-Helaire, RB,
LSU
Round 2
Willie Gay Jr., LB,
Mississippi State
Round 3
Lucas Niang, OT,
TCU
Round 4
L'Jarius Sneed, DB,
Louisiana Tech
Round 5
Mike Danna, EDGE,
Michigan
Round 7
Thakarius Keyes, CB,
Tulane

SIGNINGS
Taco Charlton, DE
Bashaud Breeland, CB

NEW DEAL
Chris Jones, DT

NO LONGER ON TEAM
Matt Moore, QB
LeSean McCoy, RB
Spencer Ware, RB
Stefen Wisniewski, OL
Cameron Erving, OL
Emmanuel Ogbah, DE
Kendall Fuller, CB
Dustin Colquitt, P

TEAM DETAILS:

Owner: Clark Hunt
General Manager: Brett Veach
Stadium: Arrowhead Stadium
Location: Kansas City, Missouri
Head Coach: Andy Reid
Offensive Coordinator:
Eric Bienemy
Defensive Coordinator:
Steve Spagnuolo
Coaching Staff:
Dave Toub (ST Coordinator / Assistant HC)
Mike Kafka (QB Coach/Passing Game Coordinator)
Deland McCullough (RB Coach)
Greg Lewis (WR Coach)
Tom Melvin (TE Coach)
Super Bowl Wins: 2 (1969, 2019)
Conference Wins: 1 (AFC, 2019)
Divisional Wins: 11 (AFL Western, 1966; AFC West, 1971, 1993, 1995, 1997, 2003, 2010, 2016, 2017, 2018, 2019)
-2019-
Record: 12-4 (Won Superbowl)
Offence Rank: Passing (5th), Rushing (23rd), Overall (5th)
Defence Rank: Passing (8th), Rushing (26th), Overall (7th)

KEY PLAYER

Patrick Mahomes: Everyone knows that the Super Bowl MVP is an elite player, you don't drag your team back into a Super Bowl and go on to win it all if not. Mahomes returns for the 2020 season with all of his weapons intact, plus a shiny new piece in Clyde Edwards-Helaire. That's a scary prospect for a league that is trying to keep up with the Chiefs. Who is betting against them this season?!

ROOKIE SPOTLIGHT

Clyde Edwards-Helaire: When the league's best quarterback hand picks you as the guy who he wants to be next to him in the offensive backfield, you have to have the spotlight on you. Edwards-Helaire is going to be a fantastic fit in Andy Reid's offense with what they can do with him in the passing game.

DEPTH CHART

Quarterback	Wide Receiver	Center	Edge	Line Backer	Cornerback
Patrick Mahomes	Tyreek Hill	Austin Reiter	Alex Okafor	Anthony Hitchens	Bashaud Breeland
Chad Henne	Sammy Watkins	Darryl Williams [R]	Frank Clark	Damien Wilson	Charvarious Ward
Jordan Ta'amu	Mecole Hardman	**Tackle**	Tanoh Kpassagnon	Willie Gay [R]	Rashad Fenton
Fullback	Demarcus Robinson	Mitchell Schwartz	Breeland Speaks	Dorian O'Daniel	Alex Brown
Anthony Sherman	Byron Pringle	Eric Fisher	**Defensive Tackle**	Darrius Harris	L'Jarius Sneed [R]
Running Back	Gehrig Dieter	Mike Remmers	Chris Jones	Free Safety	Strong Safety
Damien Williams	**Tight End**	**Guard**	Derrick Nnadi	Juan Thornhill	Tyrann Mathieu
Clyde Edwards-Helaire	Travis Kelce	Nick Allegretti	Mike Pennell	Daniel sorensen	Chris Lammons
Darwin Thompson	Deon Yelder	Laurent Duvernay-Tardif	**Kicker**	**Punter**	**Long Snapper**
Darrel Williams	Ricky Seals-Jones	Andrew Wylie	Harrison Butker	Tyler Newsome	James Winchester

NFL

1

FULL 10 YARDS

KANSAS CITY CHIEFS

2019 RANKINGS

Player	Pos	Standard			0.5PPR			PPR		
		Pts	Avg	Rank	Pts	Avg	Rank	Pts	Avg	Rank
Patrick Mahomes	QB	279.8	21.5	QB8						
Damien Williams	RB	83.7	8.4	RB41	96.7	9.7	RB42	109.7	11	RB42
LeSean McCoy	RB	90.6	7.0	RB40	104.6	8.1	RB40	118.6	9.1	RB39
Tyreek Hill	WR	124.2	11.3	WR26	151.2	14	WR29	178.2	16	WR31
Sammy Watkins	WR	85.7	6.6	WR49	111.2	8.6	WR49	136.7	11	WR46
Mecole Hardman	WR	84.5	5.6	WR51	97.0	6.5	WR59	109.5	7.3	WR64
Demarcus Robinson	WR	60.5	4.0	WR73	76.0	5.1	WR71	91.5	6.1	WR71
Travis Kelce	TE	154.9	10.3	TE1	201.9	14	TE1	248.9	17	TE1
Kansas City Chiefs	DST	129.0	8.6	DST7						
Harrison Butker	K	158.0	10.5	K1						

PATRICK MAHOMES

In 2019, Mahomes was the unanimous QB1 in ranking, averaging 25 fantasy points per game and with the current Chiefs offense, there is no reason to believe he won't repeat this in 2020. He will be one of the first 2 QB's off the board in every draft and it's only injury that will likely stop that.

ADP 2.07

CLYDE EDWARDS-HELARIE

ADP 1.07

Edwards-Helaire wouldn't have made this list in July but with Damien Williams now sitting out the 2020 season due to the coronavirus, his value has just skyrocketed! He offers Chiefs Head Coach, Andy Reid, a versatile skillset of both running and pass catching that should fit into the Chiefs offense perfectly. Edwards-Helaire may seem like a risk in the 1st Rd due to being a rookie, but he has massive potential for fantasy owners.

TYREEK HILL

Tyreek Hill could very easily finish the season as the top rated fantasy wide receiver. He has Patrick Mahomes throwing him the ball, is one of the fastest players in the NFL and at 26, is in his prime but it's not all rosy - In 2019 he had 5/11 games where he finished outside the top 37 wide receivers but he did suffer with two separate injuries. Hill is a top tier WR.

ADP 1.12

MECOLE HARDMAN

ADP 9.09

Hardman is not a guaranteed starter but in deeper fantasy leagues he is worth picking up. In 2019, he played in less than 50% of the Chiefs snaps but still ended up with six touchdowns due to his big play ability. If anything was to happen to Tyreek Hill, Hardman will step into the role.

TRAVIS KELCE

Kelce is your number 1 Tight End! He has finished atop the pile of all tight ends for the past 4 seasons and should find himself there once again in the 2020 season. Picking Kelce is all about your own draft strategy as he won't be available for too long. Constituency is the key, and Kelce delivers for fantasy owners every week!

ADP 2.08

2020 Projections

Position	Player	Standard		0.5PPR		Full PPR	
		Pts	Rank	Pts	Rank	Pts	Rank
QB	Patrick Mahomes	385.1	2				
RB	C. Edwards-Helaire	207.0	11	227.5	14	248.0	12
RB	Darwin Thompson	27.6	92	34.1	88	40.6	88
RB	D. Washington	91.9	53	99.9	56	107.9	58
WR	Tyreek Hill	179.0	3	212.0	7	245.0	11
WR	Sammy Watkins	95.9	53	119.9	53	143.9	54
WR	Mecole Hardman	91.6	58	109.6	61	127.6	64
WR	Demarcus Robinson	43.1	108	53.1	108	63.1	108
TE	Travis Kelce	159.3	1	203.8	1	248.3	1

ADP taken from Ultimate Draft Kit (PPR)

Projections by Rob Grimwood @FFBritballer

FANTASY FOOTBALL

2

KANSAS CITY CHIEFS

LAST 5 YEARS

	W	L	T	Div	P/Offs
2019	12	4	0	1st	Won SB
2018	12	4	0	1st	Lost Conf
2017	10	6	0	1st	Lost WC
2016	12	4	0	1st	Lost Div
2015	11	5	0	2nd	Lost Div

DO SAY..
Super Bowl champions!

DON'T SAY..
We are nothing without Patrick Mahomes

BETTING ODDS BY ADAM WALFORD (@TOUCHDOWNTIPS)

SUPER BOWL	13/2
AFC CONFERENCE	13/4
AFC WEST	1/4

TO MAKE PLAYOFFS
1/14
TEAM TOTAL WINS
11.5

ADAM'S BEST BET
WIN SUPER BOWL
13/2

PLEASE GAMBLE RESPONSIBLY

VIEW FROM THE SIDELINES

By Ross Stirling (@RossStrirling83)

The Chiefs offseason can be described in 3 words – Deals, Deals, Deals and the number 177. $177 was the value of cap space the Chiefs had remaining at the start of the off season despite this GM Brett Veach got deals done during the off season. Re-worked deals for Frank Clark & Sammy Watkins topped off with a blockbuster deal for Mahomes, as well as deals for Chris Jones % the league's best TE Travis Kelce. Massive respect for Laurent Duvernay-Tardif who opts out to help on the front lines during the pandemic as well. The door has been opened 1st round draft pick Clyde Edwards-Helaire who seems like a natural fit for a Reid offence. Going into the season the mantra of the team has been 'Run It Back' suggesting that with many of the team returning I wouldn't bet against another Super Bowl win. Week 3 @ Ravens and week 15 @Saints which could easily be precursors to Championship and Superbowl games respectively.

►RETRO FOCUS◄

DERRICK THOMAS – OLB

Even though Derrick Thomas has been gone for 20 years, he will never be forgotten by Chiefs fans. The OLB was one of the most dominant pass rushers in NFL history, once racking up a game-wrecking 7 sacks in a single game. 126.5 sacks in his career puts him 4th all time for all LBs. Thomas also registered three safeties and had 45 forced fumbles in his career, ranking him top in Chiefs history. Thomas was the Walter Payton Man of the Year in 1993.

DID YOU KNOW

Arrowhead Stadium holds the World Record for the loudest crowd roar at a sports stadium at 142.2 decibels. It was achieved in September 2014 when they sacked Patriots' QB Tom Brady.

KEY STAT

"On the Frontline"
Chiefs offensive lineman, Dr. Laurent Duvernay-Tardif was the first player to opt out of the 2020 NFL season due to the COVID-19 pandemic.

FULL10YARDS VERDICT

It took the Chiefs a full 50 years to win their second Super Bowl but there's a good chance it might take them just one year to seal another. They've just paid out squillions of dollars to keep Patrick Mahomes at QB for another decade and to have Chris Jones bossing the D-line for the next four years. Nearly all of last year's Super Bowl winners are still in tow, the offence is even more loaded and, if Jones's predictions on social media are right, Kansas are going to dominate the league, let alone their division, for years.

BETTING, STATS, FANS VIEW, RETRO

3

FULL 10 YARDS

LAS VEGAS RAIDERS

THE LOWDOWN:

A new city and a new beginning for the Raiders. Fans of the silver and black will be excited to see their team perform in their new state of the art arena which is located just off the world famous Las Vegas strip. Jon Gruden's men will be hoping to get off to a winning start in their new home. The raiders surprised a few people when they took Wide Receiver Henry Ruggs III. They also brought in former 2nd overall pick Marcus Mariota after his tenure ended with the Titans. The Raiders are adamant that Derek Carr is their starting QB but it wouldn't come as a surprise to see Mariota lead the Raiders as starter once or twice this season.

SCHEDULE

Week 1: @ Panthers
Week 2: Vs Saints *(MNF)*
Week 3: @ Patriots
Week 4: Vs Bills
Week 5: @ Chiefs
Week 6: BYE
Week 7: Vs Buccaneers *(SNF)*
Week 8: @ Browns
Week 9: @ Chargers
Week 10: Vs Broncos
Week 11: Vs Chiefs *(SNF)*
Week 12: @ Falcons
Week 13: @ Jets
Week 14: Vs Colts
Week 15: Vs Chargers *(TNF)*
Week 16: Vs Dolphins
Week 17: @ Broncos

2020 NFL DRAFT CLASS

Round 1
Henry Ruggs III, WR,
Alabama
Damon Arnette, CB,
Ohio State
Round 3
Lynn Bowden, RB/WR,
Kentucky
Bryan Edwards, WR,
South Carolina
Tanner Muse, LB,
Clemson
Round 4
John Simpson, IOL,
Clemson
Amik Robertson, CB,
Louisiana Tech

SIGNINGS

Nelson Agholor, WR
Prince Amukamara, CB
Maliek Collins, DT
Jeff Heath, S
Nick Kwiatkoski, LB
Marcus Mariota, QB
Carl Nassib, DE
Damarious Randall, DB
Jason Witten, TE

STAR SIGNING
Cory Littleton, LB

NO LONGER ON TEAM

Mike Glennon, QB
DeShone Kizer, QB
Vontaze Burfict, LB
Tahir Whitehead, LB
Karl Joseph, S

TEAM DETAILS:

Owner: Mark Davis
General Manager: Mike Mayock
Stadium: Allegiant Stadium
Location: Las Vegas, Nevada
Head Coach: Jon Gruden
Offensive Coordinator:
Greg Olson
Defensive Coordinator:
Paul Guenther
Coaching Staff:
Rich Bisaccia (ST Coordinator/Assistant HC)
Kirby Wilson (RB Coach)
Edgar Bennett (WR Coach)
Frank Smith (TE Coach)
Super Bowl Wins: 3 (1976, 1980, 1983)
Conference Wins: 4 (AFC, 1976, 1980, 1983, 2002)
Divisional Wins: 15 (AFL West, 1967, 1968, 1969; AFC West, 1970, 1972, 1973, 1974, 1975, 1976, 1983, 1985, 1990, 2000, 2001, 2002)
-2019-
Record : 7-9
Offence Rank: Passing (9th), Rushing (13th), Overall (24th)
Defence Rank: Passing (25th), Rushing (8th), Overall (24th)

KEY PLAYER

Darren Waller: The Raiders make the leap to Las Vegas without a whole lot of star power. What they do have is a youthful roster stacked with talent. These youngsters are going to look to the team's established veterans for leadership. Darren Waller will head up a youthful receiving core, with the Tight End looking to build on a 1323 yard season in 2019.

Henry Ruggs III: Insane speed and jumping ability is what Henry Ruggs is known for, however, he is more than just a deep ball receiver who is going to run go-routes. Ruggs can climb the ladder and get vertical and he also has huge hands and is super reliable when making big time catches.

ROOKIE SPOTLIGHT

DEPTH CHART

Quarterback	Wide Receiver	Center	Edge	Line Backer	Cornerback
Derek Carr	Henry Ruggs [R]	Rodney Hudson	Clelin Ferrell	Nick Kwiatkowski	Prince Amukamara
Marcus Mariota	Tyrell Williams	Andre James	Maxx Crosby	Cory Littleton	Trayvon Mullen
Nathan Peterman	Hunter Renfrow	**Tackle**	Carl Nassib	Nicholas Morrow	Lamarcus Joyner
Fullback	Zay Jones	Trent Brown	Arden Key	Marquel Lee	Damon Arnette [R]
Alec Ingold	Nelson Agholor	Kolton Miller	**Defensive Tackle**	Kyle Wilbur	Isaiah Johnson
Running Back	Bryan Edwards [R]	Brandon Parker	Maurice Hurst	**Free Safety**	**Strong Safety**
Josh Jacobs	**Tight End**	**Guard**	Maliek Collins	Jonathan Abram	Damarious Randall
Jalen Richard	Darren Waller	Richie Incognito	Jonathan Hankins	Erik Harris	Jeff Heath
Lynn Bowden [R]	Jason Witten	Gabe Jackson	**Kicker**	**Punter**	**Long Snapper**
Devontae Booker	Forster Moreau	Erik Magnusson	Daniel Carlson	AJ Cole III	Trent Sieg

NFL

1

FULL 10 YARDS

LAS VEGAS RAIDERS

2019 RANKINGS

Player	Pos	Standard			0.5PPR			PPR		
		Pts	Avg	Rank	Pts	Avg	Rank	Pts	Avg	Rank
Derek Carr	QB	232.9	15.5	QB17						
Josh Jacobs	RB	171.6	13.2	RB13	181.6	14	RB15	191.6	15	RB19
Jalen Richard	RB	40.9	2.7	RB66	57.9	3.9	RB60	74.9	5	RB57
Tyrell Williams	WR	101.1	7.8	WR40	122.1	9.4	WR43	143.1	11	WR43
Hunter Renfrow	WR	68.3	5.7	WR63	89.8	7.5	WR63	111.3	9.3	WR61
Zay Jones	WR	19.8	1.4	WR135	32.3	2.3	WR120	44.8	3.2	WR115
Darren Waller	WR	120.3	8.0	TE5	162.3	11	TE5	204.3	14	TE5
Foster Moreau	TE	47.4	3.7	TE33	57.9	4.5	TE36	68.4	5.3	TE37
Las Vegas Raiders	DST	65.0	4.3	DST29						
Daniel Carlson	K	88.0	5.9	K25						

DEREK CARR
ADP 18.11

Carr has thrown for less than 23 touchdowns in each of the past 3 seasons and although he has been given some offensive weapons in Henry Ruggs and Hunter Renfrow, he will need to be throwing around 30 TDs in 2020 to become a more viable option for fantasy owners. Plus Marcus Mariota is lurking...

JOSH JACOBS
ADP 2.02

Jacobs could be the fantasy break out player of 2020. He has the potential to become a top-5 fantasy running back if he is given the targets. The Raiders brought back Jalen Richard who is seen as a pass catching specialist but he should be involved more in the passing game in 2020.

HENRY RUGGS
ADP 9.12

Ruggs was the first wide receiver selected in the 2020 draft, ahead of CeeDee Lamb and Jerry Jeudy. Ruggs is a big play speedster and is likely to step into an every down role. He excels after the catch and could offer the big plays that the Raiders have been missing. As with any rookie, there may be some initial teething problems but Ruggs has a lot of upside.

HUNTER RENFROW
ADP 15.11

Renfrow finished the 2019 with a flourish finishing as the sixth best wide receiver in weeks 16 and 17. He should remain as the Raiders slot receiver and this could lead to a large number of targets. Henry Ruggs' speed on the outside could draw some coverage away from Renfrow giving him even more opportunities.

DARREN WALLER
ADP 5.10

Waller is a late bloomer, having a breakout season at 27 years of age. He had 28% of the Raiders total receiving yards in 2019, the most by any TE in the NFL. The Raiders have drafted WRs in the first and third rounds of the 2020 draft so Waller will see his targets decline but in a position that doesn't offer much outside of Kelce/Kittle, he is a solid option.

2020 Projections

Position	Player	Standard		0.5PPR		Full PPR	
		Pts	Rank	Pts	Rank	Pts	Rank
QB	Derek Carr	271.2	26				
RB	Josh Jacobs	193.7	16	205.7	16	217.7	19
RB	Jalen Richard	47.0	75	62.5	69	78.0	68
RB	Lynn Bowden Jr.	98.9	50	110.9	48	122.9	49
WR	Henry Ruggs III	82.1	66	98.1	71	114.1	75
WR	Tyrell Williams	88.8	61	107.8	63	126.8	65
WR	Hunter Renfrow	69.5	76	89.0	77	108.5	76
WR	Bryan Edwards	27.4	121	35.4	121	43.4	121
WR	Nelson Agholor	32.8	114	44.3	110	55.8	110
TE	Darren Waller	113.9	5	144.9	5	175.9	5
TE	Jason Witten	31.4	47	46.4	44	61.4	43

ADP taken from Ultimate Draft Kit (PPR)

Projections by Rob Grimwood @FFBritballer

FANTASY FOOTBALL

2

FULL 10 YARDS

LAS VEGAS RAIDERS

LAST 5 YEARS

	W	L	T	Div	P/Offs
2019	7	9	0	3rd	
2018	4	12	0	4th	
2017	6	10	0	3rd	
2016	12	4	0	2nd	Lost WC
2015	7	9	0	3rd	

DO SAY..
Knock on wood if you're with me

DON'T SAY..
Oakland

BETTING ODDS BY ADAM WALFORD (@TOUCHDOWNTIPS)

SUPER BOWL	**80/1**
AFC CONFERENCE	**30/1**
AFC WEST	**10/1**

TO MAKE PLAYOFFS
15/8
TEAM TOTAL WINS
7

ADAM'S BEST BET
HENRY RUGGS OVER 4.5 TDS
10/11

PLEASE GAMBLE RESPONSIBLY

VIEW FROM THE SIDELINES
By Tyler Arthur (@TylerJArthur)

The Raiders take on their new name & a new stadium, as they make themselves feel at home in Nevada. Their inaugural season provides many more reasons to be excited than just the new digs. The offense was already good last year & should be slightly improved and the defense has multiple new additions who should make a real impact. If nothing else changes, the pass coverage should be less frustrating, which was the biggest issue & has been for years. With better defensive output, the sky is the limit for this franchise. The AFC West always make things harder but with hype to live up to & all eyes on Las Vegas, the Raiders will look to pick up on last year's potential & push for the playoffs in 2020. Record prediction; 9-7 – 2nd in the AFC West.

►RETRO FOCUS◄
JOHN MATUSZAK – DL

If you don't recognise the name you may recognise the body, as Raiders defensive lineman John Matuszak was the person who played the disfigured monster Sloth in the iconic 80s film The Goonies. Matuszak won two Super Bowls with the Silver and Black in the 70s and 80s, the second time part of the first Wild Card team to win the Vince Lombardi trophy. As sacks were not recorded in the 70s we have no clear evidence of the chaos that 'Tooz' caused for a decade.

DID YOU KNOW
Carl Weathers played seven games for the Raiders in 1970 and 1971 before becoming boxer Apollo Creed in the Rocky films.

KEY STAT

"Vegas Baby!"
The Las Vegas Raiders are the third major sporting franchise established in Sin City since 2017, joining the NHL's Vegas Golden Knights and the WNBA's Las Vegas Aces.

FULL10YARDS VERDICT
After revamping their roster over the last couple of years, it could be time for the Raiders to wreak havoc. Derek Carr finally has weapons around him, from new speedster Henry Ruggs III to a decent tight end corps while defensively, free agency has done them no harm. If Clelin Ferrell starts to show why he was the #4 overall pick last year and fellow DE Maxx Crosby pushes on, Vegas could get lucky in their new high-tech desert home and be worthy of an outside bet to sneak into the playoffs.

BETTING, STATS, FANS VIEW, RETRO

3

FULL 10 YARDS

LOS ANGELES CHARGERS

THE LOWDOWN:

Starting fresh in a new stadium, The Chargers and their fans will be hoping this is the beginning of a new era for the team. They drafted rookie QB Justin Herbert in the first round of the draft this year and will look for him to be the teams franchise QB for years to come. He'll be joining Tyrod Taylor who will be a key role in mentoring him and shaping up to starting calibre. The Chargers offence will go through Keenan Allen and Mike Williams as they look to compete in a tough AFC West. Austin Ekeler will also play a key role. Defensively, Joey Bosa, the league's highest paid defender, will be expected to live up to the value of his contract and based on his career so far, it's clear that he will. Derwin James will command the secondary and hope to shut down the aerial attacks of teams they come up against.

SCHEDULE

Week 1: @ Bengals
Week 2: Vs. Chiefs
Week 3: Vs. Panthers
Week 4: @ Buccaneers
Week 5: @ Saints *(MNF)*
Week 6: Vs. Jets
Week 7: @ Dolphins
Week 8: Vs. Jaguars
Week 9: Vs. Raiders
Week 10: BYE
Week 11: @ Broncos
Week 12: @ Bills
Week 13: Vs. Patriots
Week 14: Vs. Falcons
Week 15: @ Raiders *(TNF)*
Week 16: Vs. Broncos
Week 17: @ Chiefs

2020 NFL DRAFT CLASS

Round 1
Justin Herbert, QB, Oregon
Kenneth Murray, LB, Oklahoma
Round 4
Joshua Kelley, RB, UCLA
Round 5
Joe Reed, WR, Virginia
Round 6
Alohi Gilman, S, Notre Dame
Round 7
K.J. Hill, WR, Ohio State

SIGNINGS

Trai Turner, OG
Bryan Bulaga, OT
Chris Harris, CB
Linval Joseph, DT

FRANCHISE TAG

Hunter Henry, TE

NO LONGER ON TEAM

Philip Rivers, QB
Melvin Gordon, RB
Derek Watt, FB
Travis Benjamin, WR
Russell Okung, OL
Brandon Mebane, DT
Jatavis Brown, LB
Thomas Davis, LB

TEAM DETAILS:

Owner: Dean Spanos
General Manager: Tom Telesco
Stadium: SoFi Stadium
Location: Los Angeles, California
Head Coach: Anthony Lynn
Offensive Coordinator:
Shane Steichen
Defensive Coordinator:
Gus Bradley
Coaching Staff:
George Stewart (ST Coordinator/Assistant HC)
Pep Hamilton (QB Coach)
Mark Ridgley (RB Coach)
Phil McGeoghan (WR Coach),
Alfredo Roberts (TE Coach)
Super Bowl Wins: 0
Conference Wins: 1 (AFC, 1994)
Divisional Wins: 10 (AFC West, 1979, 1980, 1981, 1992, 1994, 2004, 2006, 2007, 2008, 2009)

-2019-
Record: 5-11
Offence Rank: Passing (6th), Rushing (28th), Overall (21st)
Defence Rank: Passing (5th), Rushing (18th), Overall (14th)

KEY PLAYER

Derwin James: The Chargers are entering a new era without Philip Rivers under centre. However, their defense remains one of the best in the league. Derwin James burst onto the scene as a rookie in 2018, and his injury last season coincided with the Chargers' poor season. A hard-tackling Safety, James reads the game fantastically, he'll be key to the Bolts' season, along with Melvin Ingram and Joey Bosa.

Justin Herbert: The physical tools that Justin Herbert possesses are off-the-charts; arm strength is A+, he can make plays with his legs and he has the prototypical measurables that NFL teams look for in terms of height. If he can continue to develop as a passer, the Chargers could have their guy for the next 10-15 years.

ROOKIE SPOTLIGHT

DEPTH CHART

Quarterback	Wide Receiver	Center	Edge	Line Backer	Cornerback
Tyrod Taylor	Keenan Allen	Mike Pouncey	Joey Bosa	Nick Vigil	Casey Hayward
Justin Herbert [R]	Mike Williams	Scott Quessenberry	Melvin Ingram	Kenneth Murray [R]	Chris Harris
Easton Stick	Andre Patton	**Tackle**	Isaac Rochell	Denzel Perryman	Desmond King
Fullback	Joe Reed [R]	Bryan Bulagra	Uchenna Nwosu	Malik Jefferson	Brandon Facyson
Derrick Gore	Darius Jennings	Sam Tevi	**Defensive Tackle**	Emeke Egbule	Michael Davis
Running Back	Jason Moore	Trent Scott	Linval Joseph	**Free Safety**	**Strong Safety**
Austin Ekeler	**Tight End**	**Guard**	Justin Jones	Rayshawn Jenkins	Derwin James
Justin Jackson	Hunter Henry	Dan Feeney	Jerry Tillery	Nasir Adderley	Roderic Teamer
Joshua Kelley [R]	Virgil Green	Trai Turner	**Kicker**	**Punter**	**Long Snapper**
Darrius Bradwell [R]	Andrew Vollert	Forrest Lamp	Michael Badgely	Ty Long	Cole Mazza

NFL

1

FULL 10 YARDS

LOS ANGELES CHARGERS

2019 RANKINGS

Player	Pos	Standard			0.5PPR			PPR		
		Pts	Avg	Rank	Pts	Avg	Rank	Pts	Avg	Rank
Philip Rivers	QB	237.8	15.9	QB16						
Austin Ekeler	RB	208.1	13.9	RB8	249.6	17	RB5	291.1	19	RB4
Melvin Gordon	RB	120.6	11.0	RB28	138.6	13	RB26	156.6	14	RB23
Justin Jackson	RB	21.1	3.5	RB88	25.6	4.3	RB90	30.1	5	RB88
Keenan Allen	WR	143.3	9.6	WR18	190.8	13	WR12	238.3	16	WR8
Mike Williams	WR	108.5	7.8	WR37	132.0	9.4	WR39	155.5	11	WR39
Dontrelle Inman	WR	17.5	2.9	WR137	23.0	3.8	WR138	28.5	4.8	WR136
Hunter Henry	TE	85.0	7.7	TE8	110.0	10	TE8	135.0	12	TE9
Los Angeles Chargers	DST	75.0	5.0	DST27						
Michael Badgley	K	61.0	7.6	K31						

TYROD TAYLOR
ADP 19.12

Taylor is the starting QB in Los Angeles but for how long? He isn't a high fantasy scorer and may not last half a season meaning he'll be on most waivers after drafts. He does possess the ability to break the pocket and run but this isn't a player that is anything more than a possible bye week streamer, for the few weeks.

AUSTIN EKELER
ADP 2.05

Ekeler benefitted from Melvin Gordon's holdout & finished as a top-5 RB in 3 of the 4 games that Gordon missed. Seen as more of a receiving back, Ekeler is the #1 RB for the Chargers & with the uncertainty at the QB position, he may see more touches. The downside with Ekeler is at QB: Taylor doesn't throw to RBs often & Herbert is untried in the NFL.

KEENAN ALLEN
ADP 5.04

Allen is a great receiver but his current situation isn't good for fantasy numbers. Tyrod Taylor or Justin Herbert at quarterback is a downgrade from Phillip Rivers in 2020 and this will impact Allen's value. He should still lead the team in targets, receptions, yards and most measurable's but don't expect the same numbers as 2019.

MIKE WILLIAMS
ADP 14.1

Williams topped 1,000 yards in 2019 for the first time in his career averaging a massive 20.4 yards per reception on just 49 catches! He has big play ability but do the Chargers have a quarterback who can get him the ball in what will be a potentially limited offense?

HUNTER HENRY
ADP 8.12

Henry is a bit of an enigma. When he is on the field he will produce at the TE position but he finds himself injured far too often. Plus the fact the Philip Rivers is no longer under Center for the Chargers. Rivers targeted the TEs often which gave opportunities to Henry but this will happen a lot less in 2020 with the QB situation & an offense that will run the ball more.

2020 Projections

Position	Player	Standard		0.5PPR		Full PPR	
		Pts	Rank	Pts	Rank	Pts	Rank
QB	Tyrod Taylor	274.7	22				
RB	Austin Ekeler	198.8	14	229.8	10	260.8	10
RB	Justin Jackson	100.0	49	108.5	50	117.0	50
RB	Joshua Kelley	98.7	51	107.2	52	115.7	52
WR	Keenan Allen	142.4	23	182.9	19	223.4	18
WR	Mike Williams	117.6	38	144.1	41	170.6	42
WR	Joe Reed	34.3	112	43.8	111	53.3	111
TE	Hunter Henry	102.1	8	132.1	8	162.1	8

ADP taken from Ultimate Draft Kit (PPR)

Projections by Rob Grimwood @FFBritballer

FANTASY FOOTBALL

2

FULL 10 YARDS

LOS ANGELES CHARGERS

DO SAY..
Justin Herbert is the future

DON'T SAY..
Home-field advantage

BETTING ODDS BY ADAM WALFORD (@TOUCHDOWNTIPS)

SUPER BOWL **50/1**

AFC CONFERENCE **22/1**

AFC WEST **10/1**

TO MAKE PLAYOFFS
9/5
TEAM TOTAL WINS
7.5

ADAM'S BEST BET
CHARGERS TO MAKE PLAYOFFS
9/5

PLEASE GAMBLE RESPONSIBLY

VIEW FROM THE SIDELINES

By John Ayers @AdroitAyers

Last year the Chargers were dark horse Super Bowl contenders. Unfortunately, injuries and inconsistent play led to a 5-11 record. What is their 2020 outlook? With PFF top-10 defensive line and CB groups, one of the best safeties in the league, and a burgeoning LB group, the defense is ready to prove they're elite. The Chargers return some of the best weapons in the NFL at WR, RB, and TE, but failed to address one of their biggest needs at LT with a proven commodity. However, the biggest question mark is QB. Herbert needs development time, so if the Chargers are going to succeed, Taylor will have to show he's capable of leading the team to the playoffs.

►RETRO FOCUS◄

LANCE ALWORTH – WR

It's not often that being given a Disney character nickname is a term of endearment, but that was the case for Lance 'Bambi' Alworth the Chargers WR. Given the moniker because of his long legs and graceful running style, Alworth went to seven consecutive Pro Bowls in the 60s and was named a six-time All Pro. He caught 542 passes for 10,266, almost all with the Chargers, winning an AFL Championship (1963) and the AFL MVP in 1964.

DID YOU KNOW

The team played its first-ever season (1960) as the Los Angeles Chargers before moving to San Diego. They returned "home" to LA in 2016

KEY STAT

"New Kid on the Block"
The Chargers will have a new starting QB for the first time since 2004 (Drew Brees started the 2004 Wildcard game vs. Jets)

FULL10YARDS VERDICT

The Chargers are entering uncharted territory, as veteran QB Tyrod Taylor battles it out with #6 draft pick Justin Herbert to fill Philip Rivers' cleats. They also have a new home in SoFi Stadium so things might be unsettled for a while. Austin Ekeler, Keenan Allen and of course the newly minted Joey Bosa are likely to be key players, while former Broncos CB Chris Harris looks like a good addition. But even if the Bolts' report card improves from 2019's five wins, I don't think we'll be watching them in January.

BETTING, STATS, FANS VIEW, RETRO

3

FULL 10 YARDS

NFL ROOKIE SPOTLIGHT
ROOKIES TO WATCH

By Lee Wakefield (@wakefield90/@Full10yardsCFB)

Arizona Cardinals Round 4, Pick No. 114: Leki Fotu, IDL, Utah

Leki Fotu is a productive people-mover on the defensive line, he played on a strong defense in Utah and was one of the better players and bigger playmakers on it. Solid in the run game and an ability to get after the QB, would have been taken earlier if he was a little more versatile and if he was a little stronger.

Atlanta Falcons Round 2, Pick No. 47: Marlon Davidson, IDL, Auburn

A versatile lineman who can play both inside and out, Marlon Davidson is going to give the Falcons' defensive line a much needed boost. There has been some turnover in that position room but alongside Grady Jarrett and newly-acquired Dante Fowler, Davidson could form a group who could give some headaches to opposition QB's.

Baltimore Ravens Round 6, Pick No. 201: James Proche, WR, SMU

James Proche just gets open and when the ball comes his way, he doesn't drop passes at all. Proche doesn't have the size that we often look for in NFL receivers, nor does he have breakaway long speed but he sure is crafty. Proche will make his money over the middle making tough, contested catches and picking up important conversions.

Buffalo Bills Round 6, Pick No. 207: Isaiah Hodgins, WR, Oregon State

Hodgins has a long and lean frame and he possesses excellent body control and great hands. A decent route runner but not the most athletic receiver in terms of speed - He will need to improve on these aspects of his game to gain separation consistently. Could develop into a great chain-mover on 3rd down.

Carolina Panthers Round 2, Pick No. 64 : Jeremy Chinn, S, Southern Illinois

Chinn is a small school prospect who, like the Panthers, will have a lot of growing to do over the next year or two, but the exciting part is that the ceiling is sky high. Chinn already possesses an NFL body and plays with a lot of power and aggression; Phil Snow is going to have some fun developing him in Charlotte.

Cincinnati Bengals Round 6, Pick No. 180: Hakeem Adeniji, OT, Kansas

Adeniji was a tackle at Kansas but we feel like he will kick inside to guard for Cincinnati next year. Adeniji doesn't have the requisite length to survive outside in the NFL, however, he does have the power and athleticism to hold his own inside. It'll be particularly interesting to see if he is used as a pulling lineman in the run game - He was great at this in college.

Chicago Bears Round 2, Pick No. 50: Jaylon Johnson, CB, Utah

A long, lean and aggressive corner who has the potential to be a CB1 for the Bears for years to come - Kyle Fuller holds that position now and will probably do so for the next couple of years. Johnson can use this time to develop (he needs to dial down the physicality (expect DPI flags in year 1)) and then he can be the guy in the Windy City.

Cleveland Browns Round 4, Pick No. 115: Harrison Bryant, TE, Florida Atlantic

Kevin Stefanski loves to roll with 12 personnel, which involves having a couple of options at tight end - Cleveland recently acquired Austin Hooper from the Falcons and have David Njoku on the roster, who has flattered to deceive so far in his career. Bryant can put the pressure on Njoku to be that second tight end.

NFL ROOKIE SPOTLIGHT
ROOKIES TO WATCH

Dallas Cowboys Round 4, Pick No. 146 : Tyler Biadasz, IOL, Wisconsin

CeeDee Lamb headlined the Dallas draft class but one pick that could be the one to give Jerry Jones big props for is Tyler Biadasz. Dallas lost Travis Frederick and that is a huge loss this offseason, Biadasz could be the guy who steps into his shoes long term - He suffered a loss of form due to injury last year but has talent.

Denver Broncos Round 4, Pick No. 118: Albert Okwuegbunam, TE, Missouri

Okwueghunam is a quick tight end who caught the eye with his combine performance in Indianapolis prior to the draft. However, he disappointed last year for Missouri. However, he had scouts and draft gurus raving over his talent in 2017 and '18. Who was his QB in those years? Drew Lock.

Detroit Lions Round 3, Pick No. 67: Julian Okwara, LB, Notre Dame

A speedy and exciting edge rusher who can look electric on his day and whose motor almost always runs hot. There is a nice potential for Okwara to make early headway in the NFL as a situational pass rusher to start off with and he could develop into a nice option for the Lions long term.

Green Bay Packers Round 3, Pick No. 94: Josiah Deguara, TE, Cincinnati

A versatile tight end with skills in the blocking and receiving game, as well as having the capability to line up in-line and flexed out in the slot. Deguara is a nuanced route runner too who is only held back by being undersized and a relatively average athlete.

Houston Texans Round 5, Pick No. 171: Isaiah Coulter, WR, Rhode Island

Coulter is a deceptive route runner with a great deal of explosive ability to go up and get the football when it is there for the taking. Coulter excels at tracking the football as it is coming towards him and he has nice soft hands when catching the ball. Big step up for him to the NFL though.

Indianapolis Colts Round 2, Pick No. 41: Jonathan Taylor, RB, Wisconsin

I am cheating a little bit with this one as this isn't really a late pick but Jonathan Taylor is a powerful running back with excellent long speed and a long history of great production in college. Some may worry about that experience in college but he means he's going to be ready from day 1 in the NFL.

Jacksonville Jaguars Round 2, Pick No. 42: Laviska Shenault, WR, Colorado

The fit with Shenault and the kind of offense that Jacksonville runs, and the strengths of Gardner Minshew, this all looks like a match made in heaven. Minshew plays best when he can get the ball out quickly and makes short passes - Shenault is the sort of receiver who you just need to get the ball in his hands and let him create.

Kansas City Chiefs Round 3, Pick No. 96: Lucas Niang, OT, TCU

Had it not been for a hip injury that dogged him throughout his time at TCU, Niang could have been taken off the board much earlier than he was and he could end up being an absolute bargain for the Chiefs. Barely allowed a pressure, nevermind a sack in the past two years.

Las Vegas Raiders Round 3, Pick No. 80: Lynn Bowden, RB/WR, Kentucky

Bowden is one of these modern day players who can do it all and simply put, are just playmakers on the offensive side of the ball. A speedy athlete with vision to create after the catch and as a ball carrier, you'll see him lining up all over the formation for the silver and black, perhaps even as a QB at times.

Los Angeles Chargers Round 7, Pick No. 220: K.J. Hill, WR, Ohio State

K.J. Hill isn't the most explosive athlete you'll see but a player who has the most catches and is 6th all time in receiving yards in Ohio State history isn't to be sniffed at. Hill is a fantastic route runner who models his game after Chargers receiver, Keenan Allen - Hill should outperform his draft position, by a long way.

Los Angeles Rams Round 4, Pick No. 136: Brycen Hopkins, TE, Purdue

A really smooth mover who runs pretty routes and has great run-after-catch ability, Hopkins should be a receiving threat for the Rams whenever he sees the field. Another tight end who is coming into the league and will likely make his impact as a big slot receiver - Hopkins doesn't possess a lot of prowess in the run blocking game.

Miami Dolphins Round 7, Pick No. 246: Malcolm Perry, WR, Navy

The former Navy QB is looking to make his mark on the league as a wide receiver but whilst he learns the nuances of being a receiver, look for the Dolphins to use him as a running back or option QB with his own offensive package of plays. Not an amazing athlete but he can make tacklers miss and is very elusive.

Minnesota Vikings Round 5, Pick No. 169: Harrison Hand, CB, Temple

Hand transferred from Baylor to Temple for his Junior year and had an uptick in all production and generally a really nice year for the Owls, garnering a lot of attention late in the draft process from the online draft community. A zone corner who can make a play when he has his eyes on the QB.

New England Patriots Round 2, Pick No. 60: Josh Uche, EDGE/LB, Michigan

Josh Uche is such a fantastic fit for the Patriots and the sort of player they love on defense' an edge rusher and also off the ball and drop into coverage - The versatility that New England loves. Uche had a fantastic Senior Bowl week where he caused havoc off the edge, so that could be his main calling for the Patriots.

New Orleans Saints Round 3, Pick No. 74: Zack Baun, EDGE/LB, Wisconsin

Baun is another linebacker who has a diverse skill set. A fantastic athlete who deploys great hand usage and who has a wide array of pass rush moves, when hunting the QB but also has the football IQ to play in space. A great addition to an already strong linebacking group in New Orleans.

New York Giants Round 7, Pick No. 218: Carter Coughlin, EDGE, Minnesota

A quick and explosive edge rusher who will play as an outside linebacker for the Giants. Coughlin has years of production at Minnesota without registering numbers that are off the charts, whether that be a healthy number of sacks, forcing fumbles or getting his hands in passing lanes - The Giants got themselves a ball player.

New York Jets Round 5, Pick No. 158: Bryce Hall, CB, Virginia

A sticky man coverage corner who probably would have been drafted much higher had an ankle injury not robbed him of the vast majority of his senior year. The Jets have a bunch of corners occupying the depth chart of whom they have drafted precisely one of those players. Hall could be a bargain if he develops into CB1 for the Jets.

Philadelphia Eagles Round 5, Pick No. 168: John Hightower, WR, Boise State

Another one of the remodelled Philadelphia wide receiver room, John Hightower is a legitimate deep threat who can take the top off a defense. Philadelphia seems to be all about speed at the receiver position when it comes to their newly acquired talent, and they could be a big play offense, thanks to Hightower and others, in 2020.

Pittsburgh Steelers Round 4, Pick No. 124: Anthony McFarland Jr., RB, Maryland

Speed kills in the NFL these days and Anthony McFarland has an elite trait in that regard. I doubt that he will ever be a feature back due to his small stature but if he can build on his receiving prowess, he could become a fantastic change of pace back and a genuine game breaker if used in creative ways.

San Francisco 49ers Round 1, Pick No. 25: Brandon Aiyuk, WR, Arizona State

Not a late round pick but he wasn't their first pick either so allow us to cheat on this one. Brandon Aiyuk is a Kyle Shanahan receiver every day of the week. Not the biggest but incredibly dangerous after the catch and with an unbelievable ability to create separation, could see a few highlight reel plays from the outset.

Seattle Seahawks Round 4, Pick No. 133: Colby Parkinson, TE, Stanford

Parkinson is a big target down the seam at 6'7 and will give Russell Wilson another guy who he can lob it up to and ask his guy to come down with it, so with the way Seattle's offense is built - to run and work off play-action for big gains - Parkinson should fit nicely.

Tampa Bay Buccaneers Round 3, Pick No. 76: Ke'Shawn Vaughn, RB, Vanderbilt

If we know one thing about Tom Brady, it's that he loves to throw to running backs out of the backfield and the speedy Vaughn is always a threat to take the ball all the way to the house on runs and after the catch. Vanderbilt is usually overmatched in the SEC, so back-to-back 1,000 yard seasons is impressive.

Tennessee Titans Round 2, Pick No. 61: Kristian Fulton, CB, LSU

Kristian Fulton hung around on the draft board for longer than anticipated by many analysts, so with that he could end up being a great value pick for Tennessee. The Titans are well stocked at corner so the talented Fulton makes this a strong group, Malcolm Butler has an out in his contract after this year so Fulton could be blooded slowly.

Washington Football Team Round 4, Pick No. 142: Antonio Gandy-Golden, WR, Liberty

Antonio Gandy-Golden is another addition to a super young receiving group in the nation's capital. Extremely productive over the past couple of seasons with over 1,000 yards and 10 TD's in each, AGG is facing a big step up but he has great size and great hands. If he can work out how to run cleaner routes, he could be fantastic.

DALLAS COWBOYS

THE LOWDOWN:

For the first time in nine years, somebody other than Jason Garrett will be the Head Coach of the Cowboys come week one. Former Packers Head Coach Mike McCarthy is now at the reigns of Americas Team & he and his team will be aiming to bring the Cowboys back to the glory days they have so often longed for. The Cowboys have built an offence stacked with playmakers. Amari Cooper, Ezekiel Elliot, Michael Gallop & 1st round draft pick CeeDee Lamb but the surprise retirement of Travis Frederick will leave some doubts about the stability of the offensive line. After dipping in & out of the playoffs over the past few years, fans will be hoping this is the year they make a deep playoff run..

SCHEDULE

Week 1: @ Rams *(SNF)*
Week 2: Vs. Falcons
Week 3: @ Seahawks
Week 4: Vs Browns
Week 5: Vs. Giants
Week 6: Vs. Cardinals *(MNF)*
Week 7: @ Washington
Week 8: @ Eagles *(SNF)*
Week 9: Vs. Steelers
Week 10: BYE
Week 11: @ Vikings
Week 12: Vs. Washington *(Thanksgiving)*
Week 13: @ Ravens *(MNF)*
Week 14: @ Bengals
Week 15: Vs. 49ers *(SNF)*
Week 16: Vs. Eagles
Week 17: @ Giants

2020 NFL DRAFT CLASS

Round 1
CeeDee Lamb, WR,
Oklahoma
Round 2
Trevon Diggs, CB,
Alabama
Round 3
Neville Gallimore, IDL,
Oklahoma
Round 4
Reggie Robinson II, CB,
Tulsa
Tyler Biadasz, IOL,
Wisconsin
Round 5
Bradlee Anae, EDGE,
Utah
Round 7
Ben DiNucci, QB,
James Madison

SIGNINGS

Anthony Brown, CB
Ha Ha Clinton-Dix, S
Andy Dalton, QB
Gerald McCoy, DT
Dontari Poe, DT
Aldon Smith, DE
Greg Zuerlein, K
Everson Griffen, DE

FRANCHISE TAG

Dak Prescott, QB

NO LONGER ON TEAM

Tavon Austin, WR
Randall Cobb, WR
Jason Witten, TE
Travis Frederick, C (Ret.)
Michael Bennett, DE
Robert Quinn, DE
Maliek Collins, DT
Byron Jones, CB
Gerald McCoy, DT

TEAM DETAILS:

Owner: Jerry Jones
General Manager: Jerry Jones
Stadium: AT&T Stadium
Location: Arlington, Texas
Head Coach: Mike McCarthy
Offensive Coordinator: Kellen Moore
Defensive Coordinator: Mike Nolan
Coaching Staff:
Doug Nussmeier (QB Coach)
Skip Peete (RB Coach)
Adam Henry (WR Coach)
Lunda Wells (TE Cocah)
John Fassel (ST Coordinator)
Super Bowl Wins: 5 (1971, 1977, 1992, 1993, 1995)
Conference Wins: 8 (NFC,1970, 1971,1975,1977,1978,1992, 1993, 1995)
Divisional Wins: 19 (NFC East, 1970,1971,1973,1975-1979,1981, 1985,1992-1996,1998, 2007,2009, 2014, 2016, 2018)
-2019-
Record: 8-8
Offence Rank: Passing (2nd), Rushing (5th),Overall (6th)
Defence Rank: Passing (10th), Rushing (11th), Overall (11th)

KEY PLAYER

Leighton Vander Esch: The Cowboys' offence is set to be one of the most dangerous in the league this year. That'll put the onus on the defense to stamp out any offensive firepower other teams bring to the table. Leighton Vander Esch is crucial to that, with Byron Jones, Jeff Heath & Robert Quinn leaving in free agency, the hard tackling Linebacker has already established himself as a leader in the locker room.

CeeDee Lamb: A surprising pick at the time but Lamb was the best player on the board when the pick went in. A dominant receiver who has a diverse skill set - Lamb is just as likely to climb the ladder to get a ball as he is to take a quick pass & go all the way. He totaled 1,327 receiving yards in his final year at Oklahoma & even found the endzone on the ground.

ROOKIE SPOTLIGHT

DEPTH CHART

Quarterback	Wide Receiver	Center	Edge	Line Backer	Cornerback
Dak Prescott	Amari Cooper	Joe Looney	Demarcus Lawrence	Leighton Vander Esch	Chidobe Awuzie
Andy Dalton	Michael Gallup	Tyler Biadasz [R]	Tyrone Crawford	Sean Lee	Anthony Brown
Clayton Thorson	CeeDee Lamb [R]	**Tackle**	Everson Griffen	Jaylon Smith	Trevon Diggs [R]
Fullback	Devin Smith	La'el Collins	Dorance Armstrong	Joe Thomas	Jourdan Lewis
Jamize Olawale	Ventrell Bryant	Tyron Smith	**Defensive Tackle**	Luke Gifford	Maurice Canaday
Running Back	Cedrick Wilson	Brandon Knight	Dontari Poe	**Free Safety**	**Strong Safety**
Ezekiel Elliott	**Tight End**	**Guard**	Trysten Hill	Xavier Woods	Ha Ha Clinton-Dix
Tony Pollard	Blake Jarwin	Connor Williams	Neville Gallimore	Luther Kirk [R]	Darian Thompson
Jordan Chunn	Dalton Schultz	Zack Martin	**Kicker**	**Punter**	**Long Snapper**
Rico Dowdle [R]	Blake Bell	Connor McGovern	Greg Zuerlein	Chris Jones	LP Ladouceur

NFL

1

FULL 10 YARDS

2019 RANKINGS

Player	Pos	Standard			0.5PPR			PPR		
		Pts	Avg	Rank	Pts	Avg	Rank	Pts	Avg	Rank
Dak Prescott	QB	319.3	21.3	QB3						
Ezekiel Elliott	RB	233.3	15.6	RB5	258.8	17	RB4	284.3	19	RB5
Tony Pollard	RB	67.7	4.8	RB50	74.7	5.3	RB52	81.7	5.8	RB53
Amari Cooper	WR	157.7	10.5	WR9	195.2	13	WR9	232.7	16	WR10
Michael Gallup	WR	118.9	9.2	WR28	149.4	12	WR30	179.9	14	WR30
Randall Cobb	WR	91.8	6.6	WR46	116.8	8.3	WR45	141.8	10	WR45
Jason Witten	TE	74.5	5.0	TE14	104.0	6.9	TE11	133.5	8.9	TE11
Blake Jarwin	TE	54.5	3.6	TE24	70.0	4.7	TE25	85.5	5.7	TE26
Dallas Cowboys	DST	92.0	6.1	DST20						
Brett Maher	K	105.0	8.1	K19						

DAK PRESCOTT

ADP 6.01

Dak Prescott is no longer the steal in drafts he once was. After posting consistent top 10 finishes, he had a career year last year and now has another weapon to add to his arsenal in WR CeeDee Lamb. Dak will go a lot earlier this year, but still may prove a value if you can get him as the 5th QB off the board.

EZEKIEL ELLIOT

ADP 1.04

Seeing Zeke go in the top 3-5 picks is now the norm (when he isn't holding out or getting into off field skirmishes. His passing volume may suffer due to the arrival of CeeDee Lamb and Tony Pollard gaining experience, but Zeke is going to get you a solid start to your draft roster and is a set it and forget it guy and will average 15-19 pts per game again, like in 2019.

AMARI COOPER

ADP 4.02

For someone perenially drafted high since entering the league, there are a lot of people who like to swerve Amari Cooper. They'll cite that he is a boom or bust type guy and goes missing in the crunch games. That being said, he was around the WR10 mark in 2019 so if you could grab him as your 2nd WR , you won't have to worry too much if the same occurs in 2020.

MICHAEL GALLUP

ADP 7.07

Gallup for the most part, went toe to toe with Amari Cooper in terms of production, falling just shy of Cooper's totals. Gallup may fall in some drafts due to those being concerned with the number of mouths to feed. However, with an ADP in the range where he'll be a flex/early benchwarmer, that's great value for a guy that can put up another 1,000 yds.

BLAKE JARWIN

ADP 13.10

Blake Jarwin is an intriguing TE this year. Jason Witten is no longer and if you combine his and Jarwin's production last season, you get a top 10 TE. Despite CeeDee Lamb's arrivals, there are enough vacated targets in this offence to make jarwin at worst a streamable option. If he is Jason Witten 2.0, then he's an absolute steal late on for those punting TE.

2020 Projections

Position	Player	Standard		0.5PPR		Full PPR	
		Pts	Rank	Pts	Rank	Pts	Rank
QB	Dak Prescott	316.8	10				
RB	Ezekiel Elliott	290.8	2	325.8	2	360.8	2
RB	Tony Pollard	89.5	56	100.5	54	111.5	55
WR	Amari Cooper	153.6	17	191.1	17	228.6	17
WR	CeeDee Lamb	83.3	64	101.3	68	119.3	70
WR	Michael Gallup	112.2	42	138.7	44	165.2	44
TE	Blake Jarwin	88.9	14	114.9	14	140.9	14
TE	Dalton Schultz	26.6	49	37.6	49	48.6	48

ADP taken from Ultimate Draft Kit (PPR)

Projections by Rob Grimwood @FFBritballer

FANTASY FOOTBALL

2

DALLAS COWBOYS

DO SAY..
Dak Prescott is a Franchise Quarterback

DON'T SAY..
Dak Prescott contract negotiations

BETTING ODDS   BY ADAM WALFORD (@TOUCHDOWNTIPS)

SUPER BOWL **20/1**

NFC CONFERENCE **9/1**

NFC EAST **11/10**

TO MAKE PLAYOFFS
5/11
TEAM TOTAL WINS
9.5

ADAM'S BEST BET
DAK PRESCOTT OVER 4275.5 PASS YARDS
10/11

PLEASE GAMBLE RESPONSIBLY

VIEW FROM THE SIDELINES
By Tim Lees (@KMSportSigned)

My predictions for the Dallas Cowboys you ask.......Well Super Bowl champions obviously! Joking aside the cowboys have improved all areas of the field. Key additions of Griffin and Poe on cheap team friendly deals improve the defence and hopefully McCarthy manages to find consistency in the offence with the plethora of weapons he has at his disposal. While Clinton-Dix has gone under the radar he is a significant improvement in that area also. I Think the Cowboys can win the division and go far into the playoffs my biggest worry is that the defensive players brought in don't work and we can't dominate on both sides of the ball.

►RETRO FOCUS◄
DREW PEARSON – WR

Having just been told he's been shortlisted for the 2020 Hall of Fame, it is fitting to celebrate the career of Cowboys 3 time All-Pro WR Drew Pearson. In a career stretching 11 seasons in Dallas, Pearson made 22 playoff appearances & has a ring from Super Bowl XII where he made one catch against the Broncos in the 27-10 win. Pearson caught 489 regular season passes for just shy of 8,000 yards.

DID YOU KNOW
The Cowboys are the only team in NFL history to record 20 straight winning seasons (1966-1985)

KEY STAT
"Doing work in the yard"
Dallas gained the most offensive yards in the NFL in 2019 with 6904!

FULL10YARDS VERDICT
The team's fortunes will come down to QB Dak Prescott's play and whether he can once again to take this team to the playoffs. If he is able to go deep in January & maybe even February, he will be cashing in on a mega contract in 12 months time. As always with Dallas in recent seasons, there will be no hiding place if they fail to reach the playoffs yet again in a weak division. There shouldn't be any teething problems with the new faces coming in getting up to speed. They have the talent, they SHOULD have the coaching staff, but anything less late January football & the season is a failure.

BETTING, STATS, FANS VIEW, RETRO

3

FULL 10 YARDS

NEW YORK GIANTS

THE LOWDOWN:

Under the direction of first time Head Coach Joe Judge, the New York Giants will be looking to get back to winning ways after a disappointing run of seasons since their last playoff appearance. The Giants haven't been to the post season since 2013. Saquon Barkley will be the focal point of the teams attack as he and Daniel Jones work to create a winning chemistry. The NFC East has been flip-flopping between winners for the past couple of years and the men in blue will be looking to put their stamp on it and make it their own.

SCHEDULE

Week 1: Vs. Steelers *(MNF)*
Week 2: @ Bears
Week 3: Vs 49ers
Week 4: @ Rams
Week 5: @ Cowboys
Week 6: Vs. Washington
Week 7: @ Eagles *(TNF)*
Week 8: Vs. Buccaneers *(MNF)*
Week 9: @ Washington
Week 10: Vs. Eagles
Week 11: BYE
Week 12: @ Bengals
Week 13: @ Seahawks
Week 14: @ Cardinals
Week 15: @ Browns
Week 16: @ Ravens
Week 17: Vs. Cowboys

2020 NFL DRAFT CLASS

Round 1
Andrew Thomas, OT,
Georgia
Round 2
Xavier McKinney, S,
Alabama
Round 3
Matt Peart, OT,
UConn
Round 4
Darnay Holmes, CB,
UCLA
Round 5
Shane Lemieux, IOL,
Oregon
Round 6
Cam Brown, EDGE,
Penn State
Round 7
Carter Coughlin, EDGE,
Minnesota
T.J. Brunson, LB,
South Carolina
Chris Williamson, CB,
Minnesota
Tae Crowder, LB,
Georgia

SIGNINGS

James Bradberry, CB
Kyler Fackrell, LB
Cam Fleming, T
Dion Lewis, RB
Blake Martinez, LB
Levine Toilolo, TE

FRANCHISE TAG

Leonard Williams, DL

NO LONGER ON TEAM

Eli Manning, QB (Ret.)
Mike Remmers, OL
Deone Bucannon, LB
Alec Ogletree, LB
Antoine Bethea, S

TEAM DETAILS:

Owner: John Mara & Steve Tisch
General Manager: Dave Gettleman
Stadium: MetLife Stadium
Loaction: East Rutherford, NJ
Head Coach: Joe Judge
Offensive Coordinator: Jason Garrett
Defensive Coordinator: Sean Spencer
Coaching Staff:
Thomas McGaughey (ST Coordinator)
Jerry Schuplinski (QB Coach)
Burton Burns (RB Coach)
Tyke Tolbert (WR Coach)
Freddie Kitchens (TE Coach)
Super Bowl Wins: 4 (1986, 1990, 2007, 2011)
Conference Wins: 5 (NFC 1986, 1990, 2000, 2007, 2011)
Divisional Wins: 8 (1986, 1989, 1990, 1997, 2000, 2005, 2008, 2011)

-2019-
Record: 4-12
Offence Rank: Passing (18th), Rushing (19th), Overall (19th)
Defence Rank: Passing (28th), Rushing (20th), Overall (30th)

KEY PLAYER

Jabrill Peppers: The Giants will be looking to rebound from a couple of down years in 2020, a new look offense is taking shape around Daniel Jones & Saquon Barkley. But their defence will really need to kick on if they're to compete against the Eagles and Cowboys. Former first round pick, Jabrill Peppers will have increased pressure this year after a slow start to life in New York. The Safety is a potential turnover machine on his day.

Andrew Thomas: Thomas possesses the requisite length, strength and technique to be a ready made tackle from day 1 in the NFL and he should slot in on Daniel Jones' blindside and give a huge boost to that unit overall. The former Georgia man has great power when throwing his punches in pass protection and when blocking in the run game.

ROOKIE SPOTLIGHT

DEPTH CHART

Quarterback	Wide Receiver	Center	Edge	Line Backer	Cornerback
Daniel Jones	Golden Tata	Spencer Pulley	Leonard Williams	Blake Martinez	Deandre Baker
Colt McCoy	Sterling Shepard	Kyle Murphy [R]	Dexter Lawrence	Lorenzo Carter	James Bradberry
Cooper Rush	Darius Slayton	**Tackle**	BJ Hill	David Mayo	Corey Ballentine
Fullback	Cody Core	Nate Solder	Austin Johnson	Devante Downs	Sam Beal
Elijhaa Penny	Corey Coleman	Andrew Thomas [R]	**Defensive Tackle**	Tae Crowder [R]	Grant Haley
Running Back	Da'Mari Scott	Cameron Fleming	Dalvin Tomlinson	**Free Safety**	**Strong Safety**
Saquon Barkley	**Tight End**	**Guard**	Kyler Fackrell	Julian Love	Jabrill Peppers
Dion Lewis	Evan Engram	Will Hernandez	Chris Slayton	Xavier McKinney [R]	Nate Ebner
Wayne Gallman	Kaden Smith	Kevin Zeitler	**Kicker**	**Punter**	**Long Snapper**
Jonathan Hillman	Levine Toilolo	Shane Lemieux [R]	Aldrick Rosas	Riley Dixon	Casey Kreiter

NFL

1

FULL 10 YARDS

NEW YORK GIANTS

2019 RANKINGS

Player	Pos	Standard			0.5PPR			PPR		
		Pts	Avg	Rank	Pts	Avg	Rank	Pts	Avg	Rank
Daniel Jones	QB	211.3	17.6	QB22						
Saquon Barkley	RB	174.4	14.5	RB12	198.9	17	RB11	223.4	19	RB12
Wayne Gallman	RB	37.2	3.7	RB74	42.7	4.3	RB72	48.2	4.8	RB72
Darius Slayton	WR	117.0	9.0	WR30	139.0	11	WR35	161.0	12	WR37
Golden Tate	WR	90.4	9.0	WR47	112.4	11	WR47	134.4	13	WR48
Sterling Shepard	WR	80.9	9.0	WR54	106.9	12	WR51	132.9	15	WR52
Cody Latimer	WR	40.8	2.9	WR90	51.8	3.7	WR90	62.8	4.5	WR91
Evan Engram	TE	65.4	8.2	TE19	87.4	11	TE18	109.4	14	TE18
New York Giants	DST	83.0	5.5	DST25						
Aldrick Rosas	K	67.0	4.5	K30						

DANIEL JONES

Jones will be a popular pick in the later rounds due to the rushing floor he provides. It would be a surprise if he doesn't better his 2019 output ending as the QB22 (despite not starting all the games). Jones should improve and has plenty of options available, plus a poor defence meaning garbage time points!

ADP 11.5

SAQUON BARKLEY

ADP 1.03

Barkley drafters were burned a bit in 2019 as Saquon missed a few games through injury. He is still most peoples RB2 for the season & should again carry a full workload in New York. The offence on the whole should improve & hopefully will be in some high scoring games meaning there could be lots of points to go around & Barkley gets the biggest slice of pie.

DARIUS SLAYTON

Slayton came from nowhere to end up as a WR3 in 2019. It's hard to know how the Wide Receiver room will shake out in 2020 as all the receivers tend to be excellent at the same thing. Slayton will probably be the most sought after in the mid round and you'll just have to live with the weeks where the productivity just isn't there. He definitely would get a good bump if oft injured Sterling Shepard continues to struggle with health.

ADP 9.11

STERLING SHEPARD

ADP 11.8

Sterling Shepard should see a lot of targets this year, if he sees the field enough. You are getting Shepard at a heavy discount due to the injury concerns and is possibly one more concussion from hanging up his cleats. Probably a good stab to have in the later rounds if you have avoided WR early, but the risk is high in a WR room that has lots of bodies.

EVAN ENGRAM

Engram has flattered to deceive since his outlandish rookie season. Again, another hampered by injury, Engram isn't coming with an injury discount on his ADP. You'd be a brave man drafting Engram as a top 8 TE but if he sees close to 16 games, he can finish as a top 5 TE with his eyes closed and would see a fair amount of targets.

ADP 7.04

2020 Projections

ADP taken from Ultimate Draft Kit (PPR)

Projections by Rob Grimwood @FFBritballer

FANTASY FOOTBALL

Position	Player	Standard		0.5PPR		Full PPR	
		Pts	Rank	Pts	Rank	Pts	Rank
QB	Daniel Jones	297.5	15				
RB	Saquon Barkley	315.3	1	365.8	1	416.3	1
RB	Dion Lewis	19.3	102	23.8	102	28.3	102
WR	Golden Tate	156.7	16	196.7	16	236.7	16
WR	Sterling Shepard	80.9	68	97.9	72	114.9	74
WR	Darius Slayton	108.9	48	131.4	50	153.9	50
TE	Evan Engram	43.2	39	59.2	37	75.2	36

2

NEW YORK GIANTS

LAST 5 YEARS

	W	L	T	Div	P/Offs
2019	4	12	0	3rd	
2018	5	11	0	4th	
2017	3	13	0	4th	
2016	11	5	0	2nd	Lost WC
2015	6	10	0	3rd	

DO SAY..
Dave Gettleman has a plan

DON'T SAY..
Dave Gettleman has a plan

BETTING ODDS BY ADAM WALFORD (@TOUCHDOWNTIPS)

SUPER BOWL **100/1**

NFC CONFERENCE **50/1**

NFC EAST **12/1**

TO MAKE PLAYOFFS
7/2
TEAM TOTAL WINS
6

ADAM'S BEST BET
UNDER 6.5 WINS
10/11

PLEASE GAMBLE RESPONSIBLY

VIEW FROM THE SIDELINES

By Dan Hewitt (@waxpacklyrical)

Typically, in recent times the off-season follows another disappointing year with 4-12 record. Shurmur's replacement Judge prompted more questions than aspirations. Who is he? Is he capable of leading our storied franchise? Investigating Joe's work under Saban/Belichick, along with his attitude when meeting the press allayed these fears. Drafting by need rather than our antiquated best on the board approach which I feel Judge has been instrumental in, made for a pleasant outcome. For the first time in years I'm optimistic. Two O-linemen in the first 3 rounds hopefully solving a problem that's been there too long. Giving Jones better protection, running lanes for Saquon & time for the WR's, alongside bolstering a secondary with McKinney we may restore pride in being a Giants fan. Don't get carried away though, 8-8 would be progress for us.

►RETRO FOCUS◄

DEL SHOFNER – WR

Del Shofner was an absolute beast at WR in the late 1950s/early 1960s. Having gained two All-Pro shouts with the Rams (58-59), Shofner moved the Big Apple in 1961 & ripped off 3 consecutive 1,100 yard seasons, which was stunning at that time. In 1962, he averaged 21.4 yards a catch & 12 TDs. His Achilles heel was the post-season for the Giants. 3 games between 1961-63 – three losses & no TDs. Shofner's career YPC (18.5) remains in the top 20 in NFL history. To add value Shofner also spent part of his career as a punter.

DID YOU KNOW

The team's name is officially the New York Football Giants, to distinguish themselves from the Giants baseball team with which they once shared a home.

KEY STAT

"Here, you have it"
The New York Giants committed at least 1 turnover on offence in all but 2 games in 2019.

FULL10YARDS VERDICT

Joe Judge's first season as an NFL coach won't be a walk in Central Park but after going 12–36 over the last three years, a few steps in the right direction will be seen as a positive for Big Blue. To do that, the O-line needs to raise their game and the strong-armed Daniel Jones needs to cut out the fumbles under the tutelage of new OC Jason Garrett. Hopefully, Saquon Barkley has left his ankle issues behind him but even if he's back to his sizzling best, I'm expecting another tough season for the Giants.

BETTING, STATS, FANS VIEW, RETRO

3

FULL 10 YARDS

PHILADELPHIA EAGLES

THE LOWDOWN:

Considering the amount of injuries the team suffered last season, reaching the Playoffs was a fantastic feat for Carson Wentz & Doug Pederson. A depleted wide receiver core and lack of offensive weapons meant the Eagles were limited in many facets of their game. They scraped into the post season with a 9-7 record, with the Cowboys one game behind them at 8-8. 1st round receiver Jalen Reagor will be a welcomed addition to the offense as they look to keep pace in an ever changing NFC. With no fans in attendance this season, the Eagles home field advantage won't be as strong as previous seasons but fans will be cheering on from home with the same level of expectations.

SCHEDULE

Week 1: @ Washington
Week 2: Vs. Rams
Week 3: Vs. Bengals
Week 4: @ 49ers *(SNF)*
Week 5: @ Steelers
Week 6: Vs. Ravens
Week 7: Vs. Giants *(TNF)*
Week 8: Vs. Cowboys *(SNF)*
Week 9: BYE
Week 10: @ Giants
Week 11: @ Browns
Week 12: Vs Seahawks *(MNF)*
Week 13: @ Packers
Week 14: Vs. Saints
Week 15: @ Cardinals
Week 16: @ Cowboys
Week 17: Vs. Washington

2020 NFL DRAFT CLASS

Round 1
Jalen Reagor, WR,
TCU
Round 2
Jalen Hurts, QB,
Oklahoma
Round 3
Davion Taylor, EDGE,
Colorado
Round 4
K'Von Wallace, S,
Clemson
Jack Driscoll, OT,
Auburn
Round 5
John Hightower, WR,
Boise State
Round 6
Shaun Bradley, LB,
Temple
Quez Watkins, WR,
Southern Miss
Prince Tega Wanogho, OT,
Auburn
Round 7
Casey Toohill, EDGE,
Stanford

SIGNINGS
Darius Slay, CB
Javon Hargrave, DT
Nickell Robey-Coleman, CB

RE-SIGNED
Jason Peters, OL
Jalen Mills, S
Rodney McLeod, S
Nate Sudfeld, QB

NO LONGER ON TEAM
Josh McCown, QB
Jordan Howard, RB
Darren Sproles, RB (Retired)
Nelson Agholor, WR
Halapoulivaati Vaitai, OL
Vinny Curry, DE
Timmy Jernigan, DT
Ronald Darby, CB
Malcolm Jenkins, S

TEAM DETAILS:
Owner: Jeffrey Lurie
General Manager: Howie Roseman
Stadium: Lincoln Financial Field
Head Coach: Doug Peterson
Offensive Coordinator: Doug Peterson
Defensive Coordinator: Jim Schwartz
Coaching Staff:
Dave Fipp (ST Coordinator)
Duce Staley (Assistant HC/RB Coach)
Press Taylor (Passing Game Coordinator/QB Coach)
Aaron Moorehead (WR Coach)
Justin Peelle (TE Coach)
Super Bowl Wins: 1 (2017)
Conference Wins: 3 (NFC, 1980, 2004, 2017)
Divisional Wins: 11 (NFC East, 1980, 1988, 2001, 2002, 2003, 2004, 2006, 2010, 2013, 2017, 2019)

-2019-
Record: 9-7 (Lost Wildcard Rd)
Offence Rank: Passing (11th), Rushing (11th), Overall (12th)
Defence Rank: Passing (19th), Rushing (3rd), Overall (15th)

KEY PLAYER

Carson Wentz: He has, to some, become the definition of injury prone since entering the league in 2016. In reality, he's only missed 8 regular season games. Wentz is crucial to an Eagles side that has some shiny new weapons on offense. His accuracy & creativity from the pocket are amongst the best in the NFL. It's crucial that the Offensive Line do everything they can to cut down on the number of sacks Wentz takes this year.

Jalen Reagor: Reagor headlines an almost brand new group of receivers that Eagles GM, Howie Roseman constructed over draft weekend. He should give the Eagles their greatest deep threat since DeSean Jackson was in his prime. Reagor will probably operate out of the slot, at least to begin with but once Alshon Jeffrey moves on, Reagor should be the man.

ROOKIE SPOTLIGHT

DEPTH CHART

Quarterback	Wide Receiver	Center	Edge	Line Backer	Cornerback
Carson Wentz	Alshon Jeffrey	Jason Kelce	Brandon Graham	Duke Riley	Darius Slay
Jalen Hurts [R]	DeSean Jackson	Nate Herbig	Derek Barnett	TJ Edwards	Avonte Maddox
Nate Sudfeld	Jalen Reagor [R]	**Tackle**	Genard Avery	Nathan Gerry	Nickell Robey-Coleman
Fullback	JJ Arcega-Whiteside	Lane Johnson	Josh Sweat	Jatavis Brown	Sidney Jones
Mike Warren	Marquise Goodwin	Andre Dillard	**Defensive Tackle**	Davion Taylor [R]	Rasul Douglas
Running Back	John Hightower [R]	Jordan Mailata	Javon Hargrave	**Free Safety**	**Strong Safety**
Miles Sanders	**Tight End**	**Guard**	Fletcher Cox	Rodney McLeod	Jalen Mills
Boston Scott	Zach Ertz	Brandon Brooks	Malik Jackson	Marcus Epps	Will Parks
Corey Clement	Dallas Goedert	Isaac Seumalo	**Kicker**	**Punter**	**Long Snapper**
Elijah Holyfield	Joshua Perkins	Matt Pryor	Jake Elliott	Cameron Johnston	Rick Lovato

PHILADELPHIA EAGLES

2019 RANKINGS

Player	Pos	Standard			0.5PPR			PPR		
		Pts	Avg	Rank	Pts	Avg	Rank	Pts	Avg	Rank
Carson Wentz	QB	265.8	17.7	QB10						
Miles Sanders	RB	163.6	10.9	RB14	187.1	13	RB14	210.6	14	RB13
Jordan Howard	RB	101.4	11.3	RB36	106.4	12	RB39	111.4	12	RB40
Alshon Jeffery	WR	79.2	7.9	WR56	100.7	10	WR54	122.2	12	WR55
Nelson Agholor	WR	55.0	5.0	WR77	74.5	6.8	WR75	94.0	8.6	WR69
Greg Ward	WR	27.6	4.6	WR113	38.6	6.4	WR109	49.6	8.3	WR107
Zach Ertz	TE	127.6	8.5	TE4	171.6	11	TE3	215.6	14	TE2
Dallas Goedert	TE	80.2	5.7	TE9	107.2	7.7	TE10	134.2	9.6	TE10
Philadelphia Eagles	DST	100.0	6.7	DST16						
Jake Elliott	K	97.0	6.5	K22						

CARSON WENTZ

Carson Wentz is a dark horse candidate to be a top 5 Quarterback & was quietly the QB9 in 2019. There may be quite a disparity in leagues on where Wentz gets drafted but he is a fine selection for those wanting a double digit QB & despite the lack of weapons in 2019, he still mustered a top 10 finish on 50% of his games. He's not got the biggest ceiling, however.

ADP 9.08

MILES SANDERS

ADP 1.10

Miles Sanders was the RB9 in the last 8 games of 2019, averaging 15.2pts per game. Many will be debating whether he gets the keys to the Cadillac this season which differs from HC Doug Pedersen's usual Modus Operandi. His ADP indicates you are drafting him as if he is, possibly because he boomed on championship week in 2019 (24.1 0.5ppr points.

JALEN REAGOR

It's not looking good for Alshon to see the field early on in 2020 and the one player that will benefit will be Jalen Reagor. The 1st round rookie from this year's draft looks set to be in the thick of things from the outset. He's fairly priced if you want to take a shot in the dark on a player that could be the most viable option outside of the TEs.

ADP 10.10

DESEAN JACKSON

ADP 11.10

DeSean Jackson started 2019 with a bang. Both on the field and physically. He was the WR2 in week 1 before a core muscle injury all but finished his season. He'll be a late round diamond as usual and reports are he is as fast as ever. You still have the problem in trying to figure out which weeks he booms or busts, but in the double digit rounds, sign me up.

ZACH ERTZ

You can pretty much copy & paste the narrative from 2019 and paste it in here: A solid, reliable TE who has fellow TE Dallas Goedert snapping at his heels. He is Wentz's security blanket & does it all. Assuming more pass catchers stay healthy in 2020, you may see a regression in targets/receptions that you would like, but for a TE, he's as solid as they come.

ADP 5.04

2020 Projections

ADP taken from Ultimate Draft Kit (PPR)

Projections by Rob Grimwood @FFBritballer

FANTASY FOOTBALL

Position	Player	Standard		0.5PPR		Full PPR	
		Pts	Rank	Pts	Rank	Pts	Rank
QB	Carson Wentz	320.0	9				
RB	Miles Sanders	225.3	8	251.8	8	278.3	8
RB	Boston Scott	88.3	57	108.8	49	129.3	47
WR	Alshon Jeffrey	66.8	81	86.3	79	105.8	79
WR	DeSean Jackson	67.7	79	81.2	81	94.7	83
WR	Jalen Reagor	90.3	60	110.3	59	130.3	61
WR	J.J Arcega-Whiteside	57.5	85	70.5	88	83.5	91
TE	Zach Ertz	124.5	4	166.0	3	207.5	3
TE	Dallas Goedert	94.8	9	126.3	9	157.8	9

2

PHILADELPHIA EAGLES

DO SAY..
The Philly Special

DON'T SAY..
Carson Wentz is injury prone

BETTING ODDS BY ADAM WALFORD (@TOUCHDOWNTIPS)

SUPER BOWL **25/1**

NFC CONFERENCE **12/1**

NFC EAST **7/5**

TO MAKE PLAYOFFS **5/11**
TEAM TOTAL WINS **9**

ADAM'S BEST BET
JALEN REAGOR OVER 650.5 REC YARDS **10/11**

PLEASE GAMBLE RESPONSIBLY

VIEW FROM THE SIDELINES
By Ste Tough (@SteTough)

#1 priority for the Eagles this season has to be keeping the skill players on the field, which has already suffered a blow with Brooks' achilles tear. Story of the last three campaigns has been injury. Pederson has to get the WR corps rolling. Still so many questions and yet another WRs Coach to answer them - 4th in 5 years. Wentz cannot keep throwing perfect balls for them to be dropped... Also look for Sophomore RB Miles Sanders to have a break-out year. Second highest rated D-Line by PFF. They HAVE to get to the QB. If they can get the sacks and put the rock in Carson's hands, he will take care of business. With a young, inexperienced secondary and several new pass-catchers, I think 10-6 would be a terrific season.

▶RETRO FOCUS◀
HAROLD CARMICHAEL – WR

One of the most imposing WR in NFL history, the 6ft 8inch Harold Carmichael tormented smaller cornerbacks for 13 years in Philly, en-route to a bust in the Hall of Fame. Uncoverable at times, Carmichael averaged 15.2 yards a catch over his career, snagging 79 TDs. All that was missing from his resume was a Super Bowl win, losing in his only appearance to the Raiders in 1980 (SB XV). 8,985 career yards puts him in the top 70 all-time.

DID YOU KNOW

The first televised professional football game – the Eagles' 23-14 loss to the Brooklyn Dodgers in October 1939 was watched by about 500 people.

KEY STAT

"A little help from our friends"
No Wide Receiver gained over 500 receiving yards in 2019, but their 2 Tight Ends and Running back did.

FULL10YARDS VERDICT

I don't know if the Eagles have a motto but it should be "triumph over adversity", having lifted the Lombardi Trophy in 2017 with a back-up QB and won their final four games with a greatly depleted offence to take the NFC East last year. It's not clear whether second-rounder Jalen Hurts was drafted in case Carson Wentz goes down again but Philly won't keep pace with the impressive-looking Cowboys if the injury hoodoo strikes again. Alas, guard Brandon Brooks is already out for the year so the omens aren't looking good.

BETTING, STATS, FANS VIEW, RETRO

3

FULL 10 YARDS

WASHINGTON FOOTBALL TEAM

THE LOWDOWN:

In perhaps the most dramatic off season in NFL history, the Washington Football Team went through a dramatic identity change after retiring their previous name as a result of mounting pressure from sponsors, politicians & activist groups. HC Ron Rivera is entering his first season with the team & will lead them into a new era for Washington pro sports. WR Terry McLaurin looks to build on his breakout year in his rookie season. Alex Smith, who suffered a near life ending injury has been cleared for practice & will serve as a great mentor for Haskins as he enters his 2nd season in the league. 2nd overall pick Chase Young will be hoping to make an impact in his rookie season.

SCHEDULE

Week 1: Vs. Eagles
Week 2: @ Cardinals
Week 3: @ Browns
Week 4: Vs. Ravens
Week 5: Vs. Rams
Week 6: @ Giants
Week 7: Vs. Cowboys
Week 8: BYE
Week 9: Vs. Giants
Week 10: @ Lions
Week 11: Vs. Bengals
Week 12: @ Cowboys
(Thanksgiving)
Week 13: @ Steelers
Week 14: @ 49ers
Week 15: Vs. Seahawks
Week 16: Vs. Panthers
Week 17: @ Eagles

2020 NFL DRAFT CLASS

Round 1
Chase Young, EDGE,
Ohio State
Round 3
Antonio Gibson, WR,
Memphis
Round 4
Saahdiq Charles, OT,
LSU
Antonio Gandy-Golden, WR,
Liberty
Round 5
Keith Ismael, IOL,
San Diego State
Khaleke Hudson, LB,
Michigan
Round 7
Kamren Curl, S,
Arkansas
James Smith-Williams, EDGE,
N.C. State
Jonathan Garvin, EDGE,
Miami

SIGNINGS

Kyle Allen, QB
Peyton Barber, RB
Ronald Darby, CB
Sean Davis, S
Thomas Davis, LB
Kendall Fuller, CB
Kevin Pierre-Louis, LB
Wes Schweitzer, OG

FRANCHISE TAG

Brandon Scherff, OG

NO LONGER ON TEAM

Case Keenum, QB
Chris Thompson, RB
Paul Richardson, WR
Vernon Davis, TE (Ret.)
Jordan Reed, TE
Donald Penn, OT
Trent Williams, OT
Ereck Flowers, OG
Quinton Dunbar, CB
Josh Norman, CB
Dominique R-Cromartie, CB

TEAM DETAILS:

Owner: Dan Snyder
General Manager: Ron Rivera
Stadium: FedEx Field
Head Coach: Ron Rivera
Offensive Coordinator:
Scott Turner
Defensive Coordinator:
Jack Del Rio
Coaching Staff:
Nate Kaczor (ST Coordinator)
Ken Zampese (QB Coach)
Randy Jordan (RB Coach),
Jim Hostler (WR Coach)
Pete Hoener (TE Coach)
Super Bowl Wins: 3 (1982, 1987, 1991)
Conference Wins: 5 (NFC, 1972, 1982, 1983, 1987, 1991)
Divisional Wins: 8 (NFC East, 1972, 1983, 1984, 1987, 1991, 1999, 2012, 2015)
-2019-
Record: 3-13
Offence Rank: Passing (32nd), Rushing (22nd), Overall (32nd)
Defence Rank: Passing (18th), Rushing (31st), Overall (27th)

KEY PLAYER

Terry McLaurin: "Scary" Terry muscled his way in to the hearts of Washington fans and fantasy football fans with an impressive rookie season. In jsut 14 games, he hauled in 58 receptions for just under 1000 yards & had 7 opportunities to celebrate in the endzone. His chemistry with Quarterback Dwayne Haskins will need to be just as successful this year as it was in 2019 for Washington to notch any wins under new HC Ron Rivera.

Chase Young: The best player from this year's draft class in the eyes of many, Chase Young is a physical beast with immense athletic ability and an arsenal of pass rush moves. The Predator should be a problem for offensive linemen as soon as he steps on the field in the NFL - A sensible bet for Defensive Rookie of the Year.

ROOKIE SPOTLIGHT

DEPTH CHART

Quarterback	Wide Receiver	Center	Edge	Line Backer	Cornerback
Dwayne Haskins	Terry McLaurin	Chase Roullier	Ryan Kerrigan	Chase Young [R]	Kendall Fuller
Kyle Allen	Kelvin Harmon	Ross Pierschblacher	Montez Sweat	Thomas Davis	Fabian Moreau
Alex Smith	Trey Quinn	**Tackle**	Ryan Anderson	Cole Holcomb	Jimmy Moreland
Fullback	Steven Sims	Morgan Moses	Jordan Brailford	Jon Bostic	Ronald Darby
Josh Ferguson	Cam Sims	Cornelius Lucas	**Defensive Tackle**	Josh Harvey-Clemons	Aaron Colvin
Running Back	Cody Latimer	Timon Parris	Jonathan Allen	**Free Safety**	**Strong Safety**
Adrian Peterson	**Tight End**	**Guard**	Da'Ron Payne	Sean Davis	Landon Collins
Antonio Gibson [R]	Jeremy Sprinkle	Brandon Scherff	Matt Ioannidis	Deshazor Everett	Jeremy Reaves
Bryce Love	Richard Rodgers	Wes Schweitzer	**Kicker**	**Punter**	**Long Snapper**
Peyton Barber	Logan Thomas	Saahdiq Charles [R]	Dustin Hopkins	Tress Way	Nick Sundberg

NFL

1

FULL 10 YARDS

WASHINGTON FOOTBALL TEAM

2019 RANKINGS

Player	Pos	Standard Pts	Standard Avg	Standard Rank	0.5PPR Pts	0.5PPR Avg	0.5PPR Rank	PPR Pts	PPR Avg	PPR Rank
Dwayne Haskins	QB	83.7	9.3	QB35						
Adrian Peterson	RB	124.2	8.3	RB27	132.2	8.8	RB31	140.2	9.4	RB35
Derrius Guice	RB	50.4	10.1	RB59	53.9	11	RB62	57.4	12	RB65
Terry McLaurin	WR	133.9	9.6	WR22	162.9	12	WR24	191.9	14	WR25
Steven Sims	WR	62.0	4.1	WR68	76.5	5.1	WR69	91.0	6.1	WR72
Kelvin Harmon	WR	33.6	2.2	WR100	47.1	3.1	WR96	60.6	4	WR94
Trey Quinn	WR	25.8	2.2	WR119	38.8	3.2	WR108	51.8	4.3	WR103
Jeremy Sprinkle	TE	28.3	1.9	TE44	39.8	2.7	TE43	51.3	3.4	TE42
Washington Redskins	DST	85.0	5.7	DST23						
Dustin Hopkins	K	97.0	6.5	K23						

DWAYNE HASKINS

Dwayne Haskins will be nothing more than Waiver Wire fodder and best case scenario he may be usuable for a week or two during the season. The team is in a bit of disarray and with the defence being a rock solid one, expect Washington to lean heavily on the run game. Haskins has a low ceiling and a low floor. Avoid.

ADP U/D

ADP 10.0

ADRIAN PETERSON

With Guice no longer on the team, the Running Back duties are up for grabs. Peterson finished as RB30 (0.5PPR) in 2019, despite being out of favour early on. A solid add in the later rounds in most leagues but may fade as the season goes on. Draft him and trade him after a peak performance. A solid flex player that will hover around the double digits in pts but may be a bit TD dependent considering there are other pass catchers there. Gamescript will not be favourable for the majority of the season, either.

ANTONIO GIBSON

It'll be interesting to see how involved Gibson is early on and with some outlandish comparisons to Christian McCaffrey are definitely nothing more than clickbait at this present time. Could be a late round dart flyer that could turn into gold in the later part of the season but with so many question marks on the backfield and the team in general, you'll probably find him on waivers at the start of 2020 in most league.

ADP 7.12

ADP 5.06

TERRY MCLAURIN

Scary Terry took the NFL like a duck to water, finishing as the WR28 in his rookie season, despite missing 2 games. He did this with poor Quarterback play & he'll be a WR looking to break in to the top 20. The touchdowns could be scarce for a team not pulling up any trees, which limits a high ceiling but he's great value as your teams 2nd or perhaps even 3rd WR.

STEVEN SIMS JI.

Sims is another that will be left on the waiver wire come week 1. Even with 2nd year WR Kelvin Harmon out for the season, Sims will be a shot in the dark for your bye week plug and plays. Considering the team is not a highly producitve one through the air, there will be other players on waivers that will be of better quality, even in deep leagues.

ADP 16.10

2020 Projections

Position	Player	Standard Pts	Standard Rank	0.5PPR Pts	0.5PPR Rank	Full PPR Pts	Full PPR Rank
QB	Dwayne Haskins	241.0	31				
RB	Adrian Peterson	90.4	55	98.9	58	107.4	59
RB	Antonio Gibson	151.2	29	169.2	28	187.2	29
RB	Peyton Barber	42.6	80	46.1	81	49.6	83
RB	Bryce Love	57.2	67	57.2	74	57.2	77
WR	Terry McLaurin	146.1	21	181.1	20	216.1	21
WR	Steven Sims Jr.	77.8	69	102.3	67	126.8	66
WR	A. Gandy-Golden	69.1	77	88.6	78	108.1	77
TE	Thaddeus Moss	50.9	34	61.4	36	71.9	37

ADP taken from Ultimate Draft Kit (PPR)

Projections by Rob Grimwood @FFBritballer

FANTASY FOOTBALL

2

FULL 10 YARDS

WASHINGTON FOOTBALL TEAM

LAST 5 YEARS

	W	L	T	Div	P/Offs
2019	3	13	0	4th	
2018	7	9	0	3rd	
2017	7	9	0	3rd	
2016	8	7	1	3rd	
2015	9	7	0	1st	Lost WC

DO SAY..
New name, new era

DON'T SAY..
Washington Redskins

BETTING ODDS BY ADAM WALFORD (@TOUCHDOWNTIPS)

SUPER BOWL **150/1**

NFC CONFERENCE **100/1**

NFC EAST **16/1**

TO MAKE PLAYOFFS **12/1**

TEAM TOTAL WINS **5**

ADAM'S BEST BET
OVER 5 WINS
10/11

PLEASE GAMBLE RESPONSIBLY

VIEW FROM THE SIDELINES

By Scott Mackay (@scottfmackay)

The Washington Red... Football Team enters a new era this year and I fully expect 2020 to be a year of rebuilding both on and off the field. Coach Rivera is instilling a culture based on hard work and integrity which is what is needed, and I believe we will see some promising green shoots as our players get used to the new way of doing things. These values will only hold us in good stead moving into 2021 & beyond but unfortunately this year, I don't see us having many victories to shout about. Lawrence may well be in play if what I fear our record might be... But I am more than willing to be proved wrong and hope that Haskins can carry us to a positive record. As with anything, time will tell. Go Football Team!

▶ RETRO FOCUS ◀

ART MONK – WR

Long before the likes of Michael Irvin & the advent of swagger, one WR went about setting records on the field and keeping his mouth firmly closed off the field. Washington's WR Art Monk set an NFL single season record of 106 catches in 1984. In 14 seasons in the nation's capital Monk caught 888 balls for 12,026 yards, winning two Super Bowl rings. He also had the dishonour of being the 1st player to have a Super Bowl TD catch overturned by replay.

DID YOU KNOW

The Redskins hold the record for the most points scored in a regular season game, winning 72-41 against the Giants on 27 November 1966.

KEY STAT

"3 and out"
Washington ranked bottom in terms of 3rd down conversion % on both offence and defence in 2019.

FULL10YARDS VERDICT

It's a time of upheaval in the nation's capital, with a new HC in Ron Rivera and the momentous decision to erase their nickname until they decide on a new one. While second-year WR Terry McLaurin could evolve into a genuine star and #2 overall pick Chase Young has been dubbed a generational talent, it'll be another long year. Trent Williams is gone, doubts still remain about Dwayne Haskins and RB Derrius Guice needs a fair crack of the whip, after missing 27 games over two years through injury. Bottom line? Washington will be picking early again next year.

BETTING, STATS, FANS VIEW, RETRO

3

NFLUK SOCIAL MEDIA

Whichever team you follow, make sure you are following your team on social media. A lot of the accounts put time and effort in to bringing team related content. Join the highs, lows and everything in between! Can anyone catch the Jaguars? (Other handles are available)
If you aren't doing so already, the NFLUK Twitter account is @NFLUK and be sure to find the NFLUK facebook group too!

(followers are correct as of 20th August 2020)

RANK	FOLLOWERS	TEAM	HANDLE
1	18493	JACKSONVILLE JAGUARS	@JAGUARSUK
2	10761	KANSAS CITY CHIEFS	@KCCHIEFS_UK
3	10617	GREEN BAY PACKERS	@UKPACKERS
4	9939	MIAMI DOLPHINS	@MIAMIDOLPHINSUK
5	7750	DALLAS COWBOYS	@UKCOWBOYFANS
6	5237	CINCINNATI BENGALS	@WHODEY_UK
7	4657	DENVER BRONCOS	@UKDENVERBRONCOS
8	4616	NEW ENGLAND PATRIOTS	@UKPATRIOTS
9	3888	NEW YORK JETS	@UKJETSHQ
10	3747	ARIZONA CARDINALS	@BRITISHBIRDGANG
11	3454	MINNESOTA VIKINGS	@UKVIKINGS
12	3124	BALTIMORE RAVENS	@UKRAVENS
13	3116	LOS ANGELES RAMS	@LARAMS_UK
14	3036	PHILADELPHIA EAGLES	@UKEAGLES_
15	2943	SAN FRANCISCO 49ERS	@49ERFAITHFULUK
16	2930	TAMPA BAY BUCCANEERS	@BUCSUK
17	2843	NEW YORK GIANTS	@NYGIANTSFANSUK
18	2803	CAROLINA PANTHERS	@PANTHERSUK
19	2735	NEW ORLEANS SAINTS	@DOMEPATROLUK
20	2498	ATLANTA FALCONS	@ATLFALCONSUK
21	2227	HOUSTON TEXANS	@TEXANSUK
22	2211	SEATTLE SEAHAWKS	@UKSEAHAWKERS
23	1949	CLEVELAND BROWNS	@UK_BROWNS
24	1944	TENNESSEE TITANS	@TEN_TITANSUK
25	1814	CHICAGO BEARS	@BEARDOWNUK
26	1645	INDIANAPOLIS COLTS	@UKCOLTSFANS
27	1565	LOS ANGELES CHARGERS	@CHARGERS_UK
28	1543	PITTSBURGH STEELERS	@TERRIBLE_UK
29	1306	WASHINGTON REDSKINS	@WASHINGTONFTUK
30	1239	LAS VEGAS RAIDERS	@RAIDERNATION
31	1164	DETROIT LIONS	@UK_DETROITLIONS
32	727	BUFFALO BILLS	@UK_BILLS

CHICAGO BEARS

THE LOWDOWN:

Chicago's fortunes have been up & down over the past couple of seasons. After their season finished on the "Double – Doink" two years ago, many believed they were just a Kicker away from a Superbowl appearance but the 2019 season didn't go as well as many had hoped. Mitch Trubisky regressed considerably and the once feared defence didn't live up to its historic expectations. In an attempt to create healthy QB competition, the Bears have brought in former Superbowl MVP, Nick Foles to compete with Trubisky for the starting job. The Bears didn't have a 1st round pick in this year's draft so they have no big name rookies coming through the door in what is a crucial season for HC Matt Nagy.

SCHEDULE

Week 1: @ Lions
Week 2: Vs Giants
Week 3: @ Falcons
Week 4: Vs Colts
Week 5: Vs Buccaneers *(TNF)*
Week 6: @ Panthers
Week 7: @ Rams *(MNF)*
Week 8: Vs Saints
Week 9: @ Titans
Week 10: Vs Vikings *(MNF)*
Week 11: BYE
Week 12: @ Packers *(SNF)*
Week 13: Vs Lions
Week 14: Vs Texans
Week 15: @ Vikings
Week 16: @ Jaguars
Week 17: Vs Packers

2020 NFL DRAFT CLASS

Round 2
Cole Kmet, TE,
Notre Dame
Jaylon Johnson, CB,
Utah
Round 5
Trevis Gipson, EDGE,
Tulsa
Kindle Vildor, CB,
Georgia Southern
Darnell Mooney, WR,
Tulane
Round 7
Arlington Hambright, IOL,
Colorado
Lachavious Simmons, OT,
Tennessee State

SIGNINGS

Nick Foles, QB
Artie Burns, CB
Deon Bush, S
Ted Ginn Jr., WR
Jimmy Graham, TE
Danny Trevathan, LB

STAR SIGNING

Robert Quinn, DE

NO LONGER ON TEAM

Chase Daniel, QB
Taylor Gabriel, WR
Trey Burton, TE
Kyle Long, OL (Retired)
Nick Williams, DT
Nick Kwiatkoski, LB
Leonard Floyd, LB
Kevin Pierre-Louis, LB
Prince Amukamara, CB
Ha Ha Clinton-Dix, S

TEAM DETAILS:

Owner: The McCaskey Family
General Manager: Ryan Pace
Stadium: Soldier Field
Location: Chicago, Illinois
Head Coach: Matt Nagy
Offensive Coordinator: Bill Lazor
Defensive Coordinator:
Chuck Pagano
Coaching Staff:
John DeFilippo (QB Coach)
Dave Ragone (Passing Game Coordinator)
Charles London (RB Coach)
Mike Furrey (WR Coach)
Clancy Barone (TE Coach)
Chris Tabor (ST Coordinator)
Super Bowl Wins: 1 (1985)
Conference Wins:
2 (NFC, 1985, 2006)
Divisional Wins: 11 (NFC Central, 1984, 1985, 1986, 1987, 1988, 1990, 2001; NFC North, 2005, 2006, 2010, 2018)
-2019-
Record: 8-8
Offence Rank: Passing (25th), Rushing (27th), Overall (29th)
Defence Rank: Passing (9th), Rushing (9th), Overall (4th)

KEY PLAYER

Roquan Smith: The Bears offense has a lot of question marks hanging over it this season. There's no such problem on defense though, where a solid unit is led by third year pro, Roquan Smith. A torn pectoral muscle meant that Smith missed four games last year, but he still led the team in tackles. If the Bears are going to mount a playoff charge this year, they'll need the former Bulldogs' star back to full fitness.

Cole Kmet: Kmet is a smooth mover with nice soft hands and toughness to take hits over the middle. Kmet is a traditional tight end who does have some value in the blocking game as well as the passing game. In terms of routes, he'll mainly work over the middle and up the seems from an in-line start.

ROOKIE SPOTLIGHT

DEPTH CHART

Quarterback	Wide Receiver	Center	Edge	Line Backer	Cornerback
Mitch Trubisky	Allen Robinson	Cody Whitehair	Khalil Mack	Danny Trevathan	Kyle Fuller
Nick Foles	Anthony Miller	Sam Mustipher	Robert Quinn	Roquan Smith	Artie Burns
Tyler Bray	Cordarrelle Patterson	**Tackle**	Bilal Nichols	Josh Woods	Buster Skrine
Fullback	Ted Ginn	Bobby Massie	Barkevious Mingo	Joel Iyiegbuniwe	Jaylon Johnson [R]
Ryan Nall	Riley Ridley	Charles Leno	**Defensive Tackle**	James Vaughters	Duke Shelley
Running Back	Javon Wims	Alex Bars	Akiem Hicks	Free Safety	Strong Safety
David Montgomery	**Tight End**	**Guard**	Eddie Goldman	Deon Bush	Eddie Jackson
Tarik Cohen	Jimmy Graham	James Daniels	John Jenkins	Tashaun Gipson	Kentrell Brice
Artavis Pierce [R]	Cole Kmet [R]	Rashaad Coward	**Kicker**	**Punter**	**Long Snapper**
Napolean Maxwell [R]	Adam Shaheen (+6)	Corey Levin	Eddy Piniero	Pat O'Donnell	Patrick Scales

NFL

1

FULL 10 YARDS

CHICAGO BEARS

2019 RANKINGS

Player	Pos	Standard			0.5PPR			PPR		
		Pts	Avg	Rank	Pts	Avg	Rank	Pts	Avg	Rank
Mitch Trubisky	QB	206.4	14.7	QB25						
David Montgomery	RB	128.1	8.5	RB24	140.6	9.4	RB24	153.1	10	RB25
Tarik Cohen	RB	78.5	5.2	RB43	113.5	7.6	RB38	148.5	9.9	RB28
Allen Robinson	WR	149.6	10.0	WR11	194.1	13	WR10	238.6	16	WR7
Anthony Miller	WR	75.0	5.0	WR58	100.5	6.7	WR55	126.0	8.4	WR54
Taylor Gabriel	WR	61.3	6.8	WR72	75.8	8.4	WR73	90.3	10	WR74
Javon Wims	WR	22.3	1.5	WR129	29.8	2	WR124	37.3	2.5	WR123
Trey Burton	TE	8.4	0.9	TE79	15.4	1.7	TE68	22.4	2.5	TE67
Chicago Bears	DST	87.0	5.8	DST21						
Eddy Pineiro	K	90.0	6.0	K24						

MITCH TRUBISKY

Trubisky has hardly rewarded Chicago for the 2nd overall pick they traded up for to get him in 2017. He's not rewarded fantasy owners either with finishes as QB28, QB15 and QB26 since entering the league and nothing suggests to me that he has the capabilities to achieve anything higher than these finishes. To couple with his poor finishes, the Bears have brought in Nick Foles to compete with him for the starting job. Leave him on waivers.

ADP U/D

NICK FOLES

ADP U/D

The 2nd piece of the QB battle in Chiacgo. Foles is a SuperBowl winner & MVP and is now reunited with a number of former Eagles coaches – most notably, QB coach John DeFilippo. Whoever wins the camp battle between the 2 QBs, neither are fantasy competent QBs for the year – Foles is my QB29 in 2020, which is higher than Foles, likely we'll see both.

DAVID MONTGOMERY

3.7 ypc. Montgomery had the 39th highest yards per carry last year out of the 46 running backs that carried the ball 100 times. Couple that with only 3 carries of over 20 yards and 6 TDs on the ground last year, RB22 was where Montgomery finished last year. I predict Cohen to have 15 more points in PPR leagues that Montgomery this year.

ADP 4.05

ALLEN ROBINSON

ADP 3.09

Robinson had the lowest key 98/1147/7 in NFL history last year. He was the third most targeted NFL player last year behind only Michael Thomas and Julio Jones and finished as the WR8 in PPR leagues last year. Robinson is an elite talent and will have either a fired up Trubisky throwing to him or a Foles who has won the training camp battle.

ANTHONY MILLER

Miller had a funny 2019. In 2018, he had a staggering 1 TD for every 4.7 receptions. In 2019, this slipped down to 1 in 26. The league average is 1 in 20. The third most targeted Bear in 2019, I can't see this changing in 2020 but, that being said, that would only make him a WR4 dart for me at the very best.

ADP 11.11

2020 Projections

ADP taken from Ultimate Draft Kit (PPR)

Projections by Rob Grimwood @FFBritballer

Position	Player	Standard		0.5PPR		Full PPR	
		Pts	Rank	Pts	Rank	Pts	Rank
QB	Mitch Trubisky	264.8	30				
RB	David Montgomery	179.9	18	194.4	21	208.9	22
RB	Tarik Cohen	97.1	52	135.1	44	173.1	34
WR	Allen Robinson	159.5	15	204.5	11	249.5	7
WR	Anthony Miller	82.2	65	105.7	64	129.2	62
WR	Cordarelle Patterson	34.7	111	40.2	117	45.7	120
WR	Ted Ginn Jr.	45.1	106	56.6	106	68.1	106
TE	Cole Kmet	44.1	38	55.6	39	67.1	38
TE	Jimmy Graham	17.1	57	22.1	58	27.1	58

FANTASY FOOTBALL

2

FULL 10 YARDS

CHICAGO BEARS

LAST 5 YEARS

	W	L	T	Div	P/Offs
2019	8	8	0	3rd	
2018	12	4	0	1st	Lost WC
2017	5	11	0	4th	
2016	3	13	0	4th	
2015	6	10	0	4th	

DO SAY.. The '85 Bears team

DON'T SAY.. The Double Doink

BETTING ODDS BY ADAM WALFORD (@TOUCHDOWNTIPS)

SUPER BOWL **50/1**

NFC CONFERENCE **25/1**

NFC NORTH **9/2**

TO MAKE PLAYOFFS **6/4**

TEAM TOTAL WINS **7.5**

ADAM'S BEST BET
NOT TO MAKE PLAYOFFS
8/15

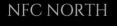

PLEASE GAMBLE RESPONSIBLY

VIEW FROM THE SIDELINES

By ClairedaBear (@Clairedabear)

I don't think our Draft was too bad but I do have the feeling that Pace doesn't have a clear plan in motion. And at one point in the offseason we had 10 TE on our roster (Please hold your laughter). Nagy has got a whole lot on this plate with the whole QB thing going down in Chi-Town at the moments. All the noisemakers say Turbisky is gonna be the starter but Big Dick Nick is not gonna go quietly. I like most sensible Bears fans just want the best man in the driving seat. Eddie Goldman is the first bears to opt out of the season completely & is a key part in our defence so this is gonna hurt us no doubt. Our defence has been the reason for winning games/keeping us in games and the general light in the dark of being a Bears fan.

►RETRO FOCUS◄

BOBBY DOUGLASS – QB

Decades before we had Michael Vick and now Lamar Jackson, there was a QB rushing for eye-popping yardage. In 1972 Bears QB Bobby Douglass rushed for 968 yards in just 14 contests. Douglass's career 6.6 yards a carry remains Chicago's all-time leader for any player who has carried the ball over 100 times. His star may have shone only briefly in the early 70s but Douglass's single season rushing total for a QB was a record that remained in place for over 30 years.

DID YOU KNOW

The Bears' 1932 Championship game vs the Portsmouth Spartans was the first playoff game, the first indoor game and the only NFL game ever played on an 80-yard field.

KEY STAT

"Legendary Field"

The Bears' home, Soldier Field is the oldest stadium in use in the NFL having been opened in 1924. It is also now the lowest capacity (61,500)

FULL10YARDS VERDICT

After 8-8 and 12-4 seasons, we shouldn't be too down on the Bears. The defence wobbled last year but that was largely due to injuries, so it's really about who wins the battle at QB. They've eaten humble pie by acquiring eight-year pro Nick Foles, admitting that Mitchell Trubisky may not be the answer. But even Foles is no sure thing, after injury and then losing out to Gardner Minshew at Jacksonville. They're also turning to old timers like Tedd Ginn Jr and Jimmy Graham in skillpositions, so I think it's a Wild Card at best here.

BETTING, STATS, FANS VIEW, RETRO

3

FULL 10 YARDS

DETROIT LIONS

THE LOWDOWN:

The Lions have suffered from mediocrity for years & last season we saw signs of life that we haven't seen in a long time! Matthew Stafford was playing at an elite level before getting injured with receivers Kenny Golladay & Marvin Jones Jr put on a show for the fans at Ford field. With HC Matt Patricia entering his third season, it's a crucial season in which he will have to produce results. The Lions held the third pick in the draft and with that they selected cornerback Jeff Okudah who will help sure up the defence after the departures of Darius Slay & Quandre Diggs. Fans will hope for an improvement on last season as they fight for a playoff spot in the very difficult NFC North.

SCHEDULE

Week 1: Vs. Bears
Week 2: @ Packers
Week 3: @ Cardinals
Week 4: Vs. Saints
Week 5: BYE
Week 6: @ Jaguars
Week 7: @ Falcons
Week 8: Vs. Colts
Week 9: @ Vikings
Week 10: Vs. Redskins
Week 11: @ Panthers
Week 12: Vs. Texans
(Thanksgiving)
Week 13: @ Bears
Week 14: Vs. Packers
Week 15: @ Titans
Week 16: Vs. Buccaneers
Week 17: Vs. Vikings

2020 NFL DRAFT CLASS

Round 1
Jeff Okudah, CB,
Ohio State
Round 2
D'Andre Swift, RB,
Georgia
Round 3
Julian Okwara, EDGE,
Notre Dame
Jonah Jackson, IOL,
Ohio State
Round 4
Logan Stenberg, IOL,
Kentucky
Round 5
Quintez Cephus, WR,
Wisconsin
Jason Huntley, RB,
New Mexico State
Round 6
John Penisini, IDL,
Utah
Round 7
Jashon Cornell, IDL,
Ohio State

SIGNINGS

Duron Harmon, DB
Geronimo Allison, WR
Chase Daniel, QB
Jayron Kearse, S
Danny Shelton, DL
Desmond Trufant, CB
Halapoulivaati Vaitai, OT

STAR SIGNING

Jamie Collins, LB

NO LONGER ON TEAM

Jeff Driskel, QB
Rick Wagner, OL
Graham Glasgow, OL
Devon Kennard, LB
Darius Slay, CB
Rashaan Melvin, CB
Tavon Wilson, S
Sam Martin, P

TEAM DETAILS:

Owner: Sheila Ford Hampton
General Manager: Bob Quinn
Stadium: Ford Field
Head Coach: Matt Patricia
Offensive Coordinator: Darrell Bevell
Defensive Coordinator: Cory Undlin
Coaching Staff:
Sean Ryan (QB Coach)
Kyle Caskey (RB Coach)
Robert Prince (WR Coach)
Ben Johnson (TE Coach)
Brayden Coombs (ST Coordinator)
Super Bowl Wins: 0
Conference Wins: 0
Divisional Wins: 3 (NFC Central, 1983, 1991, 1993)
-2019-
Record: 3-12-1
Offence Rank: Passing (10th), Rushing (21st), Overall (18th)
Defence Rank: Passing (32nd), Rushing (21st), Overall (26th)

KEY PLAYER

Matthew Stafford: When Stafford is playing, the Lions stand a chance against any team in the league. In the 8 games he missed in the 2019 season, Detroit won a total of 0 games and slumped to a 3-12-1 record. With an exciting wide receiver core and two young running backs, the former first overall pick has a bounty of weapons. If he can stay healthy, the Lions can be right in the mix for the NFC North.

ROOKIE SPOTLIGHT

Jeff Okudah: Darius Slay is now residing in Philadelphia, so 3rd overall pick, Jeff Okudah is going to have to step up and be the main man immediately for the Lions. Despite being a rookie, this shouldn't worry Lions fans too much at all - Okudah is a smooth and fluid cover man with all the skills to be absolutely lockdown.

DEPTH CHART

Quarterback	Wide Receiver	Center	Edge	Line Backer	Cornerback
Matthew Stafford	Kenny Golladay	Frank Ragnow	Trey Flowers	Jamie Collins	Jeff Okudah [R]
Chase Daniel	Marvin Jones	Beau Benzschawel	Romeo Okwara	Jarrad Davis	Desmond Trufant
David Blough	Danny Amendola	**Tackle**	Austin Bryant	Christian Jones	Justin Coleman
Fullback	Geronimo Allison	Halapoulivaati Vaitai	Julian Okwara [R]	Jalen Reeves-Maybin	Darryl Roberts
Nick Bawden	Victor Bolden	Taylor Decker	**Defensive Tackle**	Elijah Lee	Jamal Agnew
Running Back	Travis Fulgham	Tyrell Crosby	Danny Shelton	**Free Safety**	**Strong Safety**
Kerryon Johnson	**Tight End**	**Guard**	John Atkins	Tracy Walker	Duron Harmon
D'Andre Swift [R]	TJ Hockenson	Joe Dahl	Kevin Strong	Jayron Kearse	Will Harris
Bo Scarborough	Jesse James	Oday Aboushi	**Kicker**	**Punter**	**Long Snapper**
Ty Johnson	Isaac Nauta	Jonah Jackson [R]	Matt Prater	Jack Fox	Don Muhlbach

NFL

1

FULL 10 YARDS

DETROIT LIONS

2019 RANKINGS

Player	Pos	Standard			0.5PPR			PPR		
		Pts	Avg	Rank	Pts	Avg	Rank	Pts	Avg	Rank
Jeff Driskel	QB	61.2	15.3	QB37						
Kerryon Johnson	RB	63.7	9.1	RB52	68.7	9.8	RB55	73.7	11	RB58
Bo Scarbrough	RB	38.0	7.6	RB71	38.5	7.7	RB75	39.0	7.8	RB78
Ty Johnson	RB	29.7	2.0	RB77	41.7	2.8	RB73	53.7	3.6	RB68
Kenny Golladay	WR	175.8	11.7	WR3	206.8	14	WR5	237.8	16	WR9
Marvin Jones	WR	131.9	10.2	WR23	162.9	13	WR25	193.9	15	WR24
Danny Amendola	WR	72.2	5.2	WR60	102.2	7.3	WR53	132.2	9.4	WR53
T.J. Hockenson	TE	48.7	4.1	TE31	64.7	5.4	TE30	80.7	6.7	TE29
Detroit Lions	DST	63.0	4.2	DST30						
Matt Prater	K	122.0	8.1	K7						

MATTHEW STAFFORD — ADP 10.4

Stafford was the QB4 in points per game last year and looks to carry that into 2020. His rushing upside is limited but the receiving weapons around him certainly propel him to a top-10 finish. Many say the intent on running the ball in Detroit will hamper Stafford, but a running game is key to a successful passing game.

ADP 5.10 — D'ANDRE SWIFT

The "Barry Sanders curse" still looms large in Detroit and, although Kerryon managed a 100-yard rushing game last year, the Lions haven't seen a 1000-yard rusher since Reggie Bush in 2013. They're very hopeful that second round pick, D'Andre Swift, will be that guy and he should see the bulk of the carries within the first few weeks of the season.

KENNY GOLLADAY — ADP 3.02

The receiving TD leader in 2019, Golladay finished as the standard WR3 & the PPR WR9. Golladay did a heck of a lot off 65 receptions last year & we must expect some level of regression on his productivity levels. Still, he had the 3rd lowest reception vs target % last year which, with improved QB play, we'd expect to go up. Draft Kenny G as a top-10 WR with confidence this year.

ADP 8.11 — MARVIN JONES

Jones was one of only five Lions wide receivers to catch a ball last year and one of only three to catch over 10. Even with Quintez Cephus, the fifth round draft pick, entering the receiving room, Jones should still see a fair amount of the target share and turn it into top-30 production once again.

T.J. HOCKENSON — ADP 13.1

The 1.08 pick in 2019, Hock was the epicentre of a waiver wire scramble after he posted 131 receiving yards and a touchdown in his NFL debut. He then disappointed fantasy owners by only posting 1 double digit fantasy performance for the remainder of the season. He's certainly got first round talent; he'll have a top-10 QB throwing to him and he'll be a sophomore in a league where rookie TEs have never done well. Top-15 is on the cards.

2020 Projections

Position	Player	Standard		0.5PPR		Full PPR	
		Pts	Rank	Pts	Rank	Pts	Rank
QB	Matthew Stafford	275.4	21				
RB	D'Andre Swift	175.5	21	194.5	20	213.5	20
RB	Kerryon Johnson	119.6	44	131.1	45	142.6	45
RB	Bo Scarbrough	29.7	90	31.7	94	33.7	97
WR	Kenny Golladay	175.2	5	210.7	9	246.2	10
WR	Marvin Jones	110.7	46	135.2	47	159.7	47
WR	Danny Amendola	76.7	71	104.2	66	131.7	59
WR	Quintez Cephus	48.9	99	64.4	99	79.9	96
TE	TJ Hockenson	78.6	20	102.1	20	125.6	19

ADP taken from Ultimate Draft Kit (PPR)

Projections by Rob Grimwood @FFBritballer

FANTASY FOOTBALL

2

DETROIT LIONS

DO SAY..
Can't get much worse than last season

DON'T SAY..
Who remembers 2008?

BETTING ODDS
BY ADAM WALFORD (@TOUCHDOWNTIPS)

SUPER BOWL **80/1**

NFC CONFERENCE **40/1**

NFC NORTH **17/2**

TO MAKE PLAYOFFS
3/1
TEAM TOTAL WINS
6.5

ADAM'S BEST BET
MATTHEW STAFFORD OVER 4100.5 PASS YARDS
10/11

PLEASE GAMBLE RESPONSIBLY

VIEW FROM THE SIDELINES
By Chris Robin (@DetroitBeastie)

It's the same recycled nonsense every season... Once again the spring and summer is littered with the same buzz words and optimistic tones. "Matthew Stafford looks good!" Or how about this one, "The Lions rookie running back is strong and making an impression on his coaches!" I can set my watch by these comments and lazy observations. "The defensive coordinator is excited about the young athletic core!" Yeah I know, we get it. To me, its just a copy and paste job. The city of Detroit has remained unapologetically behind this organization through thick and thin. Almost to the point where it becomes harmful. Ownership seemingly doesn't care, they plug and play the same mediocre talent year in and year out. After a certain point in each season the coaching staff settles for, "that was fine." or, "that is good enough!" While the city and it's fan are clamoring for change. The definition of insanity, as I've understood it, is doing the same thing over and over again and expecting different results. The Lions should have that hanging in their locker room on a plaque they can slap above the locker room door as they take the field.

RETRO FOCUS
JASON HANSON – PK

When you spend 21 seasons suiting up for just one team, and you do not win a single playoff game (6 played), then you deserve some credit. Jason Hanson ranks 4th all-time for points scored in NFL history, having booted 495 field goals over three decades, missing just 8 extra points in 327 games. Hanson made two Pro Bowls and even accrued 27 tackles in his illustrious career. Perhaps a Hall of Fame call is due one day?.

DID YOU KNOW

In 1970, Motown star Marvin Gaye, tried out for the team.

KEY STAT

"50-50 ball? More like 70-30!"
Lions receiver Kenny Golladay may have achieved 1,190 yards, however he only averaged 1.9 yards of separation per reception.

FULL10YARDS VERDICT
The Lions had their fair share of misfortune last year. Matt Stafford and rookie tight end TJ Hockenson got injured and both deputy quarterbacks underwhelmed. Now, with Chase Daniel in the QB room and draft pick D'Andre Swift adding some RB juice, they might not finish a full five games behind the rest of the NFC North again. Defensive improvements in the form of rookie CB Jeff Okudah plus several free agency pick-ups will be vital in keeping Stafford on the field, and ensuring HC Matt Patricia avoids another losing season.

BETTING, STATS, FANS VIEW, RETRO

3

FULL 10 YARDS

GREEN BAY PACKERS

THE LOWDOWN:

The Packers reached last year's NFC Championship game with rookie Head Coach Matt LaFleur finishing with a record of 13-3. Everybody expected the Packers to try and build on this feat by bolstering their team and trying to surround Aaron Rodgers with weapons to help them reach the Superbowl. Instead, they drafted Quarterback Jordan Love in the first round. As history seems to be repeating itself in Green Bay in the QB room, many fans are hoping it doesn't derail the progress that was made last season. While the race for the best in the NFC heats up, the window for Rodgers to make a run at another ring is slowly closing.

SCHEDULE

Week 1: @ Vikings
Week 2: Vs. Lions
Week 3: @ Saints *(SNF)*
Week 4: Vs. Falcons *(MNF)*
Week 5: BYE
Week 6: @ Buccaneers
Week 7: @ Texans
Week 8: Vs. Vikings
Week 9: @ 49ers *(TNF)*
Week 10: Vs. Jaguars
Week 11: @ Colts
Week 12: Vs. Bears *(SNF)*
Week 13: Vs. Eagles
Week 14: @ Lions
Week 15: Vs. Panthers
Week 16: Vs. Titans *(SNF)*
Week 17: @ Bears

2020 NFL DRAFT CLASS

Round 1
Jordan Love, QB,
Utah State
Round 2
A.J. Dillon, RB,
Boston College
Round 3
Josiah Deguara, TE,
Cincinnati
Round 5
Kamal Martin, LB,
Minnesota
Round 6
Jon Runyan, IOL,
Michigan
Jake Hanson, IOL,
Oregon
Simon Stepaniak, OT,
Indiana
Round 7
Vernon Scott, S,
TCU

SIGNINGS

Devin Funchess, WR
Rick Wagner, OT
Marcedes Lewis, TE

STAR SIGNING

Christian Kirksey, LB

NO LONGER ON TEAM

Geronimo Allison, WR
Jimmy Graham, TE
Bryan Bulaga, OL
Blake Martinez, LB

TEAM DETAILS:

Owner: Green Bay Packers Inc.
General Manager: Brian Gutenkunst
Stadium: Lambeau Field
Location: Green Bay, Wisconsin
Head Coach: Matt LaFleur
Offensive Coordinator: Nathaniel Hackett
Defensive Coordinator: Mike Pettine
Coaching Staff:
Luke Getsy (QB Coach, Passing Game Coordinator)
Ben Sirmans (RB Coach)
Jason Vrable (WR Coach)
Justin Outten (TE Coach)
Shawn Mennenga (ST Coordinator)
Super Bowl Wins: 4 (1966, 1967, 1996, 2010)
Conference Wins: 3 (NFC, 1996, 1997, 2010)
Divisional Wins: 15 (NFL Central, 1967; NFC Central, 1972, 1995, 1996, 1997; NFC North, 2002,2003, 2004, 2007, 2011, 2012, 2013, 2014, 2016, 2019)
-2019-
Record: 13-3 (Lost NFC Title game)
Offence Rank: Passing (17th), Rushing (15th), Overall (15th)
Defence Rank: Passing (14th), Rushing (23rd), Overall (9th)

KEY PLAYER

Aaron Jones: It was a Madden like season for Running Back Aaron Jones in 2019, and it's fair to say most people are expecting regression this year. You can see why, it's not easy to replicate 1558 all purpose yards and 19(!)TDs. However, if anyone can, it's Jones, he's the secondary pass option for Aaron Rodgers, elusive in the run game and on a roster which didn't see a lot of upgrades in the off-season.

ROOKIE SPOTLIGHT

Jordan Love: Whether he likes it or not, Aaron Rodgers' replacement is in the building. Jordan Love is raw; he has all of the physical traits that you would ideally want in an NFL QB but the mental aspects of his game need some development. With a little marinating he could be special.

DEPTH CHART

Quarterback	Wide Receiver	Center	Edge	Line Backer	Cornerback
Aaron Rodgers	Davante Adams	Coret Linsley	Za'Darius Smith	Christian Kirksey	Jaire Alexander
Jordan Love	Allen Lazard	Cole Madison	Preston Smith	Oren Burks	Kevin King
Tim Boyle	Devin Funchess	**Tackle**	Dean Lowry	Curtis Bolton	Chandon Sullivan
Fullback	Marquez Valdes-Scantling	David Bakhtiari	Tyler Lancaster	Rashan Gary	Josh Jackson
Elijah Wellman	Jake Kumerow	Ricky Wagner	**Defensive Tackle**	Ty Summers	Ka'dar Hollman
Running Back	Reggie Begelton	Josh Leglue	Kenny Clark	**Free Safety**	**Strong Safety**
Aaron Jones	**Tight End**	**Guard**	Montravius Adams	Adrian Amos	Darnell Savage
AJ Dillon [R]	Marcedes Lewis	Lane Taylor	Gerald Willis III	Will Redmond	Vernon Scott [R]
Jamaal Williams	Jace Sternberger	Billy Turner	**Kicker**	**Punter**	**Long Snapper**
Dexter Williams	Robert Tonyan	Elgton Jenkins	Mason Crosby	JK Scott	Hunter Bradly

NFL

1

FULL 10 YARDS

GREEN BAY PACKERS

2019 RANKINGS

Player	Pos	Standard			0.5PPR			PPR		
		Pts	Avg	Rank	Pts	Avg	Rank	Pts	Avg	Rank
Aaron Rodgers	QB	262.3	17.5	QB11						
Aaron Jones	RB	251.5	16.8	RB2	275.0	18	RB2	298.5	20	RB2
Jamaal Williams	RB	107.3	7.7	RB34	126.8	9.1	RB33	146.3	11	RB30
Davante Adams	RB	114.4	10.4	WR33	152.4	14	WR27	190.4	17	WR26
Allen Lazard	WR	54.9	3.7	WR79	70.4	4.7	WR77	85.9	5.7	WR78
Geronimo Allison	WR	39.7	2.7	WR92	55.2	3.7	WR88	70.7	4.7	WR88
Marquez Valdes-Scantling	WR	56.2	3.8	WR75	68.2	4.6	WR79	80.2	5.4	WR83
Jimmy Graham	TE	57.8	3.9	TE22	74.8	5	TE22	91.8	6.1	TE22
Green Bay Packers	DST	104.0	6.9	DST15						
Mason Crosby	K	103.0	6.9	K20						

AARON RODGERS — ADP 8.10

Rodgers has vented his frustration his dissatisfaction at the Green Bay Packers this offseason for drafting his heir apparent, Jordan Love. He's admitted that he now probably won't play out his career for the cheeseheads so can we be sure his heart is truly there? His receiving options have certainly not improved from last year and he's all the down as my QB17 on the year.

AARON JONES — ADP 2.07

Another member of the backfield that is disgruntled by the organisation spending an early draft pick on their position. A.J. Dillon was brought in from the 2nd round of the draft & compares a likeness to Derrick Henry, who Matt LaFleur had success with during his time in Tennessee. AJ will still be a serviceable fantasy RB, but certainly don't expect him to lead the league in rushing TDs again.

DAVANTE ADAMS — ADP 1.10

The only bright fantasy spark in Green Bay this year and just about sneaks into the first round of PPR drafts. Adams will receive an abundance of targets this year but, with that, will have the very best coverage. He's a lock for a top-10 receiver but there will be weeks that he disappoints fantasy owners.

ALLEN LAZARD — ADP 12.9

Funchess, the only wide receiver brought into Green Bay this offseason, opted out of the season, leaving Lazard as the favourite option for the WR2 role this year. He'll have competition from Valdez-Scantling and Kumerow but should look to build on last year's WR67 finish. Somebody in the Green Bay receiver room has to step up.

JACE STERNBERGER — ADP U/D

Sternberger managed to grab touchdowns in both the pre and post season last year, but the only stat that he recorded in the regular season was an assist on a tackle. Jimmy Graham is out if the door and leaves behind 63 targets which will be distributed between Sternberger and Marcedes Lewis. Lewis, a former first round pick, is now 36.

2020 Projections

Position	Player	Standard		0.5PPR		Full PPR	
		Pts	Rank	Pts	Rank	Pts	Rank
QB	Aaron Rodgers	304.3	13				
RB	Aaron Jones	234.0	7	259.5	7	285.0	7
RB	A.J Dillon	101.9	47	105.9	53	109.9	56
RB	Jamaal Williams	53.9	69	64.4	68	74.9	69
WR	Davante Adams	189.4	2	239.4	2	289.4	2
WR	Allen Lazard	94.7	54	119.7	54	144.7	53
WR	M. Valdes-Scantling	49.2	98	63.2	100	77.2	99
WR	E. St. Brown	56.5	86	69.5	91	82.5	95
TE	Jace Sternberger	61.7	30	79.2	29	96.7	29

ADP taken from Ultimate Draft Kit (PPR)

Projections by Rob Grimwood @FFBritballer

FANTASY FOOTBALL

2

GREEN BAY PACKERS

LAST 5 YEARS

	W	L	T	Div	P/Offs
2019	13	3	0	1st	Lost Conf
2018	6	9	1	3rd	
2017	7	9	0	3rd	
2016	10	6	0	1st	Lost Conf
2015	10	6	0	2nd	Lost Div

DO SAY..
Back to Back HoF QBS

DON'T SAY..
Only 2 Super Bowls with those QBs?

BETTING ODDS BY ADAM WALFORD (@TOUCHDOWNTIPS)

SUPER BOWL	**28/1**
NFC CONFERENCE	**14/1**
NFC NORTH	**7/4**

TO MAKE PLAYOFFS
5/7
TEAM TOTAL WINS
8.5

ADAM'S BEST BET
AARON JONES UNDER 1325 COMBINED YARDS
10/11

PLEASE GAMBLE RESPONSIBLY

VIEW FROM THE SIDELINES
By Richard King (@RichKingFF)

Let's start with the record from last season - we aren't a 13 win team. We were lucky to pull some victories that we did in the season, and weren't overly hit with injury last season (as a whole). I don't expect either to happen again this year.

The offseason movements have been essentially flat, which is a little bit disappointing. The team have a great quarterback coming to the end of his career, but haven't opted to give him any more weapons. I can actually see a world were we play better, but end up with a worse record and either don't make the playoffs, or end up getting dumped out early.

▶RETRO FOCUS◀
FORREST GREGG – OT

There are not many offensive tackles that go from Super Bowl winner to then go and become the head coach of the team they played for, but that is the career of Packers legend Forrest Gregg. Gregg has one of the most impressive NFL C.V.s in NFL history, 9 Pro Bowls, 7 All Pro nods & 5 NFL Championships including winning the first two Super Bowls. Gregg went on to become the NFL Coach of the Year in 1974, but never repeated his playing successes.

DID YOU KNOW
The Packers are the only publicly owned franchise in the NFL, with 360,584 stockholders totaling 5,011,557 shares.

KEY STAT
"Winning at Life"
Head Coach Matt LaFleur currently owns the highest win percentage in the NFL (.778%) - The Packers HC has a combined 14-4 record.

FULL10YARDS VERDICT
With a 13-3 season under their belt, the Packers are still the ones to beat in the NFC North but they didn't help themselves this offseason. Looking to the future, they drafted Aaron Rodgers' likely replacement in Jordan Love instead of adding weapons to win with now; that had to rankle with the franchise QB. Beyond Davante Adams and Aaron Jones, the offence isn't loaded but the team have invested in the defence. Is that enough to elevate Green Bay from pretender to contender? I doubt they'll go all the way but they should extend their season into January.

BETTING, STATS, FANS VIEW, RETRO

3

FULL 10 YARDS

MINNESOTA VIKINGS

THE LOWDOWN:

The Vikings are competing in a tough NFC North division. Kirk Cousins contract has been extended and under the supervision of new offensive co-ordinator, Gary Kubiak, the team will be hoping for high levels of offensive production similar to that enjoyed under Kevin Stefanski. The loss of Stefon Diggs to the Buffalo Bills was a tough pill to swallow but Adam Thielen and rookie wide receiver Justin Jefferson are great targets for Cousins to have. The addition of rookie Jeff Gladney at will be welcomed across the Vikings defense. A big year for the Vikings as they look to keep pace with the Packers who reached the NFC Championship game last season.

SCHEDULE

Week 1: Vs. Packers
Week 2: @ Colts
Week 3: Vs. Titans
Week 4: @ Texans
Week 5: @ Seahawks *(SNF)*
Week 6: Vs. Falcons
Week 7: BYE
Week 8: @ Packers
Week 9: Vs. Lions
Week 10: @ Bears *(MNF)*
Week 11: Vs. Cowboys
Week 12: Vs. Panthers
Week 13: Vs. Jaguars
Week 14: @ Buccaneers
Week 15: Vs. Bears
Week 16: @ Saints
Week 17: @ Lions

2020 NFL DRAFT CLASS

Round 1
Justin Jefferson, WR, *LSU*
Jeff Gladney, CB, *TCU*
Round 2
Ezra Cleveland, OT, *Boise State*
Round 3
Cameron Dantzler, CB, *Mississippi State*
Round 4
D.J. Wonnum, DE, *South Carolina*
James Lynch, IDL, *Baylor*
Troy Dye, LB, *Oregon*
Round 5
Harrison Hand, CB, *Temple*
K.J. Osborn, WR, *Miami*
Round 6
Blake Brandel, OT, *Oregon State*
Josh Metellus, S, *Michigan*
Round 7
Kenny Willekes, EDGE, *Michigan State*
Nate Stanley, QB, *Iowa*
Brian Cole II, S, *Mississippi State*
Kyle Hinton, IOL, *Washburn*

SIGNINGS
Michael Pierce, DT
Tajae Sharpe, WR

FRANCHISE TAG
Anthony Harris, S

NO LONGER ON TEAM
Stefon Diggs, WR
Laquon Treadwell, WR
Everson Griffen, DE
Stephen Weatherly, DE
Mackensie Alexander, CB
Xavier Rhodes, CB
Trae Waynes, CB
Andrew Sendejo, S

TEAM DETAILS:
Owner: Zygi Wilf
General Manager: Rick Spielman
Stadium: U.S. Bank Stadium
Location: Minneapolis, MN
Head Coach: Mike Zimmer
Offensive Coordinator:
Dirk Koetter
Defensive Coordinator:
Raheem Morris
Coaching Staff:
Gary Kubiak (Assistant HC)
Klint Kubiak (QB Coach)
Kennedy Polamalu (RB Coach)
Andrew Janocko (WR Coach)
Brian Pariani (TE Coach)
Marwan Maalouf (ST Coordinator)
Super Bowl Wins: 0
Conference Wins: 4 (NFL Western 1969; NFC, 1973, 1974, 1976)
Divisional Wins: 6 20 (NFL Central, 1968, 1969; NFC Central; 1970, 1971, 1973, 1974, 1975, 1976, 1977, 1978, 1980, 1989, 1992, 1994, 1998, 2000; NFC North, 2008, 2009, 2015, 2017)
-2019-
Offence Rank: Passing (23rd), Rushing (6th), Overall (8th)
Defence Rank: Passing (15th), Rushing (13th), Overall (5th)

KEY PLAYER

Anthony Barr: A defensive overhaul is the main story of the Vikings' offseason, alongside the trade of Stefon Diggs. The departure of some of their leaders will put more pressure on the shoulders of the players such as Anthony Barr, the 7th year Linebacker. Barr and veteran Safety, Harrison Smith, will be vital if Minnesota is going to give Kirk Cousins and co time to produce on offense.

Justin Jefferson: Another team who replaced a top level veteran player with their first pick of their draft, Jefferson is a sure handed receiver who is coming off a hugely successful season with LSU. A great route runner who creates a great deal of separation and who has a nose for the endzone.

ROOKIE SPOTLIGHT

DEPTH CHART

Quarterback	Wide Receiver	Center	Edge	Line Backer	Cornerback
Kirk Cousins	Adam Thielen	Garrett Bradbury	Danielle Hunter	Anthony Barr	Mike Hughes
Sean Mannion	Justin Jefferson [R]	Brett Jones	Ifeadi Odenigbo	Eric Kendricks	Jeff Gladney [R]
Nate Stanley [R]	Olabisi Johnson	**Tackle**	Anthony Zettel	Eric Wilson	Cameron Dantzler [R]
Fullback	Tajae Sharpe	Riley Reiff	Eddie Yarborough	Ben Gedeon	Holton Hill
CJ Ham	Chad Beebe	Brian O'Neill	**Defensive Tackle**	DeMarquis Gates	Harrison Hand [R]
Running Back	JKJ Osborn [R]	Ezra Cleveland [R]	Michael Pierce	**Free Safety**	**Strong Safety**
Dalvin Cook	**Tight End**	**Guard**	Shamar Stephen	Anthony Harris	Harrison Smith
Alexander Mattison	Kyle Rudolph	Pat Elflein	Jaleel Johnson	Josh Metellus [R]	Brian Cole II [R]
Mike Boone	Irv Smith Jr	Dakota Dozier	**Kicker**	**Punter**	**Long Snapper**
Ameer Abdullah	Tyler Conklin	Aviante Collins	Dan Bailey	Britton Colquitt	Austin Cutting

NFL

1

FULL 10 YARDS

MINNESOTA VIKINGS

2019 RANKINGS

Player	Pos	Standard			0.5PPR			PPR		
		Pts	Avg	Rank	Pts	Avg	Rank	Pts	Avg	Rank
Kirk Cousins	QB	250.4	16.7	QB13						
Dalvin Cook	RB	239.4	17.1	RB3	265.9	19	RB3	292.4	21	RB3
Alexander Mattison	RB	58.4	4.5	RB54	63.4	4.9	RB57	68.4	5.3	RB59
Adam Thielen	WR	84.4	8.4	WR52	99.4	9.9	WR57	114.4	11	WR59
Stefon Diggs	WR	149.1	9.9	WR13	180.6	12	WR17	212.1	14	WR20
Olabisi Johnson	WR	44.6	3.0	WR85	58.6	3.9	WR87	72.6	4.8	WR87
Kyle Rudolph	WR	74.7	5.0	TE13	94.2	6.3	TE14	113.7	7.6	TE14
Irv Smith Jr.	TE	42.0	2.8	TE38	59.5	4	TE34	77.0	5.1	TE33
Minnesota Vikings	DST	136.0	9.1	DST4						
Dan Bailey	K	119.0	7.9	K10						

KIRK COUSINS

There's been that much happening in Minnesota this year that Kirk Cousins' contract extension fell somewhat under the radar. There's a new guy calling the plays, he's lost his WR1a and they are an offence built to run the ball. Minnesota should be playing from behind more this year which helps but he isn't a QB1 for fantasy.

ADP 14.8

DALVIN COOK

ADP 1.06

Cook has finally cleared the air about his contract situation and looks set to be the Vikings ball carrier in 2020. If we could guarantee his health, he would be drafted as a top-5 back; but he's already missed plenty of games in his young career and the Vikings have a more than competent backup in Alexander Mattison. If Cook plays 16, he's a bargain at ADP.

ADAM THIELEN

Thielen, although set to turn 30 before the start of the season, is Mr Consistent when it comes to fantasy football. Injuries ruined the second half of his season last year, but when he is on the field and healthy, he's a great PPR option every week. His target share will increase with the departure of Diggs and he'll fancy himself for a top-15 finish.

ADP 3.06

JUSTIN JEFFERSON

ADP 11.3

The first round pick out of LSU is tipped to be the most NFL ready wide receiver in this year's rookie class. That's particularly important considering the lack of time these new wideouts will have building chemistry with their quarterbacks this offseason. He'll fall straight into a WR2 role this season and will see the majority of Digg's 92 vacated targets.

IRV SMITH JR.

Irv started to plug away at Kyle Rudolph's target share last year and is tipped to increase that further this year. Minnesota will be passing the ball more and Diggs leaves behind a large number of targets. Smith Jr. is a nice tight end sleeper for this year.

ADP U/D

2020 Projections

Position	Player	Standard		0.5PPR		Full PPR	
		Pts	Rank	Pts	Rank	Pts	Rank
QB	Kirk Cousins	267.6	27				
RB	Dalvin Cook	247.3	5	271.3	5	295.3	5
RB	Alexander Mattison	78.1	63	86.1	63	94.1	63
WR	Adam Thielen	163.4	11	204.9	10	246.4	9
WR	Justin Jefferson	132.2	29	163.7	31	195.2	32
WR	Tajae Sharpe	72.3	75	89.3	76	106.3	78
TE	Kyle Rudolph	35.2	43	47.2	43	59.2	44
TE	Irv Smith Jr	66.8	24	94.3	24	121.8	21

ADP taken from Ultimate Draft Kit (PPR)

Projections by Rob Grimwood @FFBritballer

FANTASY FOOTBALL

2

FULL 10 YARDS

MINNESOTA VIKINGS

DO SAY..
The Minneapolis Miracle

DON'T SAY..
Super Bowl Record

BETTING ODDS
BY ADAM WALFORD (@TOUCHDOWNTIPS)

SUPER BOWL **33/1**

NFC CONFERENCE **16/1**

NFC NORTH **13/8**

TO MAKE PLAYOFFS
5/7
TEAM TOTAL WINS
8.5

ADAM'S BEST BET
OVER 8.5 WINS

10/11

PLEASE GAMBLE RESPONSIBLY

VIEW FROM THE SIDELINES
By Andy Henson (@AJHenson1985)

Optimism for the season has been up and down. Losing Diggs was a big blow & some experienced backs including Xavier Rhodes have moved on. However, we added smart options in free agency like Michael Pierce & Tajae Sharpe, as well as securing extensions for key players like Anthony Harris & Dan Bailey. The draft went well. Justin Jefferson is an exciting prospect at WR & we addressed the weakness at Cornerback. Securing Dalvin Cook for at least another season will be massive and it looks like Coach Zimmer is extending his own stay and his experience will be vital, overseeing a young squad. I think we will make the playoffs again this year with a 10-6 season.

▶RETRO FOCUS◀
FRAN TARKENTON – QB

QB Fran Tarkenton is a name you may have heard of, but you may not knowhe had 2 periods as the Vikings QB, with a 5 year stint at the Giants wedged in the middle. In 13 seasons with Minnesota, Fran threw for over 33,000 yards & reached 4 Super Bowls. Unfortunately just like Jim Kelly would do years later, Tarkenton was on the losing side of all 4 Lombardi contests. The Hall of Famer went to 9 Pro Bowls, but only got 1 All Pro nod.

DID YOU KNOW

The defensive line of the Vikings In the early Seventies, which took them to four Super Bowls, were known as the "Purple People Eaters".

KEY STAT
"All Day"
Kirk Cousins was afforded the most time to throw of any QB in 2019, Cousins had on average 3.01 seconds to make a pass.

FULL10YARDS VERDICT
The Vikings have much to be confident about on offense. Drafting Justin Jefferson will help fill the Stefon Diggs-shaped hole and, as long as he doesn't sulk on the sidelines waiting for a better deal, Dalvin Cook should shine once again. Minnesota are rebuilding on defence though, with wholesale changes in the secondary, and they have a tough road schedule. They will be strong enough to emerge from the NFC North, probably behind Green Bay, and play some January football but I can't see them taking the ultimate prize.

BETTING, STATS, FANS VIEW, RETRO

3

FULL 10 YARDS

STAFF PREDICTIONS

	TIM	SHAUN	LAWRENCE	LEE	ROB	ANDY M
SUPER BOWL	KC	NEW O	BAL	NEW O	NEW O	BAL
AFC	KC	KC	BAL	BAL	KC	BAL
NFC	DAL	NEW O	SF	NEW O	NEW O	LAR
AFC EAST	BUF	BUF	NEW E	BUF	NEW E	BUF
AFC NORTH	BAL	CLE	BAL	BAL	BAL	BAL
AFC SOUTH	IND	TEN	IND	IND	IND	TEN
AFC WEST	KC	KC	KC	KC	KC	KC
NFC EAST	DAL	DAL	PHI	DAL	DAL	PHI
NFC NORTH	GB	MIN	GB	GB	GB	MIN
NFC SOUTH	NEW O	NEW O	NEW O	NEW O	NEW O	TB
NFC WEST	SEA	SF	SF	SF	SEA	LAR
REG. SEASON MVP	MAHOMES	BREES	N.BOSA	BREES	BREES	JACKSON
PASSING LEADER	PRESCOTT	MAHOMES	RYAN	BREES	BREES	STAFFORD
RUSHING LEADER	COOK	CHUBB	COOK	ELLIOTT	ELLIOTT	ELLIOTT
RECEIVING LEADER	ADAMS	JONES	JONES	JONES	ADAMS	HILL
OFFENSIVE ROOKIE	BURROW	EDWARDS-H	BURROW	TAYLOR	JEUDY	BURROW
DEFENSIVE ROOKIE	YOUNG	YOUNG	SIMMONS	YOUNG	YOUNG	YOUNG
#1 PICK 2021 DRAFT	WAS	JAX	DET	CHI	CAR	JAX

	MICHAEL	JAMES	ANDY G	SEAN	DAVE
SUPER BOWL	KC	KC	KC	BAL	KC
AFC	KC	KC	KC	BAL	KC
NFC	SEA	NO	NO	NO	DAL
AFC EAST	BUF	BUF	NEW E	BUF	BUF
AFC NORTH	BAL	BAL	BAL	BAL	BAL
AFC SOUTH	IND	IND	TEN	TEN	IND
AFC WEST	KC	KC	KC	KC	KC
NFC EAST	DAL	DAL	DAL	DAL	DAL
NFC NORTH	MIN	GB	MIN	GB	MIN
NFC SOUTH	ATL	NO	NO	NO	NO
NFC WEST	SEA	SF	SF	SF	ARI
REG. SEASON MVP	WILSON	MAHOMES	BREES	JACKSON	MAHOMES
PASSING LEADER	MAHOMES	BREES	BREES	PRESCOTT	PRESCOTT
RUSHING LEADER	ELLIOTT	ELLIOTT	HENRY	HENRY	CHUBB
RECEIVING LEADER	HOPKINS	KUPP	THOMAS	THOMAS	THOMAS
OFFENSIVE ROOKIE	TAYLOR	EDWARDS-H	EDWARDS-H	BURROW	BURROW
DEFENSIVE ROOKIE	YOUNG	YOUNG	YOUNG	YOUNG	YOUNG
#1 PICK 2021 DRAFT	JAX	JAX	NYJ	JAX	JAX

ATLANTA FALCONS

THE LOWDOWN:

Playing in one of the toughest divisions in football, the NFC South, the Atlanta Falcons will have their work cut out for them this season if they want to be successful. With a loaded offense which contains several household names including Matt Ryan, Julio Jones and Todd Gurley, Falcons fans will have high hopes for what their team can produce this year. They will be facing Tom Brady and Drew Brees twice a season, so they will have to perform at an elite level to get results. Defensive End Takk McKinley had his fifth year option declined, while LB Deone Bucannon agreed to terms with Atlanta.

SCHEDULE

Week 1: Vs. Seahawks
Week 2: @ Cowboys
Week 3: Vs. Bears
Week 4: @ Packers *(MNF)*
Week 5: Vs. Panthers
Week 6: @ Vikings
Week 7: Vs. Lions
Week 8: @ Panthers *(TNF)*
Week 9: Vs. Broncos
Week 10: BYE
Week 11: @ Saints
Week 12: Vs. Raiders
Week 13: Vs. Saints
Week 14: @ Chargers
Week 15: Vs. Buccaneers
Week 16: @ Chiefs
Week 17: @ Buccaneers

2020 NFL DRAFT CLASS

Round 1
A.J. Terrell, CB,
Clemson
Round 2
Marlon Davidson, IDL,
Auburn
Round 3
Matt Hennessy, IOL,
Temple
Round 4
Mykal Walker, LB,
Fresno State
Jaylinn Hawkins, S,
California
Round 7
Sterling Hofrichter, P,
Syracuse

SIGNINGS

Charles Harris, DE
Hayden Hurst, TE
Dante Fowler Jr., DE
Tyeler Davison, DT

STAR SIGNING
Todd Gurley, RB

NO LONGER ON TEAM

Devonta Freeman, RB
Austin Hooper, TE
Wes Schweitzer, OG
Adrian Clayborn, DE
De'Vondre Campbell, LB
Vic Beasley, LB
Desmond Trufant, CB
Johnathan Cyprien, S

TEAM DETAILS:

Owner: Arthur Blank
General Manager:
Thomas Dimitroff
Stadium: Mercedes-Benz
Location: Atlanta, Georgia
Head Coach: Dan Quinn
Offensive Coordinator:
Dirk Koetter
Defensive Coordinator:
Raheem Morris
Coaching Staff:
Jeff Ulbrich (Assistant HC, LB Coach)
Greg Knapp (QB Coach)
Bernie Parmalee (RB Coach)
Dave Brock (WR Coach)
Ben Steele (TE Coach);
Ben Kotwica (ST Coordinator)
Super Bowl Wins: 0
Conference Wins: 2 (1998,2016)
Divisional Wins: 6 (NFC West: 1980, 1998; NFC South: 2004, 2010, 2012, 2016)
-2019-
Record: 7-9
Offence Rank: Passing (3rd), Rushing (30th), Overall (13th)
Defence Rank: Passing (22nd), Rushing (15th), Overall (23rd)

KEY PLAYER

Julio Jones: Not many wide receivers can boast seven 1000-yard seasons in nine years. On his day, Jones is the best receiver in the league and often provides the spark that gets the Falcons firing. The addition of former first round picks, Todd Gurley and Laquon Treadwell, should provide the veteran playmaker with space to wreak even more havoc amongst secondaries in the NFC South.

ROOKIE SPOTLIGHT

A.J Terrell: Terrell is a fantastic athlete with excellent movement skills and oily hips. He excels in man coverage and has great click and close skills with an eye for an interception - See the 2019 College Football National Championship game, and his pick-6 of Tua Tagovailoa for the first score of the game.

DEPTH CHART

Quarterback	Wide Receiver	Center	Edge	Line Backer	Cornerback
Matt Ryan	Julio Jones	Alex Mack	Takkarist McKinley	Deoin Jones	AJ Terrell [R]
Matt Schaub	Calvin Ridley	Matt Hennessy [R]	Dante Fowler	Charles Harris	Isaiah Oliver
Kurt Benkert	Russel Gage	**Tackle**	Allen Bailey	Deone Bucannon	Kendall Sheffield
Fullback	Laquon Treadwell	Jake Matthews	Austin Larkin	Foyesade Oloukon	Jordan Miller
Keith Smith	Christian Blake	Kaleb McGary	**Defensive Tackle**	Mykal Walker [R]	CJ Reavis
Running Back	Olamide Zaccheaus	John Wetzel	Grady Jarrett	**Free Safety**	**Strong Safety**
Toddy Gurley	**Tight End**	**Guard**	Tyeler Davison	Ricardo Allen	Keanu Neal
Brian Hill	Hayden Hurst	Chris Lindstrom	Marlon Davidson [R]	Sharrod Neasman	Damontae Kazee
Quadree Ollison	Khari Lee	James Carpenter	**Kicker**	**Punter**	**Long Snapper**
Ito Smith	Jaeden Graham	Justin McCray	Younghoe Koo	Ryan Allen	Josh Harris

NFL

1

FULL 10 YARDS

ATLANTA FALCONS

2019 RANKINGS

Player	Pos	Standard			0.5PPR			PPR		
		Pts	Avg	Rank	Pts	Avg	Rank	Pts	Avg	Rank
Matt Ryan	QB	267	19	QB9						
Devonta Freeman	RB	131	10	RB23	160	12	RB20	188	15	RB21
Qadree Ollison	RB	28.8	4.1	RB78	29.3	4.2	RB82	29.8	4.3	RB89
Julio Jones	WR	167	12	WR4	213	15	WR4	259	19	WR4
Calvin Ridley	WR	134	10	WR21	166	13	WR23	197	15	WR22
Mohammed Sanu	WR	61.6	4.4	WR70	89.6	6.4	WR64	118	8.4	WR57
Russell Gage	WR	43	2.9	WR86	64	4.3	WR84	85	5.7	WR80
Austin Hooper	TE	112	9.4	TE7	146	12	TE6	180	15	TE6
Atlanta Falcons	DST	76	5.1	DST26						
Younghoe Koo	K	75	11	K29						

MATT RYAN

ADP 7.12

Matty Ice is always in & around the top-10 of fantasy quarterbacks. Fantasy owners would have been disappointed last year with his QB11 finish after he finished as the QB2 last year. He has plenty of receiving options all over the field. Dirk Koetter offenses love to pass & that doesn't look to change this year.

TODD GURLEY

ADP 3.05

Gurley is splitting the fantasy world this year. He's just turned 26 and the only running back at a team with a high-powered offense. On the flip, injury concerns shroud his future and we can't be certain of his workload. Gurley looked good in the latter half of last season and the Falcons (hopefully) have done their due diligence. Top-15 is a definite possibility.

JULIO JONES

ADP 2.03

Julio has been one of the best receivers in the league for years and his fantasy production matches that. Many criticise his touchdown production but he's the only player in NFL history with multiple 250-yard receiving games. Ridley, opposite Jones, should detract from his attention which leaves the door open for another monster season.

CALVIN RIDLEY

ADP 4.05

The Ridley hype train has well and truly left the station, and many are predicting a Godwin-esque breakout season this year. Ryan will certainly throw the ball enough times to satisfy two wide receiver ones in this offense and Ridley is the clear benefactor of these targets. He was on pace for 1,000 yards last season and should break that this year.

HAYDEN HURST

ADP 7.09

Austin Hooper leaves behind 97 targets after his departure to Cleveland and Hurst looks to be the prime candidate for the majority of these. Hurst is talented but got stuck behind Mark Andrews in the Baltimore depth chart. There's enough targets to go around and Hurst has a sneaky chance at being a top-15 tight end this year.

2020 Projections

Position	Player	Standard		0.5PPR		Full PPR	
		Pts	Rank	Pts	Rank	Pts	Rank
QB	Matt Ryan	306.1	12				
RB	Todd Gurley	200.2	12	222.7	15	245.2	13
RB	Qadree Ollison	50.1	74	53.1	77	56.1	79
RB	Ito Smith	82.6	59	99.6	57	116.6	51
WR	Julio Jones	177.2	4	222.7	3	268.2	4
WR	Calvin Ridley	162.8	13	203.8	12	244.8	12
WR	Laquon Treadwell	60.0	82	78.0	82	96.0	81
WR	Russell Gage	47.5	102	68.0	93	88.5	88
TE	Hayden Hurst	88.4	15	111.9	16	135.4	16

ADP taken from Ultimate Draft Kit (PPR)

Projections by Rob Grimwood @FFBritballer

FANTASY FOOTBALL

2

FULL 10 YARDS

ATLANTA FALCONS

LAST 5 YEARS

	W	L	T	Div	P/Offs
2019	7	9	0	2nd	
2018	7	9	0	2nd	
2017	10	6	0	3rd	Lost Div
2016	11	5	0	1st	Lost SB
2015	8	8	0	2nd	

DO SAY..

Matt Ryan to Julio Jones [Ctrl] + C, [Ctrl] + V

DON'T SAY..

28th March

BETTING ODDS BY ADAM WALFORD (@TOUCHDOWNTIPS)

SUPER BOWL **50/1**

NFC CONFERENCE **25/1**

NFC SOUTH **10/1**

TO MAKE PLAYOFFS **12/5**

TEAM TOTAL WINS **7.5**

ADAM'S BEST BET

TO FINISH 2ND NFC SOUTH **5/2**

PLEASE GAMBLE RESPONSIBLY

VIEW FROM THE SIDELINES

By Danny & Cal (@ATLFalconsUK)

Following a roller coaster of a season which had the Falcons starting on a massive low and finishing on a 6-2 we are anticipating major growth. Our draft selections have covered the necessary positions even if the names that were brought in weren't all on everyone's predictions. Add to that the acquisitions of players such as Gurley, Hurst & Fowler have added the required quality/experience to our young roster so we have high expectations going into the season. We are both predicting a 10-6 finish to push the Falcons into at worst, a wildcard spot. This is a huge season for Dan Quinn & a make or break season for a few players so we are expecting everyone to step it up & play as they should, all or nothing. Don't be surprised if you see us deep into the playoffs this season.

▶RETRO FOCUS◀

MIKE KENN - OT

When Mike Kenn began life at Michigan he weighed just 220 pounds, but by the end of his 17 year NFL career he tipped the scales at 286. Arguably the greatest offensive tackle in Falcons history, Kenn went to five consecutive Pro Bowls in the 80s and was a two-time first team All-Pro (1980/1991). Kenn is renowned for starting in every single game he ever played in the NFL. His ironman-esque 251 starts ranks 2nd all-time for NFL offensive linemen, behind only Bruce Matthews (293 starts).

DID YOU KNOW

A local radio station sponsored a name the team contest. Suggestions included the Fireballs, Knights, Peaches, Vibrants, Lancers, Thrashers & Goobers.

KEY STAT

"Put that arm on Ice"
The Falcons attempted the most passes in 2019, with 684 and averaged 6.4 plays per drive (ranked 2nd).

FULL10YARDS VERDICT

It's now or never for HC Dan Quinn, who's under pressure to take the Falcons back to postseason football after back-to-back 7-9 seasons. If they come out of the traps like they finished last year, going 6-2 in their final eight games, they'll be fine but they do have a tough start. Any team containing Matt Ryan, Julio Jones, Calvin Ridley and Todd Gurley will rack up points so it'll be down to new defensive signings Dante Fowler Jr. and Takkarist McKinley, plus rookie corner AJ Terrell, to determine which side of .500 Atlanta finishes on.

BETTING, STATS, FANS VIEW, RETRO

3

FULL 10 YARDS

CAROLINA PANTHERS

THE LOWDOWN:

The 2020 Carolina Panthers will be a new look franchise compared to what fans seen last season. New Head Coach Matt Rhule, who came from Baylor University made his intentions abundantly clear at the draft. Every player the Panthers selected plays on defense. A complete haul-over and system change for one of the poorest units in the league last season. Offensively, the Panthers signed Quarterback Teddy Bridgewater as he prepares to take over the reigns as the starter. Paired with one of the best offensive weapons in the league in Christian McCaffery – The Panthers new look offense will be up to the challenge of competing in the NFC South.

SCHEDULE

Week 1: Vs. Raiders
Week 2: @ Buccaneers
Week 3: @ Chargers
Week 4: Vs. Cardinals
Week 5: @ Falcons
Week 6: Vs. Bears
Week 7: @ Saints
Week 8: Vs. Falcons *(TNF)*
Week 9: @ Chiefs
Week 10: Vs. Buccaneers
Week 11: Vs. Lions
Week 12: @ Vikings
Week 13: BYE
Week 14: Vs. Broncos
Week 15: @ Packers
Week 16: @ Washington
Week 17: Vs. Saints

2020 NFL DRAFT CLASS

Round 1
Derrick Brown, IDL,
Auburn
Round 2
Yetur Gross-Matos, EDGE,
Penn State
Jeremy Chinn, S,
Southern Illinois
Round 4
Troy Pride, CB,
Notre Dame
Round 5
Kenny Robinson, S,
West Virginia
Round 6
Bravvion Roy, IDL,
Baylor
Round 7
Stantley Thomas-Oliver, CB,
Florida International

SIGNINGS

Robby Anderson, WR
Eli Apple, CB
Pharoh Cooper, WR
Seth DeValve, TE
John Miller, G
Seth Roberts, WR
P.J. Walker, QB
Stephen Weatherly, DE
Tahir Whitehead, LB
Tre Boston, S:

STAR SIGNING

Teddy Bridgewater, QB

NO LONGER ON TEAM

Cam Newton, QB
Kyle Allen, QB
Greg Olsen, TE
Trai Turner, OL
Daryl Williams, OL
Dontari Poe, DT
Luke Kuechly, LB (Ret.)
Mario Addison, DE
Vernon Butler, DE
James Bradberry, CB
Eric Reid, S

TEAM DETAILS:

Owner: David Tepper
General Manager: Marty Hurney
Stadium: Bank of America Stadium
Location: Charlotte, NC
Head Coach: Matt Rhule
Offensive Coordinator: Joe Brady
Defensive Coordinator: Phil Snow
Coaching Staff:
Jake Peetz (QB Coach)
Jeff Nixon (RB Coach, Senior Offensive Assistant)
Frisman Jackson (WR Coach)
Brian Angelichio (TE Coach)
Chase Blackburn (ST Coordinator)
Super Bowl Wins: 0
Conference Wins: 2 (NFC, 2003, 2015)
Divisional Wins: 6 (NFC West, 1996; NFC South, 2003, 2008, 2013, 2014, 2015)
-2019-
Record: 5-11
Offence Rank: Passing (20th), Rushing (14th), Overall (20th)
Defence Rank: Passing (13th), Rushing (29th), Overall (31st)

KEY PLAYER

Christian McCaffrey: Not only did McCaffrey put up 1387 rushing yards in 2019, he also added 1005 receiving yards as well. The definition of the modern pass catching back, it's fair to say everything that the Panthers do on offense runs through him. "Run CMC" moves onto his 3rd QB this season & it appears that the short, game management style of Teddy Bridgewater could match his game perfectly.

ROOKIE SPOTLIGHT

Derrick Brown: On this game, Brown can be a game wrecker from the interior of the line. A superb athlete with first step explosion that shouldn't be possible for a man of his size. Brown is excellent at plugging up gaps as a 0-tech but can also move out to the edge and play as a big end in some situations.

DEPTH CHART

Quarterback	Wide Receiver	Center	Edge	Line Backer	Cornerback
Teddy Bridgewater	DJ Moore	Matt Paradis	Stephen Weatherly	Shaq Thompson	Donte Jackson
Will Grier	Robby Anderson	Tyler Larsen	Kawann Short	Tahir Whitehead	Eli Apple
PJ Walker	Curtis Samuel	**Tackle**	Brian Burns	Jermaine Carter	Cole Luke
Fullback	Pharoh Cooper	Russel Okung	Marquis Haynes	Andre Smith	Corn Elder
Alex Armah	Seth Roberts	Taylor Moton	**Defensive Tackle**	Christian Miller	Troy Pride [R]
Running Back	DeAndrew White	Greg Little	Derrick Brown [R]	**Free Safety**	**Strong Safety**
Christian McCaffrey	**Tight End**	**Guard**	Woodrow Hamilton	Tre Boston	Jeremy Chinn [R]
Reggie Bonnafon	Ian Thomas	John Miller	Bravvion Roy [R]	Quin Blanding	Juston Burris
Jordan Scarlett	Chris Manhertz	Dennis Daley	**Kicker**	**Punter**	**Long Snapper**
Mike Davis	Temarrick Hemingway	Branden Bowen [R]	Graham Gano	Michael Palardy	JJ Jansen

NFL

1

2019 RANKINGS

Player	Pos	Standard			0.5PPR			PPR		
		Pts	Avg	Rank	Pts	Avg	Rank	Pts	Avg	Rank
Kyle Allen	QB	182.1	14.0	QB28						
Christian McCaffrey	RB	339.4	22.6	RB1	393.9	26	RB1	448.4	30	RB1
Reggie Bonnafon	RB	19.1	1.3	RB92	21.1	1.4	RB93	23.1	1.5	RB93
D.J. Moore	WR	143.5	9.6	WR17	187.0	13	WR13	230.5	15	WR12
Curtis Samuel	WR	116.4	7.8	WR31	142.4	9.5	WR32	168.4	11	WR34
Jarius Wright	WR	27.9	1.9	WR111	40.9	2.7	WR102	53.9	3.6	WR99
Greg Olsen	TE	70.5	5.4	TE16	95.5	7.4	TE13	120.5	9.3	TE13
Ian Thomas	TE	18.4	1.2	TE56	25.9	1.7	TE53	33.4	2.2	TE54
Carolina Panthers	DST	94.0	6.3	DST18						
Joey Slye	K	126.0	8.4	K6						

TEDDY BRIDGEWATER

Two glove Teddy has his first starting job in the NFL since 2015 & has a nice crop of weapons around him. He's deputised for Drew Brees and, last year particularly, didn't look half bad (though I think I'd be OK throwing to Michael Thomas). Teddy B will likely have to throw a lot but temper expectations for a QB who hasn't thrown for more than 14 TDs in a season.

ADP 14.9

CHRISTIAN McCAFFREY

ADP 1.01

McCaffrey was a cheat code last year and, if you didn't win your league with him, something went drastically wrong. It was the best fantasy football season in history, and he's been rewarded with a big contract. He still warrants his ADP of 1.01 but expect regression from his historic 2019 season.

D.J. MOORE

Moore finished as WR16 last year and finished above some big names who played a similar number of games to him. There's an increasing number of mouths to feed in this offense, a new quarterback and a new system. It'll be difficult for Moore to crack on into the top-15 this year but has the talent and the system that plays to his strengths.

ADP 3.12

CURTIS SAMUEL

ADP 14.8

Samuel had the least receptions for any player targeted over 100 times last year. He still produced 627 receiving yards and 6 TDs on 54 receptions and, regression suggests, this production will increase. There's a lot of players to satisfy in this offense but Samuel is talented and a push for the top-25 is on the cards.

ROBBY ANDERSON

A WR40 last year, Anderson is my third (fourth if you count McCaffrey, which you should) favourite receiver on this team. He's never broken 1000 yards in his career and his career high fantasy finish is WR18. It's a new team, a new QB who isn't known for pushing the ball downfield, a new system and I'm not high on Anderson this year – at all.

ADP 14.10

2020 Projections

Position	Player	Standard		0.5PPR		Full PPR	
		Pts	Rank	Pts	Rank	Pts	Rank
QB	Teddy Bridgewater	276.4	20				
RB	Christian McCaffrey	315.3	1	365.8	1	416.3	1
RB	Reggie Bonnafon	19.3	102	23.8	102	28.3	102
WR	D.J Moore	156.7	16	196.7	16	236.7	16
WR	Curtis Samuel	80.9	68	97.9	72	114.9	74
WR	Robby Anderson	108.9	48	131.4	50	153.9	50
WR	Seth Roberts	33.6	113	43.1	113	52.6	112
TE	Ian Thomas	43.2	39	59.2	37	75.2	36

ADP taken from Ultimate Draft Kit (PPR)

Projections by Rob Grimwood @FFBritballer

FANTASY FOOTBALL

2

CAROLINA PANTHERS

LAST 5 YEARS				
	W	L	T	Div	P/Offs
2019	5	11	0	4th	
2018	7	9	0	3rd	
2017	11	5	0	2nd	Lost WC
2016	6	10	0	4th	
2015	15	1	0	1st	Lost SB

DO SAY..
Run CMC

DON'T SAY..
Super Bowl 50

BETTING ODDS BY ADAM WALFORD (@TOUCHDOWNTIPS)

SUPER BOWL **125/1**

NFC CONFERENCE **60/1**

NFC SOUTH **22/1**

TO MAKE PLAYOFFS
5/1
TEAM TOTAL WINS
5.5

ADAM'S BEST BET
C.McCAFFREY UNDER 1900.5 COMBINED YARDS
10/11

PLEASE GAMBLE RESPONSIBLY

VIEW FROM THE SIDELINES
By Rob Cowsill (@CowsillRob)

2020 is a rebuilding season for Carolina. Cam was a personality, but losing him & Luke Keuchly took away major anchor points for both sides of the team. Hopefully we build around McCaffrey & find our way after seeming a little lost last campaign. I'm also excited to see how our draft class grows into the defense. Ultimately it's a big learning experience for everyone, for fans, players - and particularly our new coaching team. It's Coach Rhule's time for the big leagues. I hope the NFL doesn't chew him up & spit him out - I think he, and Joe Brady, could go places.

▶RETRO FOCUS◀
JON KASAY - PK

When you crack the top 10 all time point scorers in NFL history you deserve some time in the spotlight. John Kasay spent 15 of his 20 NFL seasons in Carolina (1995-2010), racking up 429exps and 351 successful field goals. This is all made more remarkable when you discover he missed the 2000 season with a broken kneecap. Kasay scored 5 points in a narrow Super Bowl loss to the Patriots in 2004. He converted 92% of all playoff field goal attempts..

DID YOU KNOW

The team plays Neil Diamond's "Sweet Caroline" after home victories.

KEY STAT
"Easy, Tiger"
New Offensive Coordinator, Joe Brady, ran the LSU passing game last season where the National Championship winning Tigers averaged 401.6 yards passing in 2019.

FULL10YARDS VERDICT
With Ron Rivera, Cam Newton, Greg Olsen and Luke Kuechly gone, it's all change in Carolina. Christian McCaffery is still there though, and he's joined by incoming HC Matt Rhule, QB Teddy Bridgewater and WR1 Robby Anderson. Despite using all their draft picks on defensive players such as Derrick Brown and Yetur Gross-Matos, they might still be flaky on D. The Panthers will ship points against most of the top QBs in the NFL this year and I doubt their attack is strong enough to compensate, so expect them to prop up the NFC South again.

BETTING, STATS, FANS VIEW, RETRO

3

FULL 10 YARDS

NEW ORLEANS SAINTS

THE LOWDOWN:

The Saints are perhaps the team that is most in a "win now" mode. The Saints offense is stacked with Michael Thomas, who recorded the most receptions in a single season filling the WR1 spot while veteran playmaker Emmanuel Sanders will line up on the other side of the field. Alvin Kamara will be back to full fitness this season & will be expected to play at the high octane, explosive level we were so used to seeing from him. 3 years in a row, the Saints have suffered devastating ends to their seasons in the playoffs, a trend which the WHO DAT nation will want to come to an abrupt end this season. Drew Brees & Tom Brady is the perfect match up in the NFC South as both Hall of Famers come to the end of their Careers.

SCHEDULE

Week 1: Vs. Buccaneers
Week 2: @ Raiders *(MNF)*
Week 3: Vs. Packers *(SNF)*
Week 4: @ Lions
Week 5: Vs. Chargers
Week 6: BYE
Week 7: Vs. Panthers
Week 8: @ Bears
Week 9: @ Buccaneers *(SNF)*
Week 10: Vs. 49ers
Week 11: Vs. Falcons
Week 12: @ Broncos
Week 13: @ Falcons
Week 14: @ Eagles
Week 15: Vs. Chiefs
Week 16: Vs. Vikings
Week 17: @ Panthers

2020 NFL DRAFT CLASS

Round 1
Cesar Ruiz, IOL,
Michigan
Round 3
Zack Baun, LB,
Wisconsin
Adam Trautman, TE,
Dayton
Round 7
Tommy Stevens, QB,
Mississippi State

SIGNINGS

Malcolm Jenkins, S:
Emmanuel Sanders, WR:
D.J. Swearinger, S:
Jameis Winston, QB:

RE-SIGNED

Drew Brees, QB
Taysom Hill, QB
Andrus Peat, OT
David Onyemata, DT
P.J. Williams, CB

NO LONGER ON TEAM

Teddy Bridgewater, QB
Ted Ginn Jr., WR
A.J. Klein, LB
Eli Apple, CB
Vonn Bell, S

TEAM DETAILS:

Owner: Gayle Benson
General Manager: Mickey Loomis
Stadium: Mercedes-Benz Superdome
Location: New Orleans, LA
Head Coach: Sean Payton
Offensive Coordinator: Pete Carmichael
Defensive Coordinator: Dennis Allen
Coaching Staff:
Darren Rizzi (ST Coordinator)
Dan Campbell (Assistant HC/TE Coach)
Joe Lombardi (QB Coach)
Joel Thomas (RB Coach)
Ronald Curry (WR Coach)
Super Bowl Wins: 1 (2009)
Conference Wins: 1 (NFC, 2009)
Divisional Wins: 8 (NFC West, 1991, 2000; NFC South, 2006, 2009, 2011, 2017, 2018, 2019)
-2019-
Record: 13-3
Offence Rank: Passing (7th), Rushing (16th), Overall (4th)
Defence Rank: Passing (20th), Rushing (4th), Overall (13th)

KEY PLAYER

Alvin Kamara: Drew Brees back in town for one last hurrah, but it's his supporting cast that will prove most important this season. In Michael Thomas the Saints have an elite receiving option, but it's their go to RB who really has the potential to make a difference. As well as being effective in the run game, Kamara has caught 81 passes in each of his pro seasons, look for that to increase as they throw everything at the Super Bowl.

ROOKIE SPOTLIGHT

Cesar Ruiz: Ruiz is powerful and athletic with a thickly built frame and tonnes of power to move and redirect guys. Ruiz will probably play guard to begin his career and form an excellent guard/center combo with last year's second round pick, Erik McCoy, in what is one of the better lines in the NFL.

DEPTH CHART

Quarterback	Wide Receiver	Center	Edge	Line Backer	Cornerback
Drew Brees	Michael Thomas	Erik McCoy	Cameron Jordan	Demario Davis	Marshon Lattimore
Jameis Winston	Emmanuel Sanders	Nick Easton	Marcus Davenport	Kiko Alonso	Janoris Jenkins
Taysom Hill	Tre-Quan Smith	Tackle	Carl Granderson	Zack Baun [R]	PJ Williams
Fullback	Deonte Harris	Terron Armstead	Alex Anzalone	Anthony Chickillo	Patrick Robinson
Mike Burton	Austin Carr	Ryan Ramczyk	Defensive Tackle	Craig Robertson	Justin Hardee
Running Back	Lil'Jordan Humphrey	Will Clapp	Sheldon Rankins	Free Safety	Strong Safety
Alvin Kamara	Tight End	Guard	David Onyemata	Malcolm Jenkins	Marcus Williams
Latavius Murray	Jared Cook	Andrus Peat	Margus Hunt	DK Swearinger	Chauncey Gardner-Johnson
Ty Montgomery	Josh Hill	Cesar Ruiz [R]	Kicker	Punter	Long Snapper
Dwayne Washington	Adam Trautman [R]	James Hurst	Will Lutz	Thomas Morstead	Zach Wood

NFL

1

FULL 10 YARDS

NEW ORLEANS SAINTS

2019 RANKINGS

Player	Pos	Standard			0.5PPR			PPR		
		Pts	Avg	Rank	Pts	Avg	Rank	Pts	Avg	Rank
Drew Brees	QB	206.8	20.7	QB24						
Taysom Hill	QB	72.3	4.8	QB36	81.3	5.4	QB36	90.3	6	QB33
Alvin Kamara	RB	149.8	11.5	RB18	189.3	15	RB13	228.8	18	RB11
Latavius Murray	RB	115.7	7.7	RB31	132.2	8.8	RB30	148.7	9.9	RB27
Michael Thomas	WR	221.9	14.8	WR1	294.4	20	WR1	366.9	25	WR1
Ted Ginn	WR	54.9	3.7	WR78	69.4	4.6	WR78	83.9	5.6	WR81
Tre'Quan Smith	WR	41.8	4.2	WR88	48.3	4.8	WR95	54.8	5.5	WR97
Jared Cook	TE	114.1	8.8	TE6	134.6	10	TE7	155.1	12	TE7
New Orleans Saints	DST	117.0	7.8	DST12						
Wil Lutz	K	157.0	10.5	K2						

DREW BREES

Brees has been the most accurate passer in NFL history throughout his career but his arm strength has dwindled over the last few years. His season was cut short last year due to a thumb injury but was on pace to be QB8. Brees will be desperate to go out with a bang and he's got a tremendous supporting cast around him.

ADP 7.08

ALVIN KAMARA

ADP 1.05

Although playing the majority of games, Kamara was playing injured last year and his production showed it – particularly his receiving game. Kamara easily has 1,500 scrimmage yards and 15 TDs in the locker and 2,000 and 20 is a distinct possibility for the 4th year back. The use of Latavius Murray will be crucial to his success.

MICHAEL THOMAS

Thomas smashing the season reception record last year with 149. He was prolific with both Brees and Bridgewater throwing to him and his 1,725 yards easily earned him the WR1 spot last year. There's no reason he shouldn't get close to those numbers again this year and he'll even look to better last year's TD total of 9.

ADP 1.06

EMMANUEL SANDERS

ADP 9.01

Sanders joins his 4th NFL team & his 3rd in two seasons. He's had some incredible quarterbacks throwing to him so far in his career (Roethlisberger/ Manning) and Drew Brees will join that list of greats this year. Sanders is easily the best WR2 that Brees has had for a long while & there are plenty of targets to feed him. A top 25 finish is easily achieveable.

JARED COOK

Jared Cook was incredibly efficient last year and will likely regress to the mean. He'll also lose targets with the arrival of Sanders and he's definitely the wrong side of 30. The Saints also traded up to draft Trautman. The odds aren't stacked in Cook's favour and you definitely shouldn't be expecting another top-10 fantasy finish.

ADP 10.4

2020 Projections

Position	Player	Standard		0.5PPR		Full PPR	
		Pts	Rank	Pts	Rank	Pts	Rank
QB	Drew Brees	337.5	5				
RB	Alvin Kamara	236.4	6	277.4	4	318.4	4
RB	Latavius Murray	103.6	45	116.1	47	128.6	48
RB	Ty Montgomery	30.8	88	42.8	83	54.8	81
WR	Michael Thomas	209.3	1	274.8	1	340.3	1
WR	Emmanuel Sanders	98.8	51	125.8	51	152.8	51
WR	Tre'Quan Smith	85.9	63	104.9	65	123.9	67
TE	Jared Cook	86.9	17	104.9	17	122.9	20
TE	Adam Trautman	62.5	28	78.5	30	94.5	30

ADP taken from Ultimate Draft Kit (PPR)

Projections by Rob Grimwood @FFBritballer

FANTASY FOOTBALL

2

NEW ORLEANS SAINTS

LAST 5 YEARS

	W	L	T	Div	P/Offs
2019	13	3	0	1st	Lost WC
2018	13	3	0	1st	Lost Conf
2017	11	5	0	1st	Lost Div
2016	7	9	0	3rd	
2015	7	9	0	3rd	

DO SAY..
Drew Brees and Sean Payton

DON'T SAY..
Playoff heartbreaks

BETTING ODDS
BY ADAM WALFORD (@TOUCHDOWNTIPS)

SUPER BOWL **14/1**

NFC CONFERENCE **7/1**

NFC SOUTH **11/10**

TO MAKE PLAYOFFS **1/3**

TEAM TOTAL WINS **10.5**

ADAM'S BEST BET
WIN NFC SOUTH **11/10**

PLEASE GAMBLE RESPONSIBLY

VIEW FROM THE SIDELINES

By Ash Pimble (@DomePatrolUK)

As a Saints fan, the last few seasons have tested my sanity, caused me to have several breakdowns, heart attacks and "are you kidding me?" moments. 2017, 2018, 2019 we stride into the playoffs and come up short every time (be it our fault or certain people in white and black striped uniforms). 2020 brings a season of renewed hope, Saints got Emmanuel Sanders to give Brees more options to scores TDs & Malcom Jenkins returns to New Orleans as a 2 time super bowl winner. The players want Drew to get his 2nd ring before he rides off into the sunset; the window of opportunity is closing & closing fast. Will we see another Peyton Manning type final season? Only time will tell. All I know is 2020 season it is Super Bowl or bust.

►RETRO FOCUS◄
PAT SWILLING – LB

Linebacker Pat Swilling spent the first 7 of his 12 year career in the Big Easy. A ferocious pass rusher he was a key member of the 'Dome Patrol'. 1n 1991, his most productive season, he registered 17 sacks and 6 forced fumbles, earning AP Defensive Player of the Year. Swilling was part of a Saints team that spent many years in the doldrums, and regretfully he never won a single playoff game with the Saints (0-4). Swilling remains in the top 25 all-time sacks chart with 107.5.

DID YOU KNOW
The Saints were awarded their place as an NFL expansion team on 1 November 1966, which just happened to be All-Saints Day.

KEY STAT
"Ball Security"
The Saints ranked 1st in turnovers given up, only turning the ball over 8 times in 2019.

FULL10YARDS VERDICT
The Saints have been a stroke of bad luck away from making the last two Super Bowls so can they bounce back yet again? The elements are all there, from the mercurial Drew Brees driving a top-five offence (with Michael Thomas and Alvin Kamara now joined by Emmanuel Sanders), the best O-line in the league and a far from shoddy D. Hell, even kicker Wil Lutz is a Pro Bowler. Despite the predicted rise in Tampa's fortunes, the Saints should win the NFC South but can they finally make their dominance count and return to the league's biggest stage?

BETTING, STATS, FANS VIEW, RETRO

3

TAMPA BAY BUCCANEERS

THE LOWDOWN:

There's a new sheriff in town for Tampa Bay and his name is Tom Brady. The former Patriots Quarterback was the marquee off-season move for 2020 as his tenure in New England came to an end. The six time Superbowl winner will play for somebody other than the Patriots for the first time in his career. Alongside him will be his long time teammate and formerly retired Rob Gronkowski who is coming out of retirement for a stint in Tampa as they chase another Superbowl ring together. Paired with Head Coach Bruce Arians this Tampa offense, which also includes Mike Evans and Chris Godwin is going to be a difficult unit to defend against this season.

SCHEDULE

Week 1: @ Saints
Week 2: Vs. Panthers
Week 3: @ Broncos
Week 4: Vs. Chargers
Week 5: @ Bears *(TNF)*
Week 6: Vs. Packers
Week 7: @ Raiders *(SNF)*
Week 8: @ Giants *(MNF)*
Week 9: Vs. Saints *(SNF)*
Week 10: @ Panthers
Week 11: Vs. Rams *(MNF)*
Week 12: Vs. Chiefs
Week 13: BYE
Week 14: Vs. Vikings
Week 15: @ Falcons
Week 16: @ Lions
Week 17: Vs. Falcons

2020 NFL DRAFT CLASS

Round 1
Tristan Wirfs, OT,
Iowa
Round 2
Antoine Winfield Jr., S,
Minnesota
Round 3
Ke'Shawn Vaughn, RB,
Vanderbilt
Round 5
Tyler Johnson, WR,
Minnesota
Round 6
Khalil Davis, IDL,
Nebraska
Round 7
Chapelle Russell, EDGE,
Temple
Raymond Calais, RB,
Louisiana-Lafayette

SIGNINGS

Tom Brady, QB
Joe Haeg, OL
Rob Gronkowski, TE

FRANCHISE TAG

Shaquil Barrett, DE

NO LONGER ON TEAM

Jameis Winston, QB
Peyton Barber, RB
Breshad Perriman, WR
Demar Dotson, OL
Carl Nassib, DE

TEAM DETAILS:

Owner: The Glazer Family
General Manager: Jason Licht
Stadium: Raymond James Stadium
Head Coach: Bruce Arians
Offensive Coordinator: Byron Leftwich
Defensive Coordinator: Todd Bowles
Coaching Staff:
Keith Armstrong (ST Coordinator)
Clyde Christensen (QB Coach)
Todd McNair (RB Coach)
Kevin Garver (WR Coach)
Rick Christophel (TE Coach)
Super Bowl Wins: 1 (2002)
Conference Wins: 1 (NFC,2002)
Divisional Wins: 6 (NFC Central, 1979, 1981, 1999; NFC South, 2002, 2005, 2007)
-2019-
Record: 7-9
Offence Rank: Passing (1st), Rushing (24th), Overall (3rd)
Defence Rank: Passing (30th), Rushing (1st), Overall (29th)

KEY PLAYER

Devin White: With the addition of Brady in the offseason it's hard to overlook him as the Bucs' key player. But on the other side of the ball Tampa have built a formidable Linebacker room. Seasoned pros Lavonte David & Shaq Barrett sit either side of last year's first rounder Devin White. The LSU product was a tackle machine last year, making 91 in total. There's every chance Tampa has a playoff run this year & White will be key to it.

Tristan Wirfs: Wirfs is going to have a lot of eyes on him - Playings for the Bucs this year is going to come with a certain amount of attention, plus fans are going to be tuning in to see evidence of that freakish athleticism that we all saw in the Combine. Wirfs should be a great fit on the right side of the line to start his career, and will be a huge asset in the run game.

ROOKIE SPOTLIGHT

DEPTH CHART

Quarterback	Wide Receiver	Center	Edge	Line Backer	Cornerback
Tom Brady	Mike Evans	Ryan Jensen	Ndamukong Suh	Devin White	Carlton Davis
Blaine Gabbert	Chris Godwin	Zach Shackelford [R]	William Gholston	Lavonte David	Sean Murphy-Bunting
Ryan Griffin	Justin Watson	**Tackle**	Jason Pierre-Paul	Jack Cichy	MJ Stewart
Fullback	Tyler Johnson [R]	Donovan Smith	Shaquil Barrett	Kendell Beckwith	Jamel Dean
TJ Logan	Scott Miller	Tristan Wirfs [R]	**Defensive Tackle**	Anthony Nelson	Ryan Smith
Running Back	Spencer Schnell	Joe Haeg	Vita Vea	**Free Safety**	**Strong Safety**
Ronald Jones	**Tight End**	**Guard**	Khalil Davis [R]	Mike Edwards	Justin Evans
Ke'Shawn Vaughn	Rob Gronkowski	Ali Marpet	Patrick O'Connor	Antoine Winfield [R]	Jordan Whitehead
Dare Ogunbowale	OJ Howard	Alex Cappa	**Kicker**	**Punter**	**Long Snapper**
Raymond Calais [R]	Cameron Brate	Zack Bailey	Matt Gay	Bradley Pinion	Zach Triner

NFL

1

FULL 10 YARDS

2019 RANKINGS

Player	Pos	Standard			0.5PPR			PPR		
		Pts	Avg	Rank	Pts	Avg	Rank	Pts	Avg	Rank
Jameis Winston	QB	318.7	21.3	QB4						
Ronald Jones II	RB	125.7	8.4	RB26	140.2	9.4	RB25	154.7	10	RB24
Peyton Barber	RB	97.0	6.5	RB39	104.0	6.9	RB41	111.0	7.4	RB41
Chris Godwin	WR	190.1	13.6	WR2	233.1	17	WR2	276.1	20	WR2
Mike Evans	WR	165.7	12.8	WR5	199.2	15	WR8	232.7	18	WR11
Breshad Perriman	WR	82.7	6.4	WR53	98.2	7.6	WR58	113.7	8.8	WR60
O.J. Howard	WR	49.9	3.8	TE29	66.9	5.2	TE27	83.9	6.5	TE28
Cameron Brate	TE	48.9	3.3	TE30	66.4	4.4	TE28	83.9	5.6	TE27
Tampa Bay Buccaneers	DST	120.0	8.0	DST11						
Matt Gay	K	143.0	9.5	K3						

TOM BRADY — ADP 8.06

At the grand old age of 43, he'll be out to prove himself with a new team. Finishing as the QB12 himself last year, Brady takes over in Tampa from the QB3 of 2019, Jameis Winston. Brady certainly doesn't have the arm strength that Winston has so a QB3 finish is out of range, but top-10 is a possibility.

ADP 5.11 — RONALD JONES

Things looked murky for RoJo as Tampa Bay drafted Ke'Shawn Vaughn in the 3rd round of the NFL draft and have just signed LeSean McCoy to the running back room. But, it wasn't a disastrous season for RoJo last year, finishing as the RB25 and Bruce Arians has come out this preseason to say that RoJo will be "the main guy" in Tampa this year.

MIKE EVANS — ADP 3.03

Evans is an underrated receiver in the league & joined Randy Moss as 1 of 2 NFL WRs in history that start their career with SIX consecutive 1000-yard seasons. Many predict that Evans will struggle to stretch the field with Brady throwing but people forget that Evans can run every route. Evans is good value at his ADP & another strong season awaits.

ADP 2.09 — CHRIS GODWIN

This time last year, Godwin was tipped to break out and boy, did he do just that. He finished as the WR2 in both PPR and standard having played just 14 games. Godwin should benefit more than Evans from Brady arriving in town and another top-5 finish is firmly on the cards.

ROB GRONKOWSKI — ADP 6.12

Gronk has not played a full compliment of games in a season since 2011 and I highly question his work ethic over his 12-months away from football. When Gronk is on his game, he's arguably the best TE that the game has ever seen. In 2011, Gronk was the sixth highest scoring fantasy football player, INCLUDING QBs. However, that was nearly a decade ago.

2020 Projections

Position	Player	Standard		0.5PPR		Full PPR	
		Pts	Rank	Pts	Rank	Pts	Rank
QB	Tom Brady	320.5	8				
RB	Ronald Jones	151.5	28	167.0	29	182.5	30
RB	Ke'Shawn Vaughn	100.1	48	107.6	51	115.1	53
RB	LeSean McCoy	42.8	79	57.8	73	72.8	70
WR	Mike Evans	174.5	7	211.0	8	247.5	8
WR	Chris Godwin	163.4	10	202.4	13	241.4	13
TE	Rob Gronkowski	78.7	19	98.2	22	117.7	24
TE	O.J Howard	65.8	26	82.8	27	99.8	28
TE	Cameron Brate	31.8	45	42.3	46	52.8	45

ADP taken from Ultimate Draft Kit (PPR)

Projections by Rob Grimwood @FFBritballer

FANTASY FOOTBALL

2

TAMPA BAY BUCCANEERS

LAST 5 YEARS

	W	L	T	Div	P/Offs
2019	7	9	0	2nd	
2018	5	11	0	4th	
2017	5	11	0	4th	
2016	9	7	0	2nd	
2015	6	10	0	4th	

DO SAY..
Tom Brady is our QB

DON'T SAY..
Jameis Winston's 30 for 30

BETTING ODDS BY ADAM WALFORD (@TOUCHDOWNTIPS)

SUPER BOWL **15/1**

NFC CONFERENCE **7/1**

NFC SOUTH **13/8**

TO MAKE PLAYOFFS
5/14
TEAM TOTAL WINS
9.5

ADAM'S BEST BET
UNDER 9.5 WINS
10/11

PLEASE GAMBLE RESPONSIBLY

VIEW FROM THE SIDELINES
By Adam Murfet (@Murf_NFL)

The Bucs have given up on the "reload" & are instead trying to win now on the fly. Arians has moved on from the "Winston Experience" and has brought in QB Tom Brady, TE Rob Gronkowski & 6 time Pro Bowler RB LeSean McCoy to bring some much needed experience & winning mentality to the team. Tampa Bay addressed their holes in the NFL Draft by drafting Tristan Wirfs who can play RT/LT, as well as picking an effective pass protecting & receiving RB KeShawn Vaughn, whilst also investing in the secondary yet again in the 2nd round with the pick of S Antoine Winfield Jr. Brady makes the Bucs relevant for the first time for over a decade, which is reflected in the 5 Prime-Time games they have. Bucs fans are right to be excited but with the excitement, comes the pressure of having to deliver a playoff berth for the first time in 12 years.

▶RETRO FOCUS◀
MIKE ALSTOTT – FB

In 11 seasons in the Florida sunshine FB Mike Alstott ran like a proverbial freight train over defenders. Nicknamed the A-Train, Alstott was not so much a FB he was a human rhino with pads and a helmet. 1,664 touches of the rock puts him in the top 100, and unlike many other Buccs stalwarts, Alstott was able to retire with a ring, having been part of the winning team in Super Bowl XXXVII (2002 season). He scored on a 2 yard plunge in the second quarter.

DID YOU KNOW

The Bucs hold the record for the longest losing streak in NFL history, going 0-26 over their first two seasons before their first win.

KEY STAT
"Wrong Team!"
Jameis Winston's 30 interceptions in 2019 was the first time a QB had been picked off 30 times since Vinny Testaverde threw 35 interceptions for the 1988 Buccaneers.

FULL10YARDS VERDICT

It's been over a decade since the Bucs last enjoyed postseason football and they haven't won a playoff game since winning the title in 2002, but that could be about to change. Nailing the offseason, can Tampa now deliver on the field? Tom Brady will relish linking up with his ol' pal Gronk, let alone 2019's most productive WR pairing in Mike Evans and Chris Godwin. With an improving defence, the Bucs could be a dark horse this year, especially with Super Bowl LV being contested on home soil.

BETTING,
STATS,
FANS VIEW,
RETRO

3

FANTASY RANKINGS

	Rank
Q	
U Lamar Jackson BAL	1
Patrick Mahomes KC	2
A Deshaun Watson HOU	3
Kyler Murray ARZ	4
R Drew Brees NO	5
Russell Wilson SEA	6
T Josh Allen BUF	7
Tom Brady TB	8
E Carson Wentz PHI	9
Dak Prescott DAL	10
R Drew Lock DEN	11
Matt Ryan ATL	12
B Aaron Rodgers GB	13
Philip Rivers IND	14
A Daniel Jones NYG	15
Cam Newton NE	16
C Baker Mayfield CLE	17
Gardner Minshew JAX	18
K Joe Burrow CIN	19
Teddy Bridgewater CAR	20
S Matthew Stafford DET	21

Tyrod Taylor LAC — 22
Ryan Fitzpatrick MIA — 23
Ryan Tannehill TEN — 24
Ben Roethlisberger PIT — 25
Derek Carr LVR — 26
Kirk Cousins MIN — 27
Jared Goff LAR — 28
Jimmy Garoppolo SF — 29
Mitch Trubisky CHI — 30
Dwayne Haskins WSH — 31
Sam Darnold NYJ — 32

QUARTERBACKS

FANTASY RANKINGS

	Non PPR	0.5 PPR	PPR
Christian McCaffrey CAR	1	1	1
Ezekiel Elliott DAL	2	2	2
Saquon Barkley NYG	3	3	3
Joe Mixon CIN	4	6	6
Dalvin Cook MIN	5	5	5
Alvin Kamara NO	6	4	4
Aaron Jones GB	7	7	7
Miles Sanders PHI	8	8	8
Derrick Henry TEN	9	11	15
Nick Chubb CLE	10	13	14
Clyde Edwards-Helaire KC	11	14	12
Todd Gurley ATL	12	15	13
Le'Veon Bell NYJ	13	9	9
Austin Ekeler LAC	14	10	10
Leonard Fournette JAX	15	12	11
Josh Jacobs LVR	16	16	19
David Johnson HOU	17	17	16
David Montgomery CHI	18	21	22
Melvin Gordon DEN	19	19	18
Kenyan Drake ARZ	20	18	17
D'Andre Swift DET	21	20	20
James Conner PIT	22	23	28
Jonathan Taylor IND	23	27	31
Chris Carson SEA	24	24	26
Devin Singletary BUF	25	22	21
J.K Dobbins BAL	26	25	27
Mark Ingram BAL	27	30	35
Ronald Jones TB	28	29	30
Antonio Gibson WSH	29	28	29
Zack Moss BUF	30	32	39
Jordan Howard MIA	31	34	38
Raheem Mostert SF	32	36	40
Kareem Hunt CLE	33	26	23
Cam Akers LAR	34	37	36
Phillip Lindsay DEN	35	38	37
Tevin Coleman SF	36	35	33
Matt Breida MIA	37	40	41
Sony Michel NE	38	42	43
Darrynton Evans TEN	39	39	32
Marlon Mack IND	40	43	44
Nyheim Hines IND	41	31	24
Anthony McFarland PIT	42	41	42
James White NE	43	33	25
Kerryon Johnson DET	44	45	45
Latavius Murray NO	45	47	48

RUNNING BACKS

FANTASY RANKINGS

	Non PPR	0.5 PPR	PPR
Michael Thomas NO	1	1	1
Davante Adams GB	2	2	2
Tyreek Hill KC	3	7	11
Julio Jones ATL	4	3	4
Kenny Golladay DET	5	9	10
Cooper Kupp LAR	6	4	3
Mike Evans TB	7	8	8
DeAndre Hopkins ARZ	8	5	5
Odell Beckham Jr CLE	9	6	6
Chris Godwin TB	10	13	13
Adam Thielen MIN	11	10	9
Robert Woods LAR	12	14	14
Calvin Ridley ATL	13	12	12
DeVante Parker MIA	14	15	15
Allen Robinson CHI	15	11	7
D.J Moore CAR	16	16	16
Amari Cooper DAL	17	17	17
D.K Metcalf SEA	18	22	22
JuJu Smith-Schuster PIT	19	18	19
A.J Brown TEN	20	24	27
Terry McLaurin WSH	21	20	21
Courtland Sutton DEN	22	23	23
Keenan Allen LAC	23	19	18
T.Y Hilton IND	24	21	20
Jerry Jeudy DEN	25	27	28
Tyler Lockett SEA	26	25	24
Marquise Brown BAL	27	29	29
Jarvis Landry CLE	28	26	25
Justin Jefferson MIN	29	31	32
Stefon Diggs BUF	30	28	26
Julian Edelman NE	31	30	30
Michael Pittman Jr. IND	32	32	31
D.J Chark JAX	33	33	33
Darius Slayton NYG	34	36	39
Laviska Shenault JAX	35	34	36
A.J Green CIN	36	37	37
Will Fuller HOU	37	35	35
Mike Williams LAC	38	41	42
Brandon Aiyuk SF	39	40	41
Jamison Crowder NYJ	40	38	34
Tyler Boyd CIN	41	42	40
Michael Gallup DAL	42	44	44
John Brown BUF	43	45	45
Deebo Samuel SF	44	46	49
Golden Tate NYG	45	39	38
Marvin Jones DET	46	47	47
Preston Williams MIA	47	48	48
Robby Anderson CAR	48	50	50
Diontae Johnson PIT	49	43	43
Christian Kirk ARZ	50	49	46
Emmanuel Sanders NO	51	51	51
Brandin Cooks HOU	52	52	52
Sammy Watkins KC	53	53	54
Allen Lazard GB	54	54	53

WIDE RECEIVERS

FANTASY RANKINGS

TIGHT ENDS

	Non PPR	0.5 PPR	PPR
Travis Kelce KC	1	1	1
George Kittle SF	2	2	2
Mark Andrews BAL	3	4	4
Zach Ertz PHI	4	3	3
Darren Waller LVR	5	5	5
Jonnu Smith TEN	6	6	6
Mike Gesicki MIA	7	7	7
Hunter Henry LAC	8	8	8
Dallas Goedert PHI	9	9	9
Noah Fant DEN	10	11	13
Austin Hooper CLE	11	10	10
Evan Engram NYG	12	13	12
Dawson Knox BUF	13	15	15
Blake Jarwin DAL	14	14	14
Hayden Hurst ATL	15	16	16
Tyler Higbee LAR	16	12	11
Jared Cook NO	17	17	20
Chris Herndon NYJ	18	18	18
Rob Gronkowski TB	19	22	24
T.J Hockenson DET	20	20	19
Will Dissly SEA	21	23	23
Jack Doyle IND	22	19	17
Vance McDonald PIT	23	21	22
Irv Smith Jr MIN	24	24	21
Devin Asiasi NE	25	25	25
O.J Howard TB	26	27	28
Jordan Akins HOU	27	26	26
Adam Trautman NO	28	30	30
C.J Uzomah CIN	29	28	27
Jace Sternberger GB	30	29	29
Trey Burton IND	31	31	31
Greg Olsen SEA	32	32	33
Eric Ebron PIT	33	33	32
Thaddeus Moss WSH	34	36	37
Tyler Eifert JAX	35	34	34
Dan Arnold ARZ	36	38	40
Ryan Griffin NYJ	37	35	35
Cole Kmet CHI	38	39	38
Ian Thomas CAR	39	37	36
Darren Fells HOU	40	42	42
David Njoku CLE	41	41	41
Gerald Everett LAR	42	40	39

DEFENCE

	Rank
Baltimore Ravens	1
San Francisco 49ers	2
Los Angeles Chargers	3
Cleveland Browns	4
Buffalo Bills	5
Pittsburgh Steelers	6
Chicago Bears	7
Tennessee Titans	8
New Orleans Saints	9
Indianapolis Colts	10
Kansas City Chiefs	11
New England Patriots	12
Denver Broncos	13
Dallas Cowboys	14
Minnesota Vikings	15
Miami Dolphins	16
Philadelphia Eagles	17
Green Bay Packers	18
Los Angeles Rams	19
Seattle Seahawks	20
Tampa Bay Buccaneers	21
New York Jets	22
Washington Redskins	23
Carolina Panthers	24
Houston Texans	25
Cincinnati Bengals	26
Atlanta Falcons	27
Las Vegas Raiders	28
Arizona Cardinals	29
Jacksonville Jaguars	30
Detroit Lions	31
New York Giants	32

KICKERS

1 Justin Tucker
2 Harrison Butker
3 Wil Lutz
4 Greg Zuerlein
5 Jake Elliott
6 Zane Gonzalez
7 Matt Prater
8 Ka'imi Fairbairn
9 Matt Gay
10 Robbie Gould
11 Michael Badgley
12 Dan Bailey
13 Chris Boswell
14 R.Blankenship
15 Mason Crosby
16 Younghoe Koo
17 Jason Myers
18 Brandon McManus
19 Joey Slye
20 Stephen Hauschka

ARIZONA CARDINALS

THE LOWDOWN:

Despite finishing with a record of 5-10-1 last year, the Arizona Cardinals showed plenty of signs of promise. Rookie QB Kyler Murray excited many with his fast paced and elusive style of play and many fans will be looking forward to seeing him run an improved offence this season. With the addition of arguably the best receiver in the league in DeAndre Hopkins, the Cardinals have the talent to compete in the NFC West this season. Many will look towards Rookie Isiah Simmons who was taken in the first round and is expected to be a versatile playmaker for the Cardinals defense.

SCHEDULE

Week 1: @ 49ers
Week 2: Vs. Washington
Week 3: Vs. Lions
Week 4: @ Panthers
Week 5: @ Jets
Week 6: @ Cowboys *(MNF)*
Week 7: vs Seahawks
Week 8: BYE
Week 9: Vs. Dolphins
Week 10: Vs Bills
Week 11: @ Seahawks *(TNF)*
Week 12: @ Patriots
Week 13: Vs. Rams
Week 14: @ Giants
Week 15: Vs. Eagles
Week 16: Vs. 49ers
Week 17: @ Rams

2020 NFL DRAFT CLASS

Round 1
Isaiah Simmons, LB,
Clemson
Round 3
Josh Jones, OT,
Houston
Round 4
Leki Fotu, IDL,
Utah
Rashard Lawrence II, IDL,
LSU
Round 6
Evan Weaver, LB,
California
Round 7
Eno Benjamin, RB,
Arizona State

SIGNINGS
DeAndre Hopkins, WR
De'Vondre Campbell, LB
Devon Kennard, LB
Larry Fitzgerald, WR

TRANSITION TAG
Kenyan Drake, RB

NO LONGER ON TEAM
David Johnson, RB
Damiere Byrd, WR
Charles Clay, TE
A.Q. Shipley, C
Joe Walker, LB

TEAM DETAILS:

Owner: The Bidwill Family
General Manager: Steve Keim
Stadium: State Farm Stadium
Location: Glendale, Arizona
Head Coach: Kliff Kingsbury
Offensive Coordinator:
Kliff Kingsbury
Defensive Coordinator:
Vance Joseph
Coaching Staff:
Jeff Rodgers (ST Co-ordinator/
Assistant HC),
Tom Clements (Passing
Game Coordinator/QB Coach)
James Saxon (RB Coach)
David Raih (WR Coach)
Steve Heiden (TE Coach)
Super Bowl Wins: 0
Conference Wins: 1 (2008)
Divisional Wins: 5 (NFC
East: 1974, 1975; NFC West: 2008,
2009, 2015)

-2019-
Record: 5-10-1
Offence Rank: Passing (24th),
Rushing (10th), Overall (16th)
Defence Rank: Passing (31st),
Rushing (24th), Overall (28th)

KEY PLAYER

Kyler Murray: The 2nd year QB carries the hopes of the Cardinals franchise on his shoulders. A rookie of the year winning debut season saw Murray put up 3722 passing yards, 544 rushing yards and 24 TDs. The addition of elite receiver DeAndre Hopkins has only helped increase the expectation, but a competitive NFC West won't make it easy for Murray to take his game to the next level.

Isaiah Simmons: A versatile piece who Vance Joseph should have a lot of fun moving around his unit to neutralise opposition playmakers. Simmons will line up as the WILL linebacker in base but he'll line up as a safety, a nickel corner and occasionally rush the passer. The epitome of a defender in 2020.

ROOKIE SPOTLIGHT

DEPTH CHART

Quarterback	Wide Receiver	Center	Edge	Line Backer	Cornerback
Kyler Murray	Deandre Hopkins	Mason Cole	Corey Peters	Isaiah Simmons [R]	Patrick Peterson
Brett Hundley	Christian Kirk	Lamont Gallard	Zach Allen	Chandler Jones	Byron Murphy
Drew Anderson	Larry Fitzgerald	**Tackle**	Devon Kennard	De'Vondre Campbell	Jalen Davis
Fullback	Andy Isabella	DJ Humphries	Jonathan Bullard	Jordan Hicks	Kevin Peterson
Parker Houston [R]	KeeSean Johnson	Marcus Gilbert	**Defensive Tackle**	Haason Reddick	Robert Alford
Running Back	Trent Sherfield	Josh Jones [R]	Jordan Phillips	**Free Safety**	**Strong Safety**
Kenyan Drake	**Tight End**	**Guard**	Leki Fotu [R]	Budda Baker	Jalen Thompson
Chase Edmonds	Maxx Williams	Justin Pugh	Miles Brown	Charles Washington	Deionte Thompson
Eno Benjamin [R]	Darrell Daniels	JR Dweezy	**Kicker**	**Punter**	**Long Snapper**
DJ Foster	Dan Arnold	Max Garcia	Zane Gonzalez	Andy Lee	Aaron Brewer

NFL

1

FULL 10 YARDS

ARIZONA CARDINALS

2019 RANKINGS

Player	Pos	Standard			0.5PPR			PPR		
		Pts	Avg	Rank	Pts	Avg	Rank	Pts	Avg	Rank
Kyler Murray	QB	282	19	QB7						
Kenyan Drake	RB	161	11	RB15	173	13	RB18	197	15	RB16
Chase Edmonds	RB	70.9	5.9	RB47	76.9	6.4	RB51	82.9	6.9	RB51
Larry Fitzgerald	WR	97.9	6.5	WR43	133	8.9	WR37	169	11	WR33
Christian Kirk	WR	93.6	7.8	WR44	124	10	WR42	155	13	WR40
Andy Isabella	WR	26.4	1.9	WR116	30.9	2.2	WR123	35.4	2.5	WR126
KeeSean Johnson	WR	25	2.5	WR121	35.5	3.6	WR114	46	4.6	WR111
Maxx Williams	TE	23.9	1.6	TE48	30.9	2.1	TE49	37.9	2.5	TE49
Arizona Cardinals	DST	68	4.5	DST28						
Zane Gonzalez	K	106	7.1	K18						

KYLER MURRAY

The sophomore quarterback will be looking to build on his impressive rookie season after finishing as QB7 last year (12th in PPG). Expect a healthy dose of passing & running and a top-5 finish for the former number 1 overall pick.

ADP 6.03

KENYAN DRAKE

ADP 2.02

Drake has quietly increased his scrimmage yardage totals year on year since entering the league. He'll creep up to 1300 scrimmage yards this year with 10 total TDs which, dependent on the number of receptions that he gets, should see him finish inside the top-10.

DEANDRE HOPKINS

There's a nice shiny new toy in the desert and some will say he's the best receiver in the league. Missing the pre-season with Kyler won't help but Nuk is still a lock for the top-10 and should push the top-5 once again.

ADP 2.06

CHRISTIAN KIRK

ADP 10.8

Kirk would have been eyeing up a WR1 finish this year had it not been for the arrival of Nuk. He crept ahead of Fitzgerald in PPG last year and finished with a better PPG than the likes of OBJ, T.Y. Hilton and Adam Thielen. That being said, he's a WR2a at best and probably won't crack the top-25.

LARRY FITGERALD

The 2b to Kirk's 2a will turn 37 before the start of the season but he still demanded over 100 targets last year. He's got records to break, a HOF place to secure and, most importantly, a Superbowl to win. Fitzgerald won't retire quietly and pushes for yet another top-40 finish.

ADP 14.7

2020 Projections

Position	Player	Standard		0.5PPR		Full PPR	
		Pts	Rank	Pts	Rank	Pts	Rank
QB	Kyler Murray	341.9	4				
RB	Kenyan Drake	177.3	20	199.8	18	222.3	17
RB	Eno Benjamin	90.7	54	62.4	55	71.4	57
RB	Chase Edmonds	53.4	70	100.2	70	109.7	71
WR	DeAndre Hopkins	171.4	8	218.9	5	266.4	5
WR	Christian Kirk	106.1	50	133.6	49	161.1	46
WR	Larry Fitzgerald	81.4	67	108.9	62	136.4	57
WR	KeeSean Johnson	51.8	95	67.3	94	82.8	94
WR	Andy Isabella	26.0	124	33.0	122	40.0	125
TE	Dan Arnold	47.1	36	56.6	38	66.1	40
TE	Maxx Williams	11.2	68	17.7	66	24.2	64

ADP taken from Ultimate Draft Kit (PPR)

Projections by Rob Grimwood @FFBritballer

FANTASY FOOTBALL

2

FULL 10 YARDS

ARIZONA CARDINALS

DO SAY..
Foundations are set with Kyler, Kliff and the Air Raid

DON'T SAY..
NFC West is a difficult division to win

BETTING ODDS
BY ADAM WALFORD (@TOUCHDOWNTIPS)

SUPER BOWL **50/1**

NFC CONFERENCE **30/1**

NFC WEST **11/1**

TO MAKE PLAYOFFS
12/5
TEAM TOTAL WINS
7

ADAM'S BEST BET
OVER 7 WINS
10/11

PLEASE GAMBLE RESPONSIBLY

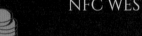

VIEW FROM THE SIDELINES
By Tom Donlan - (@BritishBirdgang)

We have strengthened all over the roster, lost very few players of note & picked up a whole host of bandwagon fans in the world of NFL media. The highlight has to be the arrival of the league's best WR, DeAndre Hopkins to the desert although the steal of Isaiah Simmons in the Draft comes in a very close second. Add to those additions the strengthening of the defensive line with Jordan Phillips & a pair of draft selections, it has been great to see Steve Keim addressing the teams' weaknesses. Having to compete in the toughest division in the entire league is not an easy prospect, but the Cardinals are definitely trending the right direction & should be competitive. Provided Vance Joseph is able to improve his unit in his second year as DC. I'm not going to say this is a Super Bowl team, but neither was the 2008 Cardinals. Make the playoffs and then, whatever happens, happens.

▶RETRO FOCUS◀
KURT WARNER – QB

The Cards have only been to one Super Bowl in their team's long history & the man who took them there was a QB that had already won a Lombardi with his first team. Now a decade after his retirement, his star WR is remarkably still playing for the Cardinals. Kurt Warner is now in the Hall of Fame and a regular TV pundit, he remains the only Cardinals player to throw a TD pass in a Super Bowl. He remains one remarkable Santonio Holmes tippy-tap from being a double Lombardi winner.

DID YOU KNOW
Founded in 1898, the Cardinals are the oldest continuously running professional football team in the US.

KEY STAT
"Door Mat"
The Cardinals gave up the most 1st downs (375) and the most yardage (6,432) on defence in 2019.

FULL10YARDS VERDICT
There's a bit of buzz about Arizona. Swapping RB David Johnson for DeAndre Hopkins was arguably the trade of the year, and he'll give Kyler Murray even more chance to blossom in his second season. Kliff Kingsbury made other decent moves on both sides of the ball, including drafting linebacker Isaiah Simmons, who should elevate the league's worst defence. Expect the Cardinals to better last year's 5-10-1 and, while they may not topple the Niners and Seahawks in the tight NFC West, they could grab one of the extra playoff berths as a third-placed team.

BETTING, STATS, FANS VIEW, RETRO

3

FULL 10 YARDS

LOS ANGELES RAMS

THE LOWDOWN:

The Rams suffered from he dreaded Superbowl hangover. Despite finishing with a winning record, the Rams were disappointing in 2019. The offence wasn't as dominant as it had been the previous year & the defence gave up a lot more points. The offence line really struggled to get into any sort of rhythm & as a result Jared Goff's play suffered. The former #1 overall pick had a tough season and will want to get back to top form and prove to people he is worthy of the price paid for him. Aaron Donald continues to be a force on the defensive line while Jalen Ramsey locks down receivers on the outside. They will need to acclimatise quickly to their new surroundings, too.

SCHEDULE

Week 1: Vs. Cowboys *(SNF)*
Week 2: @ Eagles
Week 3: @ Bills
Week 4: Vs. Giants
Week 5: @ Washington
Week 6: @ 49ers *(SNF)*
Week 7: Vs. Bears
Week 8: @ Dolphins
Week 9: BYE
Week 10: Vs. Seahawks
Week 11: @ Buccaneers *(MNF)*
Week 12: Vs. 49ers
Week 13: @ Cardinals
Week 14: Vs. Patriots *(TNF)*
Week 15: Vs. Jets
Week 16: @ Seahawks
Week 17: Vs. Cardinals

2020 NFL DRAFT CLASS

Round 2
Cam Akers, RB,
Florida State
Van Jefferson, WR,
Florida
Round 3
Terrell Lewis, EDGE,
Alabama
Terrell Burgess, S,
Utah
Round 4
Brycen Hopkins, TE,
Purdue
Round 6
Jordan Fuller, S,
Ohio State
Round 7
Clay Johnston, LB,
Baylor
Sam Sloman, K,
Miami (Ohio)
Tremayne Anchrum, IOL,
Clemson

SIGNINGS
Austin Blythe, OL
Leonard Floyd, DE
A'Shawn Robinson, DT

RE-SIGNED
Andrew Whitworth, OL
Michael Brockers, DT

NO LONGER ON TEAM
Blake Bortles, QB
Brandin Cooks, WR
Dante Fowler Jr., DE
Cory Littleton, LB
Clay Matthews, LB
Nickell Robey-Coleman, CB
Eric Weddle, S (Ret.)
Greg Zuerlein, K

TEAM DETAILS:
Owner: Stan Kroenke
General Manager: Les Snead
Stadium: SoFi Stadium
Location: Los Angeles, California
Head Coach: Sean McVay
Offensive Coordinator: Kevin O'Conell
Defensive Coordinator: Brandon Staley
Coaching Staff:
John Bonamego (ST Coordinator)
Shane Waldron (Pass Game Coordinator)
Thomas Brown (RB Coach)
Eric Yarber (WR Coach)
Wes Phillips (TE Coach)
Super Bowl Wins: 1 (1999)
Conference Wins: 4 (NFC, 1979, 1999, 2001, 2018)
Divisional Wins: 15 (NFL Coastal, 1967, 1969, NFC West, 1973, 1974, 1975, 1976, 1977, 1978, 1979, 1985, 1999, 2001, 2003, 2017, 2018)

-2019-
Record: 9-7
Offence Rank: Passing (4th), Rushing (26th), Overall (11th)
Defence Rank: Passing (12th), Rushing (19 th), Overall (17th)

KEY PLAYER

Jared Goff: A do or die year for the Quarterback who is on what is perceived as an expensive contract for what he provides to the team. However he was one of the best performing QBs on 3rd or 4th downs in 2019. He has the supporting cast but his offensive line is not the best and when pressured, Jared Goff does not look like a 4 year $134m extension worthy Quarterback.

Cam Akers: Akers will come in and form a diverse trio of backs with Malcolm Brown and Darrell Henderson. Akers should be amazed at just how many gaps and how much space is in front of him now that he isn't running behind the Florida State offensive line - A talented back who could make the RB1 job his own.

ROOKIE SPOTLIGHT

DEPTH CHART

Quarterback	Wide Receiver	Center	Edge	Line Backer	Cornerback
Jared Goff	Cooper Kupp	Brian Allen	Michael Brockers	Leonard Floyd	Jalen Ramsey
John Wolford	Robert Woods	Coleman Shelton	Samson Ebukam	Micah Kiser	Troy Hill
Bryce Perkins [R]	Josh Reynolds	**Tackle**	Terrell Lewis [R]	Kenny Young	Darious Williams
Fullback	Van Jefferson [R]	Andrew Whitworth	Morgan Fox	Travin Howard	David Long
John Kelly	Nsimba Webster	Rob Havenstein	**Defensive Tackle**	Clay Johnston [R]	Donte Deayton
Running Back	Greg Dortch	Bobby Evans	Aaron Donald	**Free Safety**	**Strong Safety**
Malcolm Brown	**Tight End**	**Guard**	A'Shawn Robinson	John Johnson	Taylor Rapp
Darrel Henderson	Tyler Higbee	Austin Corbett	Marquise Copeland	Jordan Fuller [R]	Terrell Burgess [R]
Cam Akers [R]	Gerald Everett	Austin Blythe	**Kicker**	**Punter**	**Long Snapper**
James Gilbert [R]	Brycen Hopkins [R]	Joseph Noteboom	Sam Sloman [R]	Johnny Hekker	Jake McQuaide

NFL

1

FULL 10 YARDS

LOS ANGELES RAMS

2019 RANKINGS

Player	Pos	Standard			0.5PPR			PPR		
		Pts	Avg	Rank	Pts	Avg	Rank	Pts	Avg	Rank
Jared Goff	QB	238.3	15.9	QB15						
Todd Gurley	RB	179.5	12.8	RB11	194.0	14	RB12	208.5	15	RB14
Malcolm Brown	RB	47.9	3.7	RB61	48.4	3.7	RB67	48.9	3.8	RB71
Cooper Kupp	WR	160.6	10.7	WR7	204.1	14	WR6	247.6	17	WR6
Robert Woods	WR	129.3	9.2	WR24	170.8	12	WR20	212.3	15	WR19
Brandin Cooks	WR	71.5	5.5	WR61	91.0	7	WR61	110.5	8.5	WR63
Tyler Higbee	TE	77.0	5.5	TE10	107.5	7.7	TE9	138.0	9.9	TE8
Gerald Everett	TE	52.8	4.4	TE25	71.3	5.9	TE23	89.8	7.5	TE23
Los Angeles Rams	DST	135.0	9.0	DST6						
Greg Zuerlein	K	121.0	8.1	K9						

JARED GOFF

Goff is currently my QB13 on the season, but more points separate him & the top-10 than him and the top-25. The "teen" quarterbacks are highly interchangeable and with the losses of Gurley/Cooks, Goff could very quickly slide down these rankings. He's a solid QB2 in Superflex but don't bank on him winning you a title.

ADP 13.6

CAM AKERS

ADP 6.02

The Florida state product will be the 4th youngest player in the NFL come September & incidentally, finds himself in a 4 strong RBBC (running back by committee). Although the most talented in the bunch, the lack of preseason will hinder his bid for a bell cow role & he'll struggle to crack the top-20RBs this season.

COOPER KUPP

Kupp was the WR4 in both PPR and standard scoring last year – something that is rarely mentioned and certainly not reflected in his WR15 ADP. There's no reason why Kupp shouldn't see the same amount of love from Goff and turn it into the same amount of production. Kupp is a fantasy bargain this year.

ADP 4.04

ROBERT WOODS

ADP 4.09

The only difference between Kupp & Woods last year was touchdowns (10-2 respectively) & 10 fantasy spots. Brandin Cooks leaves behind 72 targets & after Van Jefferson has had a share, Woods should match his reception/yardage totals from last year. Assuming positive TD regression, he's looking at a top-10 finish.

TYLER HIGBEE

Higbee won the TE battle in LA last year and a new contract. Higbee was able to snag a top-8 finish but his PPG finish was down to TE11. With players such as Blake Jarwin/Hayden Hurst set to take on TE1 roles in their teams, another top-10 finish might not be on the cards for Higbee in 2020 but it doesn't take much to get there.

ADP 8.04

2020 Projections

Position	Player	Standard		0.5PPR		Full PPR	
		Pts	Rank	Pts	Rank	Pts	Rank
QB	Jared Goff	267.6	28				
RB	Cam Akers	139.6	34	155.1	37	170.6	36
RB	Malcolm Brown	79.8	61	87.8	62	95.8	62
RB	Darrell Henderson	28.1	91	32.6	91	37.1	91
WR	Cooper Kupp	174.5	6	222.0	4	269.5	3
WR	Robert Woods	163.3	12	201.3	14	239.3	14
WR	Josh Reynolds	52.4	94	65.4	97	78.4	98
WR	Van Jefferson	27.5	120	37.5	120	47.5	118
TE	Tyler Higbee	87.8	16	118.8	12	149.8	11
TE	Gerald Everett	39.6	42	53.1	40	66.6	39

ADP taken from Ultimate Draft Kit (PPR)

Projections by Rob Grimwood @FFBritballer

FANTASY FOOTBALL

2

FULL 10 YARDS

LOS ANGELES RAMS

DO SAY..
The Greatest Show on Turf

DON'T SAY..
Jared Goff is worth that contract

BETTING ODDS BY ADAM WALFORD (@TOUCHDOWNTIPS)

SUPER BOWL **40/1**

NFC CONFERENCE **20/1**

NFC WEST **6/1**

TO MAKE PLAYOFFS
6/4
TEAM TOTAL WINS
8

ADAM'S BEST BET
FINISH 4TH IN NFC WEST
9/4

PLEASE GAMBLE RESPONSIBLY

VIEW FROM THE SIDELINES
By Ben Ramsdale (@benaramsdale)

Few franchises are being slept on more than the LA Rams heading into 2020. For a team full of studs and one that missed out on last year's play-offs by the finest of margins, many experts now seem to have them down as a below 500 squad. Jalen Ramsey, Aaron Donald, Cooper Kupp & the exciting new additions of Cam Akers and Terrell Lewis just to name a few, will be more than enough to see the team right and strike fear into opponents throughout the NFL. Pressure is firmly off of Sean McVay's side in comparison to the last campaign and I'd wager that this could make the Rams more dangerous than ever. Prediction: 11-5

▶RETRO FOCUS◀
JACK YOUNGBLOOD – DE

Jack Youngblood spent 14 seasons occupying QBs nightmares, playing 202 of 203 possible career games. This DE was voted on the Hall of Fame All-70s team, and if sacks would have been recorded in the 1970s Youngblood he would have been recognised as a top 5 performer in NFL history by the time he retired in 1984. Youngblood played in 17 playoff contests, including a Super Bowl loss to the Steelers at the end of the 1979 season..

DID YOU KNOW

In July 1972, Rams owner Jim Irsay decided to swap teams with Baltimore Colts owner Carroll Rosenbloom.

KEY STAT
"Go Long!"
Rams QB, Jared Goff had the joint longest pass completion by air yards, 60.5 yards (tied w/ Kirk Cousins).

FULL10YARDS VERDICT
The additional playoff space this year could work in the Rams' favour as they might struggle to do better than third in the NFL's tightest division – a long way from reaching the season finale just two years ago. With salary cap pressures contributing to the release of Todd Gurley, the trade of Brandin Cooks and loss of Cory Littleton and Dante Fowler Jr, it's hard to predict how the season might pan out. Jared Goff, Jalen Ramsey and Aaron Donald will need to do something special to get the fans at their new stadium on their feet.

BETTING, STATS, FANS VIEW, RETRO

3

FULL 10 YARDS

SAN FRANCISCO 49ERS

THE LOWDOWN:

Last year's bridesmaids in the Super Bowl. The 49ers remain vastly unchanged as they approach the 2020 season. With two 1st round picks in the draft, they added playmakers on both sides of the ball. DT Javon Kinlaw was selected 14th overall & will slot into a starting role, replacing the departed DeForest Buckner. Offensively they added wideout Brandon Aiyuk, the speedy WR from the Arizona State University. The 49ers have locked up their front office & coaching staff as both GM John Lynch and HC Kyle Shanahan signed 5 year contracts which will keep the pair until 2025. QB Jimmy Garappolo will be want to prove a lot of people wrong as he come under fire towards the end of last season.

SCHEDULE

Week 1: Vs. Cardinals
Week 2: @ Jets
Week 3: @ Giants
Week 4: Vs. Eagles *(SNF)*
Week 5: Vs. Dolphins
Week 6: Vs. Rams *(SNF)*
Week 7: @ Patriots
Week 8: @ Seahawks
Week 9: Vs Packers *(TNF)*
Week 10: @ Saints
Week 11: BYE
Week 12: @ Rams
Week 13: Vs. Bills *(MNF)*
Week 14: Vs. Washington
Week 15: @ Cowboys *(SNF)*
Week 16: @ Cardinals
Week 17: Vs. Seahawks

2020 NFL DRAFT CLASS

Round 1
Javon Kinlaw, IDL,
South Carolina
Brandon Aiyuk, WR,
Arizona State
Round 5
Colton McKivitz, OT,
West Virginia
Round 6
Charlie Woerner, TE,
Georgia
Round 7
Jauan Jennings, WR,
Tennessee

SIGNINGS
Trent Williams, OT
Travis Benjamin, WR
Jordan Reed, TE

RE-SIGNED
Ben Garland, C
Jimmie Ward, S
Arik Armstead, DL

NO LONGER ON TEAM
Emmanuel Sanders, WR
Garrett Celek, TE (Retired)
Levine Toilolo, TE
DeForest Buckner, DT

TEAM DETAILS:

Owner: Jed York
General Manager: John Lynch
Stadium: Levi's Stadium
Location: Santa Clara, California
Head Coach: Kyle Shanahan
Offensive Coordinator:
Kyle Shanahan
Defensive Coordinator:
Robert Saleh
Coaching Staff:
Rich Hightower (ST Coordinator)
Shane Day (QB Coach)
Robert Turner Jr. (RB Coach)
Wes Welker (WR Coach)
Jon Embree (Assistant HC/ TE Coach)
Super Bowl Wins: 5 (1981, 1984, 1988, 1989, 1994)
Conference Wins: 7 (1981, 1984, 1988, 1989, 1994, 2012, 2019)
Divisional Wins: 20 (NFC West, 1970, 1971, 1972, 1981, 1983, 1984, 1986, 1987, 1988, 1989, 1990, 1992, 1993, 1994, 1995, 1996, 1997, 1998, 2001, 2002, 2011, 2012, 2013, 2019)
-2019-
Record: 13-3 (Lost Super Bowl)
Offence Rank: Passing (13th), Rushing (2nd), Overall (2nd)
Defence Rank: Passing (1st), Rushing (17th), Overall (8th)

KEY PLAYER

Nick Bosa: The 49ers built their Super Bowl 54 run on the back of a solid run game and a mean defensive line. They'll be looking for more of the same this year, with Arik Armstead, Solomon Thomas and Nick Bosa at the heart of the action. Bosa's rookie year was impressive as he struck fear into Tackles across the league. With the support around him, there's no reason why he can't build on the 13 sacks he racked up in 2019.

ROOKIE SPOTLIGHT

Javon Kinlaw: Another insane athlete on the interior of the defensive line - Off the snap he is a problem from the millisecond that the ball is going back to the QB. A pass rusher from the middle with an arsenal of rush moves and counters to go along with the sheer athleticism. A worthy replacement for DeForest Buckner, not as good yet, but all the potential in the world.

DEPTH CHART

Quarterback	Wide Receiver	Center	Edge	Line Backer	Cornerback
Jimmy Garoppolo	Deebo Samuel	Weston Richburg	Arik Armstead	Kwon Alexander	Richard Sherman
Nick Mullens	Brandon Aiyuk [R]	Ben Garland	Nick Bosa	Fred Warner	Ahkello Witherspoon
CJ Beathard	Kendrick Bourne	**Tackle**	Dee Ford	Dre Greenlaw	K'Waun Williams
Fullback	Jalen Hurd	Trent Williams	Kentavius Street	Mark Nzeocha	Jason Verrett
Kyle Juszczyk	Ritchie James	Mike McGlinchey	**Defensive Tackle**	Joe Walker	Emmanuel Moseley
Running Back	Dante Pettis	Daniel Brunskill	Soloman Thomas	**Free Safety**	**Strong Safety**
Raheem Mostert	**Tight End**	**Guard**	Javon Kinlaw [R]	Jimmie Ward	Jaquiski Tartt
Tevin Coleman	George Kittle	Laken Tomlinson	DJ Jones	Tarvarious Moore	Marcell Harris
Jerrick McKinnon	Ross Dwelley	Tom Compton	**Kicker**	**Punter**	**Long Snapper**
Jeff Wilson	Daniel Helm	Ross Reynolds	Robbie Gould	Mitch Wishnowsky	Kyle Nelson

NFL

1

FULL 10 YARDS

SAN FRANCISCO 49ERS

2019 RANKINGS

Player	Pos	Standard			0.5PPR			PPR		
		Pts	Avg	Rank	Pts	Avg	Rank	Pts	Avg	Rank
Jimmy Garoppolo	QB	248.4	16.6	QB14						
Raheem Mostert	RB	131.9	8.8	RB22	138.4	9.2	RB27	144.9	9.7	RB32
Tevin Coleman	RB	112.6	8.7	RB32	122.6	9.4	RB35	132.6	10	RB38
Deebo Samuel	WR	112.6	8.0	WR35	138.6	9.9	WR36	164.6	12	WR36
Emmanuel Sanders*	WR	121.8	7.6	WR27	153.3	9.6	WR26	184.8	12	WR28
Kendrick Bourne	WR	67.8	4.5	WR64	82.8	5.5	WR66	97.8	6.5	WR67
Dante Pettis	WR	23.5	2.1	WR124	29.0	2.6	WR126	34.5	3.1	WR129
George Kittle	TE	128.2	9.9	TE3	167.2	13	TE4	206.2	16	TE4
San Francisco 49ers	DST	162.0	10.8	DST3						
Robbie Gould	K	107.0	8.9	K16						

*6 games with Denver

JIMMY GAROPPOLO

The jury is out as to whether Jimmy G is a good NFL quarterback or not but there's no denying that he's a very average fantasy quarterback. He's currently my QB24 but just 20 points accelerate him to the QB14 spot. The 49ers will run the football & win games which restricts his fantasy production but he's a safe QB2.

ADP 14.1

ADP 5.02

RAHEEM MOSTERT

Mostert, the RB26 of last year proved his credentials in the NFC Championship game (29/220/4!!) If we assign Mostert half of Breida's work & multiply it by Mostert's production from last year, he would have finished as RB9 in PPR leagues. There will be Tevin Coleman weeks however, so don't get too carried away.

DEEBO SAMUEL

All eyes will be on Deebo's recovery from his broken foot. If we see football in September, it's likely that Samuel will miss time which, of course, hampers his fantasy value. He's electric with the ball in his hands but won't be a stud every week so is best paired with a safer, high reception option like Michael Thomas.

ADP 8.06

ADP 12.2

The 49ers traded up into the first round to select Aiyuk out of Arizona State. If Shanahan/Lynch make this move, they see a role for him in their offense. With Deebo potentially side lined for the first few weeks, there's a vacant WR1 spot available which Aiyuk is surely the favourite to take.

BRANDON AIYUK

GEORGE KITTLE

Kittle is the best all round tight end in the league. Whilst Kelce's receiving just edges Kittle's, Kittle's blocking ability is greatly superior to Kelce's. That,however, hinders his potential fantasy ability. I see a slight drop off for Kittle this season but a top-3TE finish is still almost guaranteed.

ADP 2.12

2020 Projections

ADP taken from Ultimate Draft Kit (PPR)

Projections by Rob Grimwood @FFBritballer

FANTASY FOOTBALL

Position	Player	Standard		0.5PPR		Full PPR	
		Pts	Rank	Pts	Rank	Pts	Rank
QB	Jimmy Garoppolo	265.9	29				
RB	Tevin Coleman	138.1	36	156.1	35	174.1	33
RB	Raheem Mostert	145.4	32	155.4	36	165.4	40
RB	Jerick McKinnon	40.6	81	48.6	80	56.6	78
WR	Deebo Samuel	111.7	44	135.2	46	158.7	49
WR	Brandon Aiyuk	117.5	39	145.0	40	172.5	41
WR	Dante Pettis	30.1	117	40.6	116	51.1	116
WR	Kendrick Bourne	75.1	74	96.1	74	117.1	71
TE	George Kittle	155.5	2	201.0	2	246.5	2

2

FULL 10 YARDS

SAN FRANCISCO 49ERS

LAST 5 YEARS

	W	L	T	Div	P/Offs
2019	13	3	0	1st	Lost SB
2018	4	12	0	3rd	
2017	6	10	0	4th	
2016	2	14	0	4th	
2015	5	11	0	4th	

DO SAY..
Shrewd front office

DON'T SAY..
Super Bowl hangover

BETTING ODDS
BY ADAM WALFORD (@TOUCHDOWNTIPS)

SUPER BOWL **10/1**

NFC CONFERENCE **6/1**

NFC WEST **6/5**

TO MAKE PLAYOFFS
5/18
TEAM TOTAL WINS
10.5

ADAM'S BEST BET
WIN NFC WEST
6/5

PLEASE GAMBLE RESPONSIBLY

VIEW FROM THE SIDELINES
By Jacob Barner (@JBBFootball)

Fresh off a disappointing Super Bowl loss, the 49ers look to get back to the big game with retention. Despite losing big name players, we rank 4th in number of snaps retained in the NFL. The key for the off-season was replacing the big names lost. Joe Staley was replaced with Trent Williams, whom they traded from Washington. Buckner, who was traded for the 13th pick, was replaced with Javon Kinlaw & 1st round WR Brandon Aiyuk was drafted to replace Sanders. The 49ers also tied up their prized assets, giving long term extensions to John Lynch, Kyle Shanahan & George Kittle, now the highest paid TE in the NFL. 49ers fans will be in good spirits this year, but they will keep their eyes on injuries amongst the WR room with Deebo Samuel & Jalen Hurd already looking like they'll miss some time.

►RETRO FOCUS◄
RONNIE LOTT – S

Arguably the toughest most hard-nosed safety in NFL history, Ronnie Lott was an enforcer that helped turn the 49ers into the Team of the 80s. He helped San Francisco to four Super Bowls in a single decade, transitioning effortlessly from CB to S in his sixth season. Lott returned five pickoffs for TDs in his career, accrued 10 Pro Bowl nods, 6 All Pro berths and an inevitable call up by the Hall of Fame. He also was one of the first names on the NFL's 100 Year anniversary team.

DID YOU KNOW

The name "49ers" comes from the prospectors who arrived in Northern California in the 1849 Gold Rush.

KEY STAT

"Need for Speed"
49ers running back, Matt Breida hit the top speed carrying the ball in 2019, 22.3mph.

FULL10YARDS VERDICT
The NFC champions kept most of their starters, but with DeForest Buckner now a Colt, Emmanuel Sanders going to the Saints and Joe Staley retiring, they've still lost some serious talent – even with Trent Williams, Javon Kinlaw and Brandon Aiyuk coming in. If Jimmy G can ease back on the interceptions, George Kittle rumbles on and their second-ranked D maintains their standards, the ghosts of their Super Bowl loss to the Chiefs can be exorcised. Losers of the title game rarely return to the scene of the crime at the first attempt but the 49ers could be an exception.

BETTING, STATS, FANS VIEW, RETRO

3

SEATTLE SEAHAWKS

THE LOWDOWN:

Russell Wilson is playing at his peak right now and the Seahawks are doing what they can to build a Championship winning squad around him. The Quarterback carried the team on his back last season and was many peoples pick for League MVP in the early parts of the season before eventually losing out to Lamar Jackson. The Seahawks completed a block buster trade this off season as they acquired Pro-Bowl safety Jamal Adams from the Jets. They gave up a couple of first rounders in the process but with the "win – now" window closing, Seattle are all in on the 2020 Season. CenturyLink Field has been a fortress but without fans this season, could that change the Seahawks fortunes?

SCHEDULE

Week 1: @ Falcons
Week 2: Vs. Patriots *(SNF)*
Week 3: Vs. Cowboys
Week 4: @ Dolphins
Week 5: Vs. Vikings *(SNF)*
Week 6: BYE
Week 7: @ Cardinals
Week 8: Vs. 49ers
Week 9: @ Bills
Week 10: @ Rams
Week 11: Vs. Cardinals *(TNF)*
Week 12: @ Eagles *(MNF)*
Week 13: Vs. Giants
Week 14: Vs. Jets
Week 15: @ Washington
Week 16: Vs. Rams
Week 17: @ 49ers

2020 NFL DRAFT CLASS

Round 1
Jordyn Brooks, LB,
Texas Tech
Round 2
Darrell Taylor, EDGE,
Tennessee
Round 3
Damien Lewis, IOL,
LSU
Round 4
Colby Parkinson, TE,
Stanford
DeeJay Dallas, RB,
Miami
Round 5
Alton Robinson, EDGE,
Syracuse
Round 6
Freddie Swain, WR,
Florida
Round 7
Stephen Sullivan, TE,
LSU

SIGNINGS

Quinton Dunbar, CB
Phillip Dorsett, WR
B.J. Finney, OL
Carlos Hyde, RB
Bruce Irvin, EDGE
Greg Olsen, TE

STAR SIGNING

Jamal Adams, SS

NO LONGER ON TEAM

Josh Gordon, WR
Ed Dickson, TE
George Fant, OL
Al Woods, DT
Ezekiel Ansah, DE
Quinton Jefferson, DE
Mychal Kendricks, LB
Jadeveon Clowney, LB
Bradley McDougald, CB

TEAM DETAILS:

Owner: The Allen Family
General Manager: John Schneider
Stadium: CenturyLink Field
Location:
Head Coach: Pete Carroll
Offensive Coordinator: Brian Schottenheimer
Defensive Coordinator: Ken Norton Jr.
Coaching Staff:
Brian Schneider (ST Coordinator)
Austin Davis (QB Coach)
Chad Morton (RB Coach)
Nate Carroll (WR Coach)
Pat McPherson (TE Coach)
Super Bowl Wins: 1 (2013)
Conference Wins: 3 (2005, 2013, 2014)
Divisional Wins: 10 (AFC West, 1988, 1999; NFC West, 2004, 2005, 2006, 2007, 2010, 2013, 2014, 2016)
-2019-
Record: 11-5 (Lost Divisional Rd)
Offence Rank: Passing (14th), Rushing (4th), Overall (9th)
Defence Rank: Passing (27th), Rushing (22nd),Overall (22nd)

KEY PLAYER

Russell Wilson: Before the 2019 season kicked off, Russell Wilson signed a monster four-year deal with the Seahawks. He lived up to that deal throughout the season, and goes into 2020 firmly in the elite tier of NFL Quarterbacks. In the eight seasons Wilson has been in the league, the Seahawks have had a winning record in every single one of this. His influence is hard to understate, that surely won't change in 2020.

Jordyn Brooks: After being the shock pick of the first round, Jordyn Brooks is going to have a lot of people looking at his performances and looking to say, I told you so. Brooks is a speedy linebacker who fits the mould of a Seahawks defender, he uses that speed to make tackles from sideline to sideline.

ROOKIE SPOTLIGHT

DEPTH CHART

Quarterback	Wide Receiver	Center	Edge	Line Backer	Cornerback
Russel Wilson	Tyler Lockett	BJ Finney	Bruce Irvin	Bobby Wagner	Shaquill Griffin
Geno Smith	DK Metcalf	Jordan Roos	LJ Collier	KJ Wright	Tre Flowers
Anthony Gordon [R]	Phillip Dorsett	**Tackle**	Benson Mayowa	Jordyn Brooks [R]	Ugochukwu Amadi
Fullback	David Moore	Duane Brown	Rasheem Green	Shaqueem Griffin	Neiko Thorpe
Nick Bellore	John Ursua	Cedric Ogbuehi	**Defensive Tackle**	Cody Barton	Quinton Dunbar
Running Back	Freddie Swain [R]	Jamarco Jones	Jarran Reed	**Free Safety**	**Strong Safety**
Chris Carson	**Tight End**	**Guard**	Poona Ford	Quandre Diggs	Jamal Adams
Carlos Hyde	Greg Olsen	Ethan Pocic	Demarcus Christmas	Marquise Blair	Delano Hill
Rashaad Penny	Will Dissly	Phil Haynes	**Kicker**	**Punter**	**Long Snapper**
DeeJay Dallas [R]	Luke Willson	Mike Iupati	Jason Myers	Michael Dickson	Tyler Ott

NFL

1

FULL 10 YARDS

2019 RANKINGS

Player	Pos	Standard			0.5PPR			PPR		
		Pts	Avg	Rank	Pts	Avg	Rank	Pts	Avg	Rank
Russell Wilson	QB	313.3	20.9	QB5						
Chris Carson	RB	195.6	13.0	RB9	214.1	14	RB10	232.6	16	RB10
Rashaad Penny	RB	67.3	6.7	RB51	71.3	7.1	RB53	75.3	7.5	RB55
Tyler Lockett	WR	142.1	9.5	WR19	180.1	12	WR18	218.1	15	WR17
D.K. Metcalf	WR	115.0	7.7	WR32	141.0	9.4	WR34	167.0	11	WR35
David Moore	WR	39.6	2.8	WR93	47.1	3.4	WR97	54.6	3.9	WR98
Will Dissly	TE	50.9	8.5	TE27	62.4	10	TE32	73.9	12	TE34
Jacob Hollister	TE	50.4	5.0	TE28	68.9	6.9	TE26	87.4	8.7	TE24
Seattle Seahawks	DST	116.0	7.7	DST13						
Jason Myers	K	114.0	7.6	K13						

RUSSELL WILSON — ADP 5.09

Danger Russ actually just misses out on my tier 1 QBs this year – that being said, he's still QB55 in my rankings. Wilson threw a 3-year high completion % and a career low 5 interceptions last year so accuracy is not something you should be worried about. Plenty of talent for him to throw to & a top-10 finish is a LOCK.

CHRIS CARSON — ADP 3.05

There's plenty of splinters in bottoms with Carson. He finished as RB12 last year but was probably 1 fumble away from the bench. He's got high RB2 upside, but the addition of Carlos Hyde is a worrying one. I believe that Penny will one day take the role but for now, Carson is the guy making his RB20 ADP a good value.

TYLER LOCKETT — ADP 5.03

Lockett is easily one of the most underrated receivers in the league in both real life and fantasy. He had his first 1,000 yard receiving season last year and will benefit further from having Metcalf opposite him. He finished as WR13 last year and is currently being drafted as the WR23. Get him EVERYWHERE that you can.

D.K. METCALF — ADP 4.11

The 1a to Lockett's 1b will be looking to improve on his impressive rookie season. However, he's currently being drafted ahead of Lockett which is CRAZY! He'll certainly push to crack the top-25 this season but he's still only the second-best receiving option in the Pacific North West this year.

GREG OLSEN — ADP U/D

We haven't seen Olsen finish inside the top-10 since 2016 and, at 35, I don't think he'll even make the top-15 this season. Dissly was incredible during his short playing time last year and I'm sure that Hollister will want a piece of the pie too. I wouldn't be surprised to see Olsen finish as the third best fantasy TE in Seattle.

2020 Projections

Position	Player	Standard		0.5PPR		Full PPR	
		Pts	Rank	Pts	Rank	Pts	Rank
QB	Russell Wilson	329.1	6				
RB	Chris Carson	165.1	24	178.6	24	192.1	26
RB	Carlos Hyde	78.8	62	82.8	64	86.8	65
RB	Rashaad Penny	82.5	60	89.5	61	96.5	61
WR	D.K Metcalf	146.5	18	179.0	22	211.5	22
WR	Tyler Lockett	134.7	26	169.7	25	204.7	24
WR	David Moore	48.1	101	58.6	105	69.1	105
WR	Phillip Dorsett	50.8	97	61.3	101	71.8	102
TE	Will Dissly	77.4	21	97.9	23	118.4	23
TE	Greg Olsen	57.6	32	73.6	32	89.6	33

ADP taken from Ultimate Draft Kit (PPR)

Projections by Rob Grimwood @FFBritballer

FANTASY FOOTBALL

2

FULL 10 YARDS

SEATTLE SEAHAWKS

LAST 5 YEARS

	W	L	T	Div	P/Offs
2019	11	5	0	2nd	Lost Div
2018	10	6	0	2nd	Lost WC
2017	9	7	0	2nd	
2016	10	5	1	1st	Lost Div
2015	10	6	0	2nd	Lost Div

DO SAY..

Russell Wilson future HoF

DON'T SAY..

The ball is at the 1 yard line, Lynch is in the backfield

BETTING ODDS BY ADAM WALFORD (@TOUCHDOWNTIPS)

SUPER BOWL **22/1**

NFC CONFERENCE **11/1**

NFC WEST **11/4**

TO MAKE PLAYOFFS
10/13
TEAM TOTAL WINS
9.5

ADAM'S BEST BET

DK METCALF OVER 850.5 REC YARDS
10/11

PLEASE GAMBLE RESPONSIBLY

VIEW FROM THE SIDELINES

By Neill Elliot (@NeillElliot)

After a quiet draft the Seahawks then did a very un-Seahawk move in trading for Adams. A good move as our secondary was a glaring weakness last season. A fully fit Lockett and breakout DK could be difference between RW3 working miracles to grab single score wins and sitting comfortably ahead with 2 minutes on the clock. Time will tell if our annual o-line problems and pass rush issues from last year have been resolved. If they have been and we can keep our running backs out of the treatment room then the Seahawks are well placed to come through, arguably, the toughest division in the league.

►RETRO FOCUS◄

JOE NASH - DT

An unsung position on an unsung team, NT Joe Nash was a fixture on the Seahawks defensive line for 15 seasons and 218 games. Nash battled through offensive linemen for 47.5 career sacks, and in 1989 he recorded a gaudy 92 tackles – incredible for a defensive lineman. Nash wasn't really recognised during his playing days, with only one Pro Bowl and one All Pro appearance, but his 779 tackles places him in the top 200 people stoppers in NFL history..

DID YOU KNOW

Thanks to some conference swapping in the 1970s & 2000s, Seattle is the only NFL team to have competed in both AFC & NFC championship games.

KEY STAT

"Tis the (post)season to be jolly"
The Seahawks have been in the playoffs 8 out of the 10 seasons Pete Carroll has been Head Coach of the team.

FULL10YARDS VERDICT

Despite Russell Wilson's fine season, Seattle couldn't reach the Super Bowl last year. The NFL's highest-paid player (a cool $35m a year) is in his prime and steered the 'Hawks into the playoffs, even with several key injuries. Wilson took 48 sacks last year so they beefed up the O-line in free agency and added Greg Olsen and Phillip Dorsett to their offensive arsenal. Even with a defence that's adequate rather than amazing – albeit boosted by Jets safety Jamal Adams recently – a ninth postseason run under Peter Carroll is the very least they expect.

BETTING, STATS, FANS VIEW, RETRO

3

FULL 10 YARDS

WHERE TO FIND US

www.Full10Yards.com

@Full10Yards
@Full10YardsCFB
@F10YFantasy
@F10YBritball
@F10YRetro

 **Full10Yards**

Full10Yards American Football Podcast
Full10Yards College Football Podcast
Full10Yards Britball Podcast

DISCOUNT CODE

10% off with code FULL10
at checkout

Discount on selected products which may vary
throughout the year.

SUPPORT THE BRITISH GAME

Make sure that when American football returns on these shores, that you get down an support your local football team, whether it be full adult contact,youth teams, women's teams and don't forget Flag football!

Fot more information on the grassroots game in this country, be sure to checkout the following websites, groups and social media accounts:

-Websites-

Official British American Football Website

https://www.britishamericanfootball.org/

Coaching Information

http://www.bafca.co.uk/

Officiating Information

https://www.bafra.info/

SUPPORT THE BRITISH GAME

Here are just a handful of social media outlets you can find that can give you all the latest information on the British American football scene.

-Facebook Groups-

General Groups

- https://www.facebook.com/britballcommunity
- https://www.facebook.com/UKamericanfootballscene

Flag Football

- https://www.facebook.com/groups/151215275013151

Women's Football

- https://www.facebook.com/groups/womensamericanfootball

Other groups

- https://www.facebook.com/groups/hailmaryhits

Plus many many more!

-Twitter-

@bafaofficial

@BAFCAOfficial

@bafraofficial

Printed in Great Britain
by Amazon